CINEPHILIA IN THE AGE OF DIGITAL REPRODUCTION

For My Father,
'I'm your Huckleberry'
– SB

CINEPHILIA IN THE AGE OF DIGITAL REPRODUCTION

Film, Pleasure and Digital Culture, Vol.1

Edited by Scott Balcerzak & Jason Sperb

WALLFLOWER PRESS
LONDON & NEW YORK

First published in Great Britain in 2009 by
Wallflower Press
6 Market Place, London W1W 8AF
www.wallflowerpress.co.uk

A catalogue record for this book is available from the British Library

ISBN 978-1-905674-83-1 (pbk)
ISBN 978-1-905674-84-8 (hbk)

Book design by Elsa Mathern

Printed in India by Imprint Digital

CONTENTS

CONTEXTS

AFFECTS

ONTOLOGIES

BODIES

NOTES ON CONTRIBUTORS

Scott Balcerzak, is Assistant Professor of Film and Literature in the Department of English at Northern Illinois, University in DeKalb, Illinois. He has published articles on cinema and performance for such publications as the *Journal of the Midwest Modern Language Association* and *Post Script*.

Robert Burgoyne is Professor of English and Film Studies at Wayne State University. He is the author of *Bertolucci's 1900: A Narrative and Historical Analysis* (1991) and *The Hollywood Historical Film* (2008).

Zach Campbell has BFA and MA degrees from New York University and is a doctoral student at Northwestern University, Chicago. He has published in *Rouge*, *Framework*, *Cineaste* and *Slant*. He blogs at elusivelucidity.blogspot.com.

Tobey Crockett is an artist and theorist, researching roles for play, community and the possibility that cyberspace is indeed indigenous space. She is currently at work on a series of books on how to build community, has several forthcoming essays addressing the emergent subjectivities of cyberspace and is hatching a large multimedia arts project.

Brian Darr is a cinephile and San Francisco native. His particular cinematic interests include, but are certainly not limited to, silent films, East Asian cinema, animation and classic films shot in his hometown.

Kevin Fisher is a Lecturer at the University of Otago in New Zealand. His essays have appeared in anthologies such as *Meta-Morphing: Visual Transformation and the Culture of Quick-Change* (1999) and *The Lord of the Rings: Studying the Event Film* (2008), as well as *Junctures: The Journal for Thematic Dialogue*.

Andy Horbal currently works as the Media Acquisition Co-ordinator for the Stark Media Services Center at the University of Pittsburgh's Hillman Library while he pursues a Masters degree in Library and Information Science. He blogs at http://thepartingglass.wordpress.com.

Christian Keathley is Associate Professor in the Film and Media Culture Programme at Middlebury College in Middlebury, Vermont. He is the author of *Cinephilia and History, or The Wind in the Trees* (2006), and has contributed to *Art Papers* and *Framework*, as well as *The Last Great American Picture Show: New Hollywood Cinema in the 1970s* (2004).

Adrian Martin is Senior Research Fellow, Film and Television Studies, Monash University, Melbourne. He is the author of *Phantasms* (1994), *The Mad Max Movies* (2003) and *Qué es el cine moderno?* (2008). He is the co-editor of *Movie Mutations: The Changing Face of World Cinephilia* (2003) and the Internet film journal *Rouge* (www.rouge.com.au).

Jenna Ng is a PhD candidate in Film Studies at University College London where she is researching temporalities and ontology of the moving image in the digital era. She is also a contributor to the well-received compilation, *Cinephilia: Movies, Love and Memory* (2005) among other journals and collections.

Lisa Purse is Lecturer in Film in the Department of Film, Theatre and Television at the University of Reading, UK. She has published essays on the presence of digital imaging in popular cinema, and is contributing a forthcoming study entitled 'Reading the Digital' to Wallflower Press's annual *Close-Up* series, exploring the challenges that digital elements of the film frame pose for interpretation.

Dan Sallitt is a filmmaker and film writer living in New York. He was the film critic for the *Los Angeles Reader*, and his writings have appeared in the *Chicago Reader*, *Slate*, *Wide Angle*, *Senses of Cinema*, the *Nashville Scene*, the *Minneapolis City Pages* and other venues. He blogs at http://sallitt.blogspot.com.

Girish Shambu is a chemical engineer and an Associate Professor of production/operations management at Canisius College in Buffalo, New York. He is also a cinephile who runs a community-oriented film culture blog at http://www.girish-shambu.com/blog.

Jason Sperb is a PhD candidate in the department of Communication and Culture at Indiana University, Bloomington. In addition to contributing to such journals as *Bright Lights Film Journal*, *Culture, Theory and Critique*, *Quarterly Review of Film and Video*, *Biography* and *Film Criticism*, he is also the author of *The Kubrick Façade* (2006).

ACKNOWLEDGEMENTS

The following is a collection of essays on the fluid, unbroken, presence of cinephilia in the age of digital reproduction. As such, this eclectic mix of work reflects the different agendas and forms through which critics and scholars have tackled the issue of cinephilia in our current historical moment. In short, how is cinephilia still present, and what does it present to us? Most are original articles written for this collection; some are reproductions of published work with the author's expressed consent; some originated as blog entries and personal Internet publications, reproduced here with permission; others still began as essays with online journals. Though each piece is different in form and content, the collective research here speaks to the enduring, and also diverse, work cinephilia does in the age of digital reproduction.

The editors wish to express gratitude to the following individuals, without whom *Cinephilia in the Age of Digital Reproduction* would not have thrived in the manner it has: Dudley Andrew, Robert Burgoyne, Chris Cagle, Zach Campbell, Barry Keith Grant, Joan Hawkins, Christian Keathley, Barbara Klinger, Lloyd Michaels, James Naremore, Jenna Ng, Eyal Peretz, Ted Pigeon, Robert Ray, Jonathan Rosenbaum, Catherine Russell, Girish Shambu, Steven Shaviro, Vivian Sobchack, Maureen Turim, Gregory Waller and Kristin Whissel.

Credits:
A shorter version of chapter five originally appeared as 'Sensing an Intellectual Nemesis', *Film Criticism*, 32, 1, (2007), 49–71. Original versions of Zach Campbell's 'Floating Hats: A Mere Diversion?' and 'Swimming' originally appeared on elusivelucidity.blogspot.com. Girish Shambu's '*Code Unknown*: An Auto-Dialogue' was originally published on www.girishshambu.com/blog. An abbreviated version of Robert Burgoyne's chapter was published in both English and Portuguese as '"Super Mario Clouds" and the John Ford Sky: Love and Loss in the Work of Douglas Gordon and Cory Arcangel', in *TXT Leituras Transdisciplinaires se Telas e Textos* (August 2008) at http://www.letras.ufmg.br/site/.

THE TWENTY-FIRST-CENTURY CINEPHILE
Christian Keathley

Cinema's first century has shown that there is no better formula for stirring up cinephiliac discourse than the introduction of new technologies into the film experience. The transition to sound and colour in the 1930s, the development of widescreen formats in the 1950s, and the introduction of home video and pay/cable TV in the 1970s all prompted cries of despair from one group of cinephiles and shouts of joy from another over what the latest technological 'advance' meant for the art of cinema. And the reasons for objection or support were not always unified.

For example, while Hollywood was quick to exploit the potential of synchronous sound for the enrichment of the entertainment experience, the European avant-garde – as well as some of the earliest film theorists, like Rudolf Arnheim (see 1933) – lamented that synch sound would halt filmmakers' crafting of a 'pure' (that is, exclusively visual) cinema, deadening it into nothing more than canned theatre. The Soviet filmmakers (such as Sergei Eisenstein, Vsevolod Pudovkin and Grigori Alexandrov (see 1928)) understood this danger as well, but were more alert to the formal possibilities offered by the new technology; they saw the potential for another level of montage in the contrapuntal use of sound and image. In the mid-1940s, André Bazin offered yet still a different argument: firstly, that sound did not mark the aesthetic break that many claimed it would (or did), and secondly, that synch sound engaged with film's ontology to extend the realist effect of cinema.

It is this issue of ontology that has become especially urgent in our present context. While the ever-expanding use of digital effects has been one issue in the recent cinephiliac debate, it hasn't been the only one, or even the primary one – after all, special effects have been around almost from the birth of the movies. Rather, it is the alleged extinction of film and its replacement by digital video technologies that has caused the most concern – the worry here being over the loss of film's ontology. Of course, as the argument goes, that ontology rested largely on the film image's status as an index – the mark of a prior presence – something that is maintained in many digitally-based visual representations. Nevertheless, the increased use of digital technologies in motion picture production has had an important psychological effect on many viewers (cinephiles especially, perhaps) and psychology was the key point of Bazin's cornerstone essay, 'The Ontology of the Photographic Image' (1945). The force of the real in a film image ultimately has less to do with the truth of the origins of its production than with our belief in its having emanated from reality. Troubled questioning has been prompted less by films in which we know that digital effects are on display – like *Jurassic Park* (1993) – than by those films that don't appear to be employing them. Many films might have, secretly, used such effects in order to cinematically 'airbrush' a change into an actor's expression or into an uncontrolled background action. Digital technologies have cast deep doubt on our faith in film images, and we must reflect on the ways in which these new technologies have changed our relationship to the movies.

But new technologies of production have not been the only developments in recent years. Indeed, as one critic put it, 'The future historian must pay greater attention to the stunning revolution which is in the process of unfolding in the *consumption* of films than in the technological developments during these same years' (in de Baecque and Frémaux 1995: 134). The critic was André Bazin, writing in the 1950s, but his words are just as relevant today. For in the past twenty years, the ways in which both cinephiles and ordinary viewers consume films have been transformed far more radically, and more conspicuously, than have the movies themselves. Of course, these changes in film consumption are not separate from technological developments; they are enabled by them. And as a result, we have experienced dramatic changes in how films are able to be watched: we can watch them at the movie theatre or at home – in the latter on small monitors or quite large ones; we can check out movies on DVD from our local library, rent them from a local video store or from NetFlix, order them up via pay-per-view, or download them (often illegally) from the Internet; we can watch a film straight through or in multiple sittings, pausing it momentarily for snack and bathroom breaks; we can screen DVD chapters out of order, or select one chapter for repeated viewing; we can elect to watch different versions of the same film, with our choice guided by MPAA rating (R or PG-13), screen format (full screen or letterbox), or preferred cut (director's or studio's); we can listen to the film's original soundtrack, or we can select an alternate one dubbed into another language or a director's commentary; we can watch films not only at home, but also in our car while travelling, on our computer while (supposedly) working, on our iPod while commuting. As late as 1977, the year *Star Wars* appeared and initiated the post-classical cinema of spectacle and effects, none of these ways of watching described above was a possibility. The effect that these changes – both good and bad – have had on the cinephile's love affair with the cinema cannot be overstated.

Of course, how we watch and what we watch are not the only factors contributing to the state of cinephilia. Antoine de Baecque and Thierry Frémaux define cinephilia not only as 'a way of watching films', but also as a way 'of speaking about them and then of diffusing this discourse.'[3] Here again, the change in cinephiliac discourse – or, we might say, the reinvigoration and expansion of cinephiliac discourse – has been, in the past two decades, astounding. When I was in high school in the late 1970s, growing up in West Palm Beach, Florida, I was able to keep up with the state of cinema by reading Pauline Kael, Vincent Canby and Richard Corliss because the *New Yorker*, the *New York Times* and *Time* were easy to get. Other than that, I was limited to local reviewers. When I stumbled across a small newsstand that carried the *Village Voice*, I was elated. I knew of Andrew Sarris and his importance to American film criticism, but I had never read his reviews. This access to his weekly column had a profound effect on my burgeoning cinephilia. Today, thanks to the Internet, a budding cinephile can read all the finest critics from across the country and, indeed, around the world, and obtain a broad range of perspectives on individual films and on the entire state of cinema.

But perhaps more important than the Internet's access to 'official' film reviewers via their host periodical's website, it is the development of the Internet blog that has most changed the landscape of cinephiliac discourse. These blogs, in effect, offer something that is in between the formal discourse of writing and the informal discourse of talking. The finest bloggers (like Girish Shambu, for example, whom I read as devotedly as I read any official critic) offer reflection, commentary, analysis and critique of films old and new, in what is a highly sophisticated fanzine style of writing. Furthermore, these bloggers invite readers to respond with comments of their own, thus enabling cinephiles in distant locales to 'talk' to one another – to share ideas, information, resources and, most of all, their passion for the cinema. It is in this kind of talking that one can offer half-baked ideas or make bold assertions, either of which someone otherwise might be too cautious to put into formal print.[1] This intermediate process – in between the watching of a film and the formal critical evaluation of it in hard print – has long been a distinguishing feature of the life of the cinephile. But one cannot depend upon the fact, as one once could, that if you went to enough movies in your town, stood in line enough times, that you would start to see the same faces, and then eventually, one day, fall into conversation with those people about your shared passion for the cinema. Blogs offer the virtual equivalent of that experience, which is as crucial for the health of cinephilia as a whole as it is for the health of the individual cinephile.

The essays in this volume are organised around distinctive experiential aspects of the cinephiliac existence. First, the contributors consider certain *affective* qualities of the cinephile's encounter with the movies – an encounter often characterised in terms of pleasure and epiphany, but certainly not limited to those positive experiences. Next, the contributors examine – and in some cases, rigorously interrogate and challenge – the claim that film's *ontology* is at the heart of the cinephiliac experience; indeed, the changes brought by new technologies demand a reexamination of whether this was in fact ever the case. Finally, if there is one site where almost all the issues raised in the consideration of cinephilia's encounter with new technologies converge, that site is the presentation (or non-presentation) of the human *body* on screen; a number of the essays in this volume explore how and why the body is such a complex topic for consideration.

Each of the issues that I have discussed above – technological change and film's ontology, the accessibility of individual titles and practices of viewing, the varieties of public discourse about cinema – cut across this volume's organisational categories. Most important is that these essays are varying examples of what cinephiles do best: watch, think, talk, rethink and write in ways that demonstrate a passionate commitment to the cinema, and that stimulate that passion in others.

NOTE

1   David Bordwell's blog is a perfect example of this phenomenon. See http://www.david-bordwell.net/blog/index.php

REFERENCES

Arnheim, Rudolf (2004a [1933]) 'Film and Reality', in Leo Braudy and Marshall Cohen (eds) *Film Theory and Criticism*. Sixth edition. New York: Oxford University Press, 322–8.

____ (2004b [1933]) 'The Making of a Film', in Leo Braudy and Marshall Cohen (eds) *Film Theory and Criticism*. Sixth edition. New York: Oxford University Press, 329–31.

Bazin, André (2004 [1950–55]) 'The Evolution of the Language of Cinema', in Leo Braudy and Marshall Cohen (eds) *Film Theory and Criticism*. Sixth edition. New York: Oxford University Press, 41–53.

____ (1967 [1945]) 'The Ontology of the Photographic Image', in *What is Cinema?* Volume 1, trans. Hugh Gray. Berkeley: University of California Press, 9–16.

de Baecque, Antoine and Thierry Frémaux (1995) 'La Cinéphilie ou L'Invention d'Une Culture', trans. Timothy Barnard. *Vingtième Siècle* 46, 134.

Eisenstein, Sergei, Vsevolod Pudovkin and Grigori Alexandrov (2004 [1928]) 'Statement on Sound', in Leo Braudy and Marshall Cohen (eds) *Film Theory and Criticism*. Sixth edition. New York: Oxford University Press, 370–2.

CONTEXTS

INTRODUCTION
PRESENCE OF PLEASURE
Jason Sperb & Scott Balcerzak

> I recall a late 1990s rental video [VHS] copy of the erotic thriller *Wild Things* (USA: John MacNaughton, 1998) with the tape all wrinkled by frequent application of the still and review functions during the scene of the 'threesome' between Matt Dillon, Denise Richards and Neve Campbell. Of course, I didn't hesitate to add a few wrinkles myself.
>
> – Drehli Robnik, 'Mass Memories of Movies'[1]

In a 2005 essay on cinephilia and blockbuster culture, Drehli Robnik beautifully articulates how the lasting memories and material effects of cinema's power had been altered fundamentally with the advent of new home video technologies – 'the isolated favourite image as a textual ruin becomes literalised in epiphanies specific to video', he writes. 'Rental videos confront you with traces, ruined images, left behind by someone else's fascination by a moment' (2005: 59). As has become more common, or at least more overt, in recent discussions of cinephilia, Robnik focuses on home video's relation to fragments or isolated images in a particular film. Yet if one skips to the end of the essay to pursue the particulars of the accompanying endnote to this statement about 'textual ruins', the reader will be greeted with a more explicit example (the reception of the tape quality of *Wild Things*' threesome) of the sort of extra-textual work that Robnik wishes to study and perform.

There are many fascinating and telling lessons to be drawn from what is otherwise a minor note in Robnik's argument – beyond just the useful reminder that it always pays to read the endnotes. At least a couple of the points are touched upon above. For one, the emergence and ubiquity of home video viewing technologies – Beta, VHS, laserdisc, DVD, iPods, online file-sharing – have permanently entered any thorough discussion of cinephilia today (even while one is compelled to point out that earlier technologies, such as private 16mm projectors, complicate any simplistic, linear narrative about the evolution of 'home' or even 'extra-theatrical' viewing). As writers such as Uma Dinsmore-Tuli (2000) and Barbara Klinger (2006) have previously noted, contemporary cinephilia is unthinkable outside of the repetition of home viewing, the avid movie collectors and the general fascination with the always already evolving technology and its potential link to watching films.

Robnik's anecdote speaks to this new reality, and to its fleeting temporality. It also speaks to the power of fragments for many (but not all) cinephiles. The particular cinematic images, or even just a part of those particular images, maintain a powerful affective hold on people, and serve well as a manifestation of their intense emotional, intellectual and even, at times, nostalgic attachment to film. Ironically, though, that damage done to the videotape would seem to foreground the *inability* to hold onto the moment, as each return to that notorious sequence in *Wild Things* produces further ruin to the image. Of course, the issue is nearly moot now, as the emergence of DVD makes the quality of the ruined VHS tape partially irrelevant to the discussion. Then again, VHS does remain a valuable, if more rare, medium for the circulation of particular titles for cinephiles. In any case, the symbolic value of Robnik's note remains, as the repeated viewings of MacNaughton's film speak to both the possibilities and the limitations of cinephilic pleasures in our current digital culture. Technological advances should allow greater access, greater possibilities for holding on to the cinephiliac text. And yet, sometimes, the closer we move to the cinephiliac object, the further away it feels. To a certain degree, this ambivalence of contemporary digital culture – both cinephilia's inexhaustible possibility and its often material restrictions – must be always kept in mind.

Of course, Robnik's note is also a passage about masturbation. Literally. Yet before we close the figurative door and turn away in awkward discomfort (think Joel Barrish's (Jim Carrey) embarrassed mother in *Eternal Sunshine of the Spotless Mind* (2004) – a true cinephiliac text *du jour*), it is perhaps important to note that cinephilia is itself often symbolically masturbatory. Scholars, critics, bloggers and so forth seek intellectual and emotional self-gratification through the act of writing about the intense pleasures and ideas (importantly, *the pleasure of ideas*) that film affords us. Of course, this is not to denigrate the cinephile, as almost all film criticism and scholarship is blissfully and unapologetically self-indulgent – as well it should be. But the cinephile's condition is more pronounced, more acute. Noted filmmaker, critic and scholar Peter Wollen has previously identified the cinephile as possessing 'a desire to remain within a child's view of the world, always outside, always fascinated by a mysterious parental drama, always seeking to master one's anxiety by compulsive repetition' (2001: 119) – and, of course, this is also partly a self-diagnosis. The cinephile's own love – the awareness of that love and the anxieties it produces – takes precedence in writing.

With the increasing ubiquity of digital culture – digital effects, digital playbacks, digital Internet – this love materialises itself in ever-expanding ways, such that the lonely cinephile, sitting in Henri Langlois' Cinémathèque Français, could not have begun to imagine. Moreover, a keen awareness of this expansion provokes further hope and desire on the part of cinephiles for a new kind of digital cinephilia only now being envisioned. The modern cinephile is the one most intensely interested in the medium's potential, which by extension best maps onto the seemingly limitless promise of new technologies which our present digital culture offers. The cinephile pushes further than the typical moviegoer, manifesting her filmic passion into production and language, and transcending the bounded intensity of the cult fan. The cinephile simply loves the cinema – *the cinephile loves the medium* – but this love today cannot be fully understood without accounting for the technologies which best harness and expand this passion. New digital technologies have radically shifted the possibilities for acting out and fleetingly satisfying what Wollen has identified as a 'compulsive repetition' in their behaviour.

And yet repetition too is based on something more, something which exceeds that repeated text. Repetition is centred on the promise of something not yet achieved. What else can technology provide? No cinephile has better summed up film's present condition than French film critic Nicole Brenez, who writes in Jonathan Rosenbaum and Adrian Martin's touchstone collection, *Movie Mutations*, that 'in the end, the cinema seems to me above all inexhaustibly generous' (in Rosenbaum *et al.* 2003: 27). For the contributors to *Cinephilia in the Age of Digital Reproduction*, the literal and symbolic effects of digital culture present the lover of film with such a state of limitless cinematic clarity. The unlimited possibilities of digital culture remind us that, in short, cinephilia has not yet been invented!

ORIGINS

But before moving towards those discursive horizons, it is important to look briefly back. The first seeds of this project might have been planted during our early days in the film studies programme at Oklahoma State University – where, besides finding our footing in the Masters programme, we helped to establish an eccentric film club called 'The Claude Rains Appreciation Society'. As its esoteric name might suggest, the club prided itself in blurring the line between the cinephilic and scholarly through its viewings and discussions of rare films. When we each moved on to faraway PhD programmes, we found ourselves respectively beginning to question cinephilia in new ways. At the University of Florida, Scott enrolled in Robert Ray's seminar on Classic Hollywood and Cinephilia, where he had the good fortune to read an early manuscript of Christian Keathley's *Cinephilia and History, or the Wind in the Trees* (2006). At Wayne State University, the influence of Steven Shaviro had Jason considering theories of affect, which soon opened out to a reinterrogation of personal cinephiliac experiences. In early 2005, on a long elevator ride in the WSU Maccabees Building, Jason began a casual conversation with Robert Burgoyne on some of the recent 'hot topics' at the annual meetings of the Society for Cinema and Media Studies (SCMS). Burgoyne mentioned digital effects and the topic stuck in Jason's mind as something to remember in connection to his recent forays into affect theory.

By then – with all these various seeds planted from Oklahoma to Florida to Michigan, along with a mutual passion for the blissful work of Roland Barthes – we decided to co-chair an SCMS panel called (in a playful nod to Walter Benjamin) 'The Work of Cinephilia in the Age of *CGI* Reproduction'. At this time, the focus was squarely on defining 'pleasure' through digital imagery as seen in spectacle films like the *Lord of the Rings* trilogy (2001, 2002, 2003), *The Polar Express* (2004), *Sky Captain and the World of Tomorrow* (2004) and *Sin City* (2005). Since these cinematic effects were denigrated by many academic and popular writers as 'ruining' film by making Hollywood products even more hollowly 'affect-less', we believed that championing the potential (if not always the 'reality') of these images would prove a welcome new take on the subject. At the time, we used 'cinephilia' largely metaphorically to connote a broadly-defined pleasure. Two of the essays which appear in this volume – Tobey Crockett's and Jenna Ng's – began as presentations on that panel, which eventually convened in Vancouver, British Columbia, in March 2006.

After the overwhelming response we received to our initial call for papers, we realised we had hit upon a provocative topic. The largely positive feedback the panel also gathered from the scholars in attendance only confirmed that we had something special. So, while sharing a cheap pot of coffee in Vancouver, we began brainstorming how to turn the panel into a collection of essays, possibly broadening the topic beyond just the special effects film. Luckily, we had the early commitment of panellist Ng, who had already established herself as a cinephile scholar in the well-received collection, *Cinephilia: Movies, Love and Memory* (de Valck & Hagener 2005), and helped organise a cinephilia conference during that collection's development. In the following months, we started to look for inspiration on another digital frontier – the Internet. During the same summer the SCMS panel was coming together, Jason – following Shaviro (creator of blog *The Pinocchio Theory*) – began his own film blog, *Jamais Vu*. That autumn, we helped create the group media blog *Dr. Mabuse's Kaleido-Scope*. Although the actual production of the group blog was a mixed bag of results, the membership quickly grew to include many other academics. Also joining and reading the blog were prolific and respected bloggers such as Girish Shambu and Zach Campbell, both of whom have contributed to this collection.

By early 2006, a new phase of our engagement with cinephilia had begun. Almost by sheer chance, we began to see how the 'digital' could have a much more expansive meaning than we originally conceived. We became aware of the immense amount of filmic writing being done online – and in time this development became as exciting as the need to champion digital effects. The project now covered key subjects we noted being discussed online – which not only explored the theatrical film, but digitised home viewing and the status of filmic discourse itself. Our own process of blogging, implicitly and explicitly about cinephilia, affected the scholarship – for example, Jason's second piece in this volume, '*Déjà Vu* for Something that Hasn't Happened Yet', began first as a *Mabuse* post in February 2006. Although blogging was the last thing on our minds when we began this process, it is impossible today to imagine this book without those valuable contributions.

Grounded in friendships and close collegiality, it might be obvious that this book is a labour of love for us. In all, much of this project grew from a fairly well-connected network of individuals, who have been pulled even closer by the simultaneity made possible through digital culture itself. We are scholars, theorists, critics and bloggers who believe cinephilia very much remains not only a (pleasurable) mode of perception but a collective (now digital) movement. These pages contain a variety of types of film writing from the rigorously theoretical to the passionately cinephilic. Reflecting the evolution of this project, this variety shows the far-reaching influences of our digital moment – as it affects academic film studies programmes, film publications and online communities. Therefore, the contributors to this volume are not only contemplating cinephilia as a concept. Through all these various incarnations, we are also *performing* 'the work of cinephilia in the age of digital reproduction'. In many ways, this book itself is an undeniable product of the digital age's limitless possibilities.

TRADITIONS OF CINEPHILIA

One of the problems found in many discussions of *cinephilia* is an inability simply to define the word in concrete terms. During the various stages of this project, we would often post on *Dr. Mabuse's Kaleido-Scope* discussions of cinephilia in direct relationship to the digital age and, sometimes, in relation to personal viewing experiences. A recurring question from readers was, essentially, what do we *mean* by 'cinephilia'? In what context are we employing the word? Did it connote a strong cinematic experience, a movement of viewership, or even an anticipation of an upcoming release? Some of the problems with getting a handle on how to properly use the word might simply be based in its irreducibly dual connotation as both a historical notion and a sensorial concept.

The word 'cinephilia' historically has most potently been linked to a diverse range of nearly ritualistic filmgoing habits of cinema connoisseurs throughout the middle part of the twentieth century – extending off-and-on from the 1920s to the 1970s in, mainly, urban centres like Berlin, New York City and, especially, Paris. Derived from this movement came the written product of cinephilia in the form of critical yet intensely personal responses to film as an art form and, more importantly, as an experience. From this writing came what might be viewed as cinephilia's more conceptually-ambiguous meaning as an abstract mode of pleasure usually discussed with passion as unrepeatable moments by the proponents of these movements. After Antoine de Baecque and Thierry Frémaux organised a conference on the history of cinephilia at the Lumière Institute in 1995, they published a definition of the word as, firstly, a way of watching films and, secondly, as a method of 'speaking about them and then diffusing this discourse' (trans. Timothy Barnard in Keathley 2006: 6). After the deliberations of the conference, they validly yet somewhat broadly defined cinephilia as 'a system of cultural organisation that engenders rituals around the gaze, speech and the written word' (in ibid.). From this expansive significance of the word, we found ourselves sometimes using 'cinephilia' in our *Mabuse* posts as some kind of lexical catchall in our ruminations over powerful moments of cinema and, conversely, to define ourselves as a type of filmgoer. No wonder readers found themselves sometimes asking what we meant by the use of the word 'cinephilia'.

But we also found that it is within the word's multiplicity that some of its most exciting possibilities reside. Confusion over what cinephilia means can extend beyond clarifying this dual significance, to exist as something much more provocative, since most recent noteworthy discussions of the phenomenon often result in asking *why* is it a topic worthy of examination. What often becomes most crucial in re-examining these mid-twentieth-century movements and their writings is how later, more 'academic' scholars (a label itself open to much debate) viewed this work in dismissive terms – or, conversely, as exemplifying something missing from more recent, supposedly 'objective' scholarship. In the 1920s, European avant-garde artists and intellectuals embraced film as the most completely modernist of art forms and the first wave of cinephilia began, with ciné-clubs and the earliest film journals becoming established through the works of such figures as Ricciotto Canudo, René Schwob, René Clair, Louis Delluc and Jean Epstein. This first wave of cinephilia was cut short by the oppressive fascist forces of mid-1930s Europe and, in a formal sense, did not fully recover until the 1950s with the birth of various specialised film publications – the most famous being based in France with the magazine *Cahiers du cinéma* and its discussions of the auteur through the writings of Jean-Luc Godard, François Truffaut, Jacques Rivette, André Bazin and others.

When Andrew Sarris brought this concept of film authorship to the United States in 1962 with his famous 'Notes on the Auteur Theory', it initiated a tradition of American cinephilia with the work of such figures as Pauline Kael and the film-focused writings of Susan Sontag. It also opened the doors for film studies in academic institutions where literary authorial scholarship ruled. As noted by Dudley Andrew, this can be seen as the first of three stages of academic film studies in America. The second occurred when cinema studies embraced – long before literary studies – the post-May 1968 influx of the continental theories of Marxism, semiotics, structuralism, psychoanalysis and poststructuralism. The third stage (while never really cancelling out the second) began in the 1980s when many scholars moved away from the idea of a 'grand theory' to return to history through exploring issues of reception – dominated by a cultural studies approach focusing on a greater awareness of race, gender, sexuality, and, in general, a sense of political urgency. While certainly there are numerous potent exceptions to these trends (like David Bordwell and Kristen Thompson's explorations of neo-formalism, for example), Andrew's three stages illustrate how and why academic film studies moved away from the impassioned cinephilic writings of its earliest days towards less emotionally-based scholarship. With these second and third stages came a supposed need to *objectify* the position of the scholar by distancing her or him from previous, less theoretically rigid, approaches that, to these newer scholars, failed to look at the 'bigger picture' beyond the text itself. Notably, though, Andrew's stages also illustrate how film studies itself was born out of the initial, less academically rigorous, movements of cinephilia.

We can see this institutional objectification occur early in the 1970s as theory was being more implicitly embraced by a newer academically-based generation of film scholars. For example, with the writings of the 1920s and 1930s, the appeal of cinema was often described as *photogénie*, a mysterious, nearly hypnotic, quality created by what was then viewed as the most innovative of art forms. As David Bordwell explained in 1974, the word grew 'out of an attempt to account for the mysteriously alienating quality of cinema's relation to reality' (in Willemen 1994a: 124), where the earliest of film scholars often stressed the enigmatic in their descriptions of cinema's power. But to Bordwell, even for the most mature of these early writers such as Epstein and Canudo, this embracement of *photogénie* created scholarship that is 'unsupportable theoretically' and often filled with idealistic contractions based in 'various assumptions never raised to theoretical self-consciousness' (in Willemen 1994a: 125).

More influentially during the 1970s, the Lacanian theories of Laura Mulvey and Christian Metz seemed to suggest to many a more detached approach to film scholarship that truly ran counter to the 1960s focus on auteurism and its impassioned celebration of the artist. Metz famously writes in *The Imaginary Signifier: Psychoanalysis and the Cinema* (1975) what could be viewed as a direct challenge to earlier cinephilic scholarship: 'To be a theoretician of the cinema, one should ideally no longer love the cinema and yet still love it: have loved it a lot and only have detached oneself from it by taking it up again from the other end, taking it as the target for the very same scopic drive which had made one love it' (1977: 15). In essence, Metz's position was influential in the way that it was an implicit attempt to demystify the appeal of cinema – essentially a reversal of the earlier proponents of *photogénie* and the *Cahiérs du cinema* critics who viewed the filmgoing experience as somewhat transcendent and born out of the auteur's inspirations. Such a move to objectify the film scholar was an attempt to see her/his love of cinema as not necessarily unimportant but as something requiring theoretical validation and, possibly, something to be distrusted during one's analytical pursuits. But there were notable exceptions to these trends as others were attempting to rescue some of the earliest film scholarship as something truly worthy of re-examination. Paul Willemen wrote a powerful defence of Jean Epstein and *photogénie* itself in 1982, stating that such writings might be 'theoretically insupportable and hopelessly idealist, but this is no reason to assume that they are devoid of logic' nor should we 'abandon which principle(s) of coherence ... can account for precisely these assemblages' (1994: 125).

By the 1980s, even outside of academia, cinephilia as a movement of impassioned filmgoing was starting to be viewed as a dying concept. The ardent 1960s cinemagoing faded from vogue with the birth of the blockbuster, multiplexes and the easy accessibility of films thanks to video. By the mid-1990s, Susan Sontag famously lamented cinephilia's death in her *New York Times Magazine* piece 'The Decay of Cinema', writing that 'the love of cinema has waned. People still like going to the movies, and some people still care about and expect something special, necessary from a film' (1996: 61). While admitting that important films were still being produced, Sontag suggested that cinephilia itself 'has come under attack as something quaint, outmoded, snobbish. For cinephilia implies that films are unique, unrepeatable, magic experiences ... Cinephilia has no role in the era of hyperindustrial films' (ibid.). Her views were understandable, as, generally, impassioned viewing born out of the 1960s *Cahiers du cinéma*-influence felt all but dead. As the film industry was now moving into a truly 'hyperindustrial' form of production in America, an impassioned cinema connoisseur would logically be dying since such films suffered in quality or, more specifically, seemingly lost the individualistic touch of the auteur. Also, such a change supposedly devalued a key ingredient in the cinematic experience for cinephiles – the movie theatre itself, which was shrinking and often overshadowed by home viewing. However, not all agreed with this bleak assessment of the era and essentially pointed out that such views are reductive. 'I've also been told over and over again that much of the blame for this sad state of affairs lies with spectators in their twenties or early thirties who purport to be cinephiles but think film history began with *Star Wars* (1977)', writes Steve Erickson (1999). 'While there are plenty of people who fit this stereotype, patronising an entire generation doesn't take into account how its critics or cinephiles are responding to (or even trying to resist) the worst aspects of our film culture.'

Such proclamations (or, in Sontag's case, obituaries) during the 1980s and 1990s also forced a wider re-examination of what cinephilia once was – and, more provocatively, what it continues to be or could become in the future. Once again, Willemen was instrumental in framing these questions when he and Noel King provided one of the most thoughtful discussions of cinephilia thus far as an accountable experience in 'Through the Glass Darkly: Cinephilia Reconsidered'. Noticing a trend in earlier *photogénie* and later *Cahiers du cinéma* film scholarship, Willemen identifies cinephilic pleasures as 'something to do with what you perceive to be the privileged, pleasure-giving, fascinating *moment* of a relationship to what's happening on a screen' (1994: 232; emphasis added), a fetishising of fleeting details as opposed to examining the film as a whole. This privileging of the moment became key in future discussions of the phenomenon, especially in relation to understanding how experiencing a film moment itself changes due to technology. The question arose if Sontag's mourning had been somewhat premature or, simply, a mourning over the passing of a phase of cinephilia – which had to fade away due to technological innovation. After all, the relatively quiet years between the 1920s and 1950s/1960s schools of cinephilia notably occurred not only during the rise of fascism, but during film's technological transition from silents to sound to colour (not to mention the emergence of television). As the 1990s came to a close, the online journal *Senses of Cinema* published a series of articles provocatively titled 'Permanent Ghosts: Cinephilia in the Age of the Internet and Video', which attempted to reposition (or, at least, reconsider) cinephilia in the age of instant replay and home viewing where 'the moment' no longer seems as fleeting.

Soon after, noted cinephiles Rosenbaum and Martin co-edited the first major discussion of cinephilia as a phenomenon not only centred now in selected urban centres, but as something worldwide and expanding in exciting new directions. Central to their collection *Movie Mutations: The Changing Face of World Cinephilia* – which was born out of five years of correspondences and interactions between international film critics, filmmakers and scholars – is the idea of a new global film community made more accessible through the proliferation of film festivals, print and online publications and a wider distribution of world cinema through DVD. Within this broadening of the cinephilic community, Rosenbaum and Martin tellingly regard academia as an important factor by including a noteworthy series of correspondences between Martin and James Naremore which question how cinephilic writing and academic film studies both correspond and, at times, dispute.

Such discussions ushered in a re-establishment of cinephilia as a worthwhile topic of discussion in academic circles. Christian Keathley provided a re-examination of cinephilia as defining a history of cinema in *Cinephilia and History, or The Wind in the Trees*, a book that overtly challenges other established trends in film scholarship and in film theory. Here, Keathley greatly expands Willemen's moment-based observations of the cinephiliac experience to recontextualise it as a 'historiographic' exercise that can be used to reintegrate 'the cinephilic spirit into critical and historical writing' (2006: 10). In essence, Keathley's approach defies a new generation of scholars to capture the fleeting cinephilic moment in an attempt to produce worthwhile and vibrant scholarship that he calls 'cinephiliac anecdotes'.

Also promoting a rebirth of cinephilia during this time, Marijke de Valck and Malte Hagener co-edited *Cinephilia: Movies, Love and Memory*, a collection of essays that set out to embrace a supposed new generation of cinephilia by continuing some of the reinventions of the concept explored by Rosenbaum and Martin, but here in a decidedly more academic manner. Of particular interest, the collection contains Thomas Elsaesser's proclamation of a current historical moment that he calls 'cinephilia take two'. This is found in two notable variations, one that has kept 'aloof of academic curriculum and kept its faith with auteur cinema' and one consisting of candidates that embrace 'the new technologies, such as DVDs and the Internet, finding communities and shared experiences through gender-bending *Star Trek* episodes and other kinds of textual poaching' (2005: 36). Of course, it is with this second classification that a new form of cinephilia feels particularly ground-breaking. It is defined by the cinephile's ability to sample, rewatch, freeze, re-edit, or remount cinema – which gives a new approach towards what Elsaesser describes as all cinephilia's 'anxious love of loss and plentitude' (2005: 40), something he sees as persuasive in not only earlier cinephilic discourses but present throughout the decades of film studies that essentially were spawned from these movements. With Elsaesser's piece, we find cinephilia now being fully considered as a digital phenomenon, one that fully suggests Sontag's lament as being, possibly, misplaced mourning.

CINEMA (AND CINEPHILIA) IN THE AGE OF DIGITAL REPRODUCTION

This rebirth of interest in cinephilia at the start of the new millennium had much to do with the rise of an undeniable technological revolution that was changing the way people made, watched and discussed cinema. Of course, fully outlining the 'digital' and all its effects upon cinema and, generally, culture, is worthy of multiple volumes of a reference work. In what follows, we will simply provide some of the most intriguing aspects of recent scholarship on cinema and, particularly, cinephilia in the digital age. We organise these in the three areas that feel most central to this collection: digital imagery, DVDs and blogging (perhaps the most popular form of online cinephilic film discourse).

DIGITAL IMAGERY

> In this more baroque cinema of effects we move towards an appreciation of the beauty of the indeterminate...
>
> – Sean Cubitt, 'Phalke, Méliès, and Special Effects Today'[2]

Not surprisingly, the 'digital' in film was first notably discussed within the realm of special effects where the Bazinian notions of the cinematic image were clearly being challenged in such series as the *Jurassic Park* movies (1993, 1997, 2001), the *Matrix* trilogy (1999, 2003, 2003), the *Lord of the Rings* trilogy (2001, 2002, 2003) and numerous other blockbuster fantasy and science fiction films. In their 1990s scholarship, Scott Bukatman (1993) and Vivian Sobchack (1998) often employed digital effects examples as a springboard to contemplate larger phenomenological issues of space and the postmodern body in their discussions of the science fiction genre. These initial forays later resulted in even more ambitious examinations of digital images, body and affect in a collection of essays edited by Sobchack, *Meta-Morphing: Visual Transformation and the Culture of Quick-Change* (2000), which features key essays covering 'morphing' in such digitally-heavy texts as *Terminator 2* (1991), *Star Trek: Deep Space Nine* (1993–99) and *Forrest Gump* (1994). Later, in *Matters of Gravity: Special Effects and Supermen in the 20th Century* (2003), Bukatman presents a wider cultural study of technological spectacle, with a firm focus on special effects (digital and otherwise) in key chapters. As found in much of this phenomenological approach to such images, he suggests viewer responses to effects sequences are both potently affective and bodily, writing: 'Special effects emphasise real time, shared space, perceptual activity, kinesthetic sensation, haptic engagement, and an emphatic sense of wonder' (2003: 115). While historically evident since the earliest innovations of cinema, Bukatman suggests that the impact of such 'spectacles' has only heightened in the era of digital effects and 'theme park attractions and other themed environments' (2003: 116).

Also historically contextualising the place of digital effects in cinema and entertainment history, Sean Cubitt (1999) explored the supposedly 'new' phenomenon of such effects as actually a continuation of silent-era attractions of magic tricks seen in George Méliès and Dadasaheb Phalke. Cubitt later applied some concepts rooted in 'digital aesthetics' – usually left to the realm of special effects study, but something he had already explored in a larger cultural manner in his *Digital Aesthetics* (1998) – to provide a far-reaching history of cinematic images and commodity in his ambitious *The Cinema Effect*. As he reflects in his opening, his study of special effects led him to question cinema itself as a historical and sensorial object, contextualising it as 'a series of "effects"' (2005: 1). Such exciting avenues of thought essentially illustrate how some of the exploration of the digital that began with special effects is itself morphing into a re-examination of all cinema. Though, as the focus on 'spectacle' suggests, most discussions of digital effects focus upon the phenomenon onscreen as sometimes diegetically excessive, in Cubitt's original suggestion, as imagery in the realm of Méliès and Phalke. Digital effects films, to many, constitute updated examples of Tom Gunning's original 'cinema of attractions', with the 'ability to show something'

(1990: 56) as opposed to providing narrative absorption. In fact, when in 2007 Gunning and others, including Sobchack, were contributing to a collection (edited by Wanda Strauven) reflecting upon the 'cinema of attractions' and its now wide-ranging use beyond discussing the earliest of cinema, the book was titled *The Cinema of Attractions Reloaded*. Significantly, this played off the second film in the special effects-heavy *Matrix* series, entitled *The Matrix: Reloaded* (2003), and even featured an image from the film series on its cover. (It can be said that the *Matrix* films, which are analysed in some chapters of this collection, have cer-tainly emerged at the turn of the century as points of fascination within the study of digital effects and affect.)

Sadly, though, less has been written about digital imagery as a *subtle* manipu-lation of the cinematic image. This is surprising since one of the undeniable truths of digital imagery is that it influences filmic images in ways often not recognised by viewers as 'spectacle'. As Stephen Prince outlined in 2004, a newly digitalised landscape greatly influenced movies within their production and distribution in a variety of subtle and even less than subtle ways:

> Recognising that there are counter-trends, in what ways is this digital turn reconfig-uring the meaning and experience of cinema, altering its nature, at a deeper struc-tural level than the provision of special effects signifiers? In its first century of exis-tence, cinema was a photo-mechanical medium, its images arising from chemistry, darkroom and processing lab, fixed in analogue form on a celluloid surface, and then trucked around the country for exhibition. This paradigm is changing because of the influx of digital tools in all phases of film production: set design, cinematog-raphy, editing, sound, post-production, distribution and exhibition. (2004: 24)

Prince essentially suggests that the digital revolution has affected the image beyond what was seen in spectacle entertainment, which, in post-production, could involve the tweaking of colour to the smallest dubbing. Even though such observations suggest a major, far-reaching revolution in what we have long conceptualised as 'film', few outside of blockbuster filmmakers like George Lucas suggested that we were soon to experience a total transition to a widely-embraced 'digital cinema' (where every element of film would be digitally pro-duced). John Belton suggested in 2002 that there could never be a total transition since numerous (sometimes non-digital) technologies influenced film as well and could also change how we view cinema.

Despite this, the monumental impact of the digital revolution upon film as text and as culture is without debate. Consequently, its influence has now been noted by even the most basic of film studies texts – prompting two essays on the topic (Belton's among them) to be added to Leo Braudy and Marshall Cohen's *Film Theory and Criticism: Introductory Readings* in 2004, along with a chapter entitled 'Film and Changing Technologies' by Laura Kipnis in *The Oxford Guide to Film Studies* (see Hill & Church Gibson 1998). Thus, film studies has had to embrace this technological revolution – but, as we will see, the changes extend far beyond the filmic image itself. Surprisingly, it is within these digital frontiers that exist away from the multiplex that we see how the digital more overtly affects cinephilia as both a concept and a movement.

DVDs

As Keathley's preface to this collection points out, various periods of cinephilia are inseparable from the particular technologies of those periods. Present cinephilias remain no different. Yet, ironically (or perhaps appropriately) many have posited technology in the past as contributing to the end of a particular brand or period of cinephilia. For example, Bill Flavell, in his *Senses of Cinema* essay 'Cinephilia and/or Cinematic Specificity' (2000), explores the importance of 35mm projection to what he calls the 'golden age' of cinephilia – again, Paris during the 1950s. He posits a very nostalgic and historically specific form of cinephilia and argues that this cinephilia did not end, as some believe, with the advent of home video. Rather, he suggests that this period of cinephilia ended with the emergence of the less technologically advanced insertion of 16mm prints into the viewing process at the Cinémathèque Français, which resulted in a less 'cinematically-specific' form of the moviegoing and perception experience. Meanwhile, James Morrison writes about cinephilia in relation to the advent of home video technologies. In a 2005 essay for *Michigan Quarterly Review* entitled, 'After the Revolution: On the Fate of Cinephilia',[3] Morrison also begins by returning to the high French period of cinephilia in the mid-twentieth century. He defines 'cinephilia' as a social movement according to that particular period. He then posits a cinephilia that was to some extent predicated on that special, unique ability to experience a film within an exact period and time. This is because cinephilia was based on the idea of traveling to out-of-the-way theatres to see a movie that could not be seen anywhere else. Thus, video (VHS) permanently changed the nature of cinephilia because, Morrison suggests, this newfound ubiquity undermined the film's previous uniqueness in place and time as a theatrical experience. Both Morrison's and Flavell's respective work foregrounds the ways in which the particulars of technology have always been a part of the discussion of cinephilia and (for some) its perceived passing(s).

Beyond Robnik's work cited in the introduction, scholars have steadily explored home viewing technologies' influence on cinephilia, a phenomenon still regarded by some as an essentially big-screen experience. In 1991, Charles Shiro Tashiro offered one of the earliest examinations of how home viewing was changing the nature of cinephilia. Looking in particular at the old videodisc format (a larger and less efficient predecessor to the DVD) as the preferred technology for home exhibition, Tashiro argues that a new cinephilia – what he prefers to call 'videophilia' – entails the consumption of film in such a way as to fundamentally alter the text itself. The physical dimensions and ratios of film change (hence the need for widescreen 'letterboxing', even though it still does not match the theatrical experience); the ability to watch the film in the order one wishes, to skip or rewind, suddenly becomes a very real possibility. 'The discs' high-tech insouciance offers, despite their truckling to the capitalist realities', he writes, 'a revolutionary hope: the destruction of classical cinema' (1991: 16). This means, for him, the removal once and for all of both the technological and experiential parameters of traditional cinephilia – that is, being forced to watch in the manner in which the multiplexes force us to watch them. Tashiro's polemical account was counterbalanced by Uma Dinsmore-Tuli (2000), who referenced his work specifically as too abstract and empirically unsound. Rather, her research suggested that certain British cinephiles[4] still preferred to watch films from beginning to end without the interruptions to or fragmentations of the experience that Tashiro suggests. Dinsmore-Tuli's subjects, in fact, claimed to never skip around during a movie, or pause it and come back later. Rather, they only wished to watch a film in its entirety, in large part because of their investment in the narrative, and perhaps as a means to mimic the theatrical experience of the movies, which in itself would reinscribe the importance of older viewing methods in an age of new technological possibilities. There is an interesting tension here, one which must remain unexplored for the time being – while recent cinephiliac scholars (Willemen, Keathley, Sperb) have increasingly privileged the emergence of fragments, in excess of the narrative, as a significant part of the modern cinephile's experience, Dinsmore-Tuli's research insists that such disruption is an uncommon practice among at least some cinephiles.

More recently, reception theorist Barbara Klinger examined how technology has completely redefined the nature of the cinephile – although the scope here is largely confined to the DVD *collecting* habits of the modern cinephile, rather than the mode of cinematic experience for the film-lover. In her book, *Beyond the Multiplex: Cinema, New Technologies and the Home* (2006), Klinger discusses how crucial and intimate private collections of texts are for today's cinephile – value is placed on the size of the collection, its particulars and how they are organised. This immense treasure trove, meanwhile, reinforces the importance of the home as a primary site for viewing and reviewing. In addition, this too perpetuates a sense of 'cultural capital' (using Pierre Bourdieu's term) for the collectors themselves. The practice of collection, however, is not strictly the domain of the private viewer or cinephile. Klinger is careful to also point out that the practice of collecting is something actually catered to and constructed by the industries, who are very conscious of (and indeed explicitly help to perpetuate) the collector's desire for the films, through such devices as the latest DVD editions, the newest audio and picture qualities and the more interesting special features that accompany it. This later qualification returns to one of Klinger's larger claims – that the 'private' home sphere is not private at all. Media institutions and producers actively cultivate it. While earlier cinephile scholars have talked about home viewing in the wake of the movie theatre's immense shadow, Klinger appears to be one of the first to suggest that studios are very conscious of, and adaptable to, cinephile behaviour, while also foregrounding an important concept – a form of cinephilia in no way tied to going to the theatre. The emergence of Internet cinephilia, meanwhile, challenges this position even further (as Zach Campbell's piece, 'Floating Hats: A Mere Diversion?', will reinforce later in this collection).

INEXHAUSTIBLE GENEROSITY: CINEPHILIA AND THE BLOGS

Bloggers are the minutemen of the digital revolution.
– Henry Jenkins, 'Blog This!'[5]

While blogging certainly is not the only form of online activity, it does seem to be the one which grants individual users the most focused voice and agency. Even if one is reluctant to embrace Jenkins' characteristically bold and certainly overstated declaration, the point remains the same – blogs are an indispensable aspect of digital culture, and it would be impossible to imagine the past articulation of (cinematic) criticism without their presence. While the term continues to gain quite a bit of currency, media scholars have only begun to explore the importance of blogs in understanding the current state of how various film, television, music and new media texts are received and processed. 'Blog' is short for 'web log', a sort of online diary/journal where people can record their daily thoughts on any range of subjects and, importantly, link their sites up with other 'bloggers'. While it may be a temptation to think that bloggers are isolated from the world, ranting to an empty audience, in fact blogging communities – while shifting, contradictory and rhizomatic – are very necessary to the success of an individual blog. Although bloggers work outside traditional channels of information distribution, they are in a sense much more hyper-conscious of the immediate audiences for which they write, and often actively nurture. Blogs live and die not on the production of the author, but on the *mutual* cultivation and engagement of their readers.

Moreover, most have been even slower to foreground how blogs are their own site of meaning production, and not just a venue for responding to dominant media industries. So far, the most prominent media scholar to engage with the subject of blogs is Jenkins. His particular interest in this subject is to be expected, given that Jenkins' ground-breaking research, *Textual Poachers: Television Fans* and Participatory Culture (1992), rethought the question of agency ascribed to fans of television shows and movies – arguing that these particular audiences participated in the reception of media by actively appropriating, rearranging and even reconstructing content to alter readings, or to highlight meanings not explicit in the master text itself. Given this fascination, it is little wonder that Jenkins gravitated to blogging – both as a subject of inquiry and as his own intellectual outlet.[6] As the formation of this collection itself highlights, every scholar with an interest in blogging invariably *becomes* a blogger her/himself – and indeed such an evolution is necessary to write with any credibility about the subject.

Although *Convergence Culture: Where New and Old Media Collide* (2006d) emerged as Jenkins' most visible and well-received recent bit of scholarship, his most interesting work on blogs in particular exists in large measure elsewhere, such as *Fans, Bloggers and Gamers* (2006a) – though some of that research overlaps with his more famous work, and vice versa. In one chapter, 'Interactive Audiences? The "Collective Intelligence" of Media Fans', Jenkins writes that 'bloggers take knowledge into their own hands, enabling successful navigation within and between these emerging knowledge cultures' (2006b: 151). While Jenkins is aware that such behaviour can be quickly appropriated by corporations and various media producers for their own capitalist ends, he also embraces the potential which blogging presents fans and consumers to diversify their engage-ment with the texts in question. Jenkins is keenly aware of how much autho-rial power blogging can wield. In 'Blog This!' (2006c) – his initial thoughts on the subject, first published in early 2002 – he writes about the emergence of blogs and how they too can become active producers of meaning. Throughout this brief piece, Jenkins becomes increasingly meta-reflective, recognising that bloggers can and would reappropriate even his own discussion of the blogs. 'Once this column appears', Jenkins writes, 'my authorial control ends and theirs begins' (2006c: 180). This in turn explains the title, 'Blog This!', which could be interpreted as either a challenge to bloggers, or as permission from Jenkins to the blogging community. It is, in some sense, an ironic move from someone who had claimed to break down power hierarchies in the construction of knowledge. By instructing, or permitting, bloggers to 'blog this', Jenkins reinscribes his own position of authority – whether intentionally or not.

Although another of his books, *The Wow Climax: Tracing the Emotional Impact of Popular Culture* (2006e), focuses on the affective and emotional investments fans make in media texts, Jenkins has yet to discuss the topic of cinephilia. Perhaps, this is because his work has typically centred on television studies and not on film. Or, it may be because of the tensions which persist between the perceived democratic tendencies of 'fan cultures' (perpetuated by himself and followers such as Matt Hills (2002) and Jason Mittell (2004)) and the continuing presence of elitism in cinephilia. Or, it may just be because Jenkins hasn't yet thought of it. In any case, the blogs represent a central means for non-professional fans and cinephiles to express their passion for the texts which they so adore. For example, blogs can and will shift how cinephilia is defined – more so than the reverse – every bit as much as digital effects and home viewing have.

Few within academia have yet to fully acknowledge how blogging is fundamentally changing the nature of cinephilia, in ways nearly impossible to articulate here. As Julia Lesage (2007) has previously noted in what is perhaps the first scholarly discussion of online academic film communities, 'the film studies profession itself has been slow to embrace new media in practice, which will probably only come with the ascendance of younger Internet-generation academics in the field.' Of course, it needs to be emphasised again that blogging is not the only form of online cinephilia, even if it may be the most acute. Lesage herself is ultimately more interested in the practice of 'bookmarking', of programming a single page, such as 'del.icio.us', to keep track of the activity occurring on her personal favourite websites. Melis Behlil has previously noted that 'For cinephiles around the world, the Internet is the only place where one can find fellow film lovers' (2005: 121). Her article foregrounds the emergence of online forums or chatrooms as a means for film discussion on the Internet, while also relaying the story of the rise of one particular film blog – *Milk Plus* (http://www.milkplus. blogspot.com/). Interestingly, this blog seems to have come about as a response to the perceived mindlessness and immaturity displayed on many other Internet fan forums. According to Behlil, the site's founder, Albert Goins, started *Milk Plus* with the hope of 'cutting out the moronic trolls that plague the NYT [*New York Times*] Forum as well as the endless white noise chatter', with this new forum encouraging 'a more fruitful and efficient way for all of us to communicate' (2005: 118). Such a development (hinted at above) speaks to the continuing tensions between cinephiles and more broadly defined fan communities. Moreover, the materialisation of the blog as a response to the logistical and temperamental inadequacies of the Internet forums suggest that blogging may indeed remain the primary outlet for the cinephile for the foreseeable future.

More importantly for our purposes, no one has yet looked at what the cinephile bloggers themselves are saying. In some respects, others outside the university and similar research institutions (such as bloggers and *Senses of Cinema*, for example) have no doubt begun to define cinephilia instead of academics. Bloggers remind us that the critical study of cinephilia is crucial because the term has very real currency and effects among people who write and talk about film today, and yet many academic institutions believe it is at the very least irrelevant or (politically) destructive, if not entirely non-existent. Bear in mind again that this project began at the annual SCMS Conference, and thus it would be foolish not to confess to our own academic bias. That said, it is not our intention to define cinephilia as academic, or for academics, but rather to put academia's finger back onto the new digital pulses throbbing with cinephilia. As scholars, we are also cinephiles. As Lesage (2007) notes, 'Media studies academics keep blogs to a lesser degree than one might anticipate, although there is a wonderful community of film bloggers[7] who can best be called "lovers of cinema" and is composed largely of cinephiles, media makers and media teachers. This community regularly discuss [sic] each others' entries and often write on the same topic one day a month'. *Cinephilia in the Age of Digital Reproduction* is, first and foremost, a project by and for cinephiles, and it is past time to acknowledge the bloggers' significance in this community.

PRESENCE OF PLEASURE

The cinema is always as perfect as it can be.

– Gilles Deleuze, *Cinema 1: The Movement Image*[8]

We are proud that what you are about to read in this collection, and in subsequent volumes, encompasses a variety of types of cinephilic discourses – from the heavily theoretical to the emotionally personal to something in between. In designing a collection with such a variety, the goal was always – as much as our limited space affords – to pay proper respect to all approaches and to celebrate the uniqueness of each writer's voice. This is a commitment which we also hope will expand with future volumes. For the time being, for this first volume, we have divided the contributions into four conceptually ambitious takes on cinephilia as social movement, practice and theory. Starting with this introduction, we begin by considering the phenomenon's social position in 'Contexts' and then move into sensational areas of fascination for the cinephile: categorised here as 'Affects', 'Ontologies' and 'Bodies'.

Beginning with 'Contexts', the contributors contemplate cinephilia's current role in digital culture. In 'Beyond the Fragments of Cinephilia: Towards a Synthetic Analysis', Adrian Martin posits a synthesis of methods from the two broad tendencies in the field of film analysis (the classical tradition and the poststructural tradition) in order to acknowledge the rich complexity of the cinematic medium. Setting out the possible conditions for the fruitful encounter of these tendencies through analysing such films as David Cronenberg's *A History of Violence* (2005) and Jean-Luc Godard's *Vivre se vie* (1962), Martin eventually considers the promise of such a synthesis in our current moment of cinephilia. Next, we offer the personal correspondences between five of the Internet's most prolific film bloggers – Girish Shambu, Dan Sallitt, Andy Horbal, Brian Darr and Zach Campbell – in 'The Digital Cine-Club: Letters on Blogging, Cinephilia and the Internet'. This engaging and eclectic dialogue was commissioned specifically for the collection. Through this epistolary conversation, the authors dissect their positions as supposedly 'amateur' film writers and question how they fit into a larger history of cinephilia. Along the way, they also discuss the undeniable influences of the Internet's technological advancements upon their roles as creators of a new type of cinematic discourse.

In 'Affects' the contributors use personal cinephiliac responses to films as springboards to contemplate larger issues of pleasure. We begin with Jenna Ng's 'A Point of Light: Epiphanic Cinephilia in Mamoru Oshii's *Avalon* (2001)', which argues for a cinephilia that is revelatory in nature, yet appropriate precisely for Computer-Generated Imagery (CGI). This concept gives rise to a singular ruptured response that Ng terms *epiphanic cinephilia*, a sensation she applies to her own cinephiliac experience in viewing the above-named film. Next, the original blog post 'Floating Hats: A Mere Diversion?' is reproduced, where Zach Campbell contemplates the various taste-dictated connotations of downloadable video clips. In 'Sensing an Intellectual *Nemesis*', Jason Sperb dissects his own cinephiliac reaction to a pleasurable digital moment in *Star Trek: Nemesis* (2002). In doing so, he explores a new form of virtual pleasure for CGI that suggests a utopian cinema of possibilities – a new trajectory for cinephilia.

With the section 'Ontologies' the contributors analyse a variety of visual texts that challenge previous theorisations of the image. First, Tobey Crockett's 'The "*Camera* as Camera": How CGI Changes the World as We Know It' reconfigures what has historically been meant by 'camera' to examine how cinema has moved into CGI worlds where all space contains potential 'cameras' – points with their own perspectives. Crockett employs her cinephiliac responses to CGI-heavy films to contemplate pleasure within this '*camera* as camera' phenomenon. Next, Sperb explores how cinephilia can be based on images and ontologies yet to occur in '*Déjà Vu* for Something That Hasn't Happened Yet / Time, Repetition and *Jamais Vu* within a Cinephilia of Anticipation'. While still considering issues of affect, Sperb looks at the film *Final Destination 3* (2006), and then its DVD incarnation (which allows the viewer to change events as they occur in the film) to suggest how competing notions of repetition and difference open up spectatorship to a 'cinephilia of anticipation'. Next, Campbell's original blog posting 'Swimming' provides insights into the onscreen placement and perceptual functions of swimming pools in films such as *Pat's Birthday* (1962) and *The St. Valentine's Day Massacre* (1969), among others. Finally, in 'Customising Pleasure: "Super Mario Clouds" and the John Ford Sky', Robert Burgoyne examines reconceptions of preserved cinephilia within the art installation pieces 'The Five Year Drive-By' (1995) by Douglas Gordon and 'Super Mario Clouds' (2003) by Cory Arcangel. Through these two works, Burgoyne explores how the artists reformulate well-known films, video games and television broadcasts as a way of personally customising industrially-produced pleasures.

The book ends with the section 'Bodies', which takes the discussion into the realm of physicality and phenomenology – exploring the possibilities of 'embodied cinephilia'. In 'Cinephilia as Topophilia in *The Matrix* (1999)', Kevin Fisher examines a key moment of cinephilic fascination from *The Matrix* (Neo's awaking) and uses it to contemplate realist and psychoanalytic schools of film theory. Ultimately, Fisher transcends these readings to embrace a fuller 'embodied' assessment of the filmic experience based on the theories of Vivian Sobchack. Next, in the blog post '*Code Unknown*: An Auto-Dialogue', Girish Shambu *embodies* the possibilities of cinematic discourse by adopting the voices of two imaginary figures in a dialogue about Michael Haneke's *Code Unknown* (2000). Then in 'Andy Serkis as Actor, Body and Gorilla: Motion Capture and the Presence of Performance', Scott Balcerzak explores the technology of 'mo-cap' as it complicates our perceptions of acting as a process and as an onscreen construct. Reading Serkis's 'performance' in Peter Jackson's *King Kong* (2005), Balcerzak suggests that the actor can now exist within new conceptions of 'presence', moving the body fully into the realm of the spectral. The collection concludes with 'Gestures and Postures of Mastery: CGI and Contemporary Action Cinema's Expressive Tendencies', where Lisa Purse employs sequences from the *Matrix* trilogy and *X-Men: The Last Stand* (2006) to suggest new 'body forth' fantasies of physical achievement and mastery written across the cinematic hero's body. Through these examples, Purse asks how the embodied spectator engages with this 'expressive turn' in recent action cinema.

We have titled this introduction 'Presence of Pleasure', a concept meant to evoke the underlying philosophy of this collection. Since, from its conception, this project has been dedicated to the digital possibilities of cinephilia, we wish to stress that in some way pleasure is still present. It has not evaporated with the passing of Susan Sontag. It has not dissipated after the 'Langlois affair' or the symbolic (and temporary) closing of the Cinémathèque Français in 1968. It has not become unattainable with the ubiquity of laserdiscs, VHS tapes and now DVDs. Pleasure remains; it is not absent. And pleasure *presents* material to us – ideas, memories, challenges, possibilities, only beginning to be actualised. In short, cinephilia is a present, a gift, one which only asks in exchange our commitment to discursive excellence.

Finally, it should be stressed that the word 'digital' is used, ultimately, metaphorically. It does not represent any particular technological development as much as it is a figuration for the complex, even contradictory, potential that such developments promise. And with that potential, and with the continuing presence of pleasure, the discussions presented in the following pages are meant to be part of a fluid discussion. A second volume is currently in the works, which will offer ideas to clarify, solidify and/or challenge some of the thoughts put forward here. The cinephile is invited to reflect on these possibilities by visiting the blogs themselves – responding, writing and pushing the lines of flight further. The particular pleasure of cinephilia in our digital culture is that it continues to be as perfect as it can be.

NOTES

1 See Robnik (2005: 64, n.19).

2 See Cubitt (1999: 118).

3 This article is planned for republication in Volume 2 of *Cinephilia in the Age of Digital Reproduction*.

4 It is important to note here that it's unclear as to whether Dinsmore-Tuli's subjects, a small sample of British citizens, are indeed *cinephiles*, even though they make the assumption that they are. Because they collect and consume a significant number of films at home, she reasons that they are. However, several cinephiles have insisted that the active process of writing about cinema (as well as making films) is a crucial part of being a cinephile.

5 See Jenkins (2006c: 179).

6 See Jenkins' *Confessions of an Aca-Fan* at: http://www.henryjenkins.org. 'Aca-Fan' is shorthand for 'academic fan', and descends from Jenkins' early work on the difficulty of being both an objective scholar and subjective fan of the texts he explores.

7 As of December 2008, Lesage's detailed list of academic film blogs is located here: http://del.icio.us/jlesage/film_blogs. Accessed 2 November 2007.

8 See Deleuze (2005: xii).

REFERENCES

Andrew, Dudley (2000) 'The "Three Ages" of Cinema Studies and the Age to Come', *PMLA*, 115, 3, 341–51.

Behlil, Melis (2005) 'Ravenous Cinephiles: Cinephilia, Internet, and Online Film Communities', in Marijke de Valck and Malte Hagener (eds) *Cinephilia: Movies, Love and Memory*. Amsterdam: Amsterdam University Press, 111–23.

Belton, John (2004 [2002]) 'Digital Cinema: A False Revolution', in Leo Braudy and Marshall Cohen (eds) *Film Theory and Criticism: Introductory Readings*. Sixth edition. New York: Oxford University Press, 901–13.

Bordwell, David (1974) 'French Impressionist Cinema: Film Culture, Film Theory and Film Style', unpublished PhD Thesis, University of Iowa.

Braudy, Leo and Marshall Cohen (eds) (2004) *Film Theory and Criticism: Introductory Readings*. Sixth edition. New York: Oxford University Press.

Bukatman, Scott (1993) *Terminal Identity: The Virtual Subject in Postmodern Science Fiction*. Durham, NC: Duke University Press.

____ (2003) *Matter of Gravity: Special Effects and Supermen in the 20th Century*. Durham, NC: Duke University Press.

Cubitt, Sean (1998) *Digital Aesthetics*. London: Sage.

____ (1999) 'Phalke, Méliès, and Special Effects Today', *Wide Angle*, 21, 1, 115–30.

____ (2005) *The Cinema Effect*. Cambridge, MA: The MIT Press.

de Baecque, Antoine and Thierry Frémaux (1995) 'La Cinéphilie ou L'Invention d'Une Culture'. *Vingtiéme Siéle*, 46, 133–42.

Deleuze, Gilles (2005) *Cinema 1: The Movement Image*, trans. Hugh Tomlinson and Barbara Habberjam. London: Continuum International Publishing Group.

Dinsmore-Tuli, Uma (2000) 'The Pleasures of "Home Cinema", or Watching Movies on Telly: An Audience Study of Cinephiliac VCR Use', *Screen*, 41, 3, 315–27.

Elsaesser, Thomas (2005) 'Cinephilia or the Uses of Disenchantment', in Marijke de Valck and Malte Hagener (eds) *Cinephilia: Movies, Love and Memory*. Amsterdam: Amsterdam University Press, 27–43.

Erickson, Steve (1999) 'Permanent Ghosts: Cinephilia in the Age of the Internet and Video, Essay 1', *Senses of Cinema*. Online. Available at: http://www.sensesofcinema.com/contents/00/4/cine1.html. Accessed 6 June 2007.

Flavell, Bill (2000) 'Cinephilia and/or Cinematic Specificity', *Senses of Cinema*. Online. Available at: http://www.sensesofcinema.com/contents/00/7/cinephilia.html. Accessed 6 June 2007.

Gunning, Tom (1990 [1981]) 'The Cinema of Attractions: Early Film, Its Spectator and the Avant-Garde', in Thomas Elsaesser (ed.) *Early Cinema: Space, Frame, Narrative*. London: British Film Institute, 56–67.

Hill, John and Pamela Church Gibson (eds) (1998) *The Oxford Guide to Film Studies*. New York: Oxford University Press.

Hills, Matt (2002) *Fan Cultures*. New York: Routledge.

Jenkins, Henry (1992) *Textual Poachers: Television Fans and Participatory Culture*. New York: Routledge.

____ (2006a) *Fans, Bloggers, and Gamers: Exploring Participatory Culture*. New York: New York University Press.

____ (2006b [2002] 'Interactive Audiences? The "Collective Intelligence" of Media Fans', in *Fans, Bloggers, and Gamers*. New York: New York University Press, 134–51.

____ (2006c [2002]) 'Blog This!', in *Fans, Bloggers, and Gamers*. New York: New York University Press, 178–81.

____ (2006d) *Convergence Culture: Where New and Old Media Collide*. New York: New York University Press.

____ (2006e) *The Wow Climax: Tracing the Emotional Impact of Popular Culture*. New York: New York University Press.

Keathley, Christian (2006) *Cinephilia and History, or The Wind in the Trees*. Bloomington: Indiana University Press.

Kipnis, Laura (1998) 'Film and Changing Technologies', in John Hill and Pamela Church Gibson (eds) (1998) *The Oxford Guide to Film Studies*. New York: Oxford University Press, 595–604.

Klinger, Barbara (2006) *Beyond the Multiplex: Cinema, New Technologies, and the Home*. Berkeley: University of California Press.

Lesage, Julia (2007) 'The Internet Today, or I got involved in Social Bookmarking', *Jump Cut*,

49. Online. Available at: http://www.ejumpcut.org/currentissue/links.html. Accessed 2 November 2007.

Metz, Christian (1977) *The Imaginary Signifier: Psychoanalysis and the Cinema*, trans. Celia Britton, Annwyl Williams, Ben Brewster and Alfred Guzzetti. Bloomington: Indiana University Press.

Mittell, Jason (2004) *Genre and Television: From Cop Shows to Cartoons in American Culture*. New York: Routledge.

Morrison, James (2005) 'After the Revolution: On the Fate of Cinephilia', *Michigan Quarterly Review*, 44, 3, 393–413.

Prince, Stephen (2004) 'The Emergence of Filmic Artifacts', *Film Quarterly*, 57, 3, 24–33.

Robnik, Drehli (2005) 'Mass Memories and Movies: Cinephilia as Norm and Narrative in Blockbuster Culture', in Marijke de Valck and Malte Hagener (eds) *Cinephilia: Movies, Love and Memory*. Amsterdam: Amsterdam University Press, 55–64.

Rosenbaum, Jonathan, Adrian Martin, Kent Jones, Alexander Horwath, Nicole Brenez and Raymond Bellour (2003) 'Movie Mutations: Letters from (and to) Some Children of 1960', in Jonathan Rosenbaum and Adrian Martin (eds) *Movie Mutations: The Changing Face of World Cinephilia*. London: British Film Institute, 1–34.

Sobchack, Vivian (1998) *Screening Space: The American Science Fiction Film*. New Brunswick: Rutgers University Press.

____ (ed.) (2000) *Meta-Morphing: Visual Transformation and the Culture of Quick-Change*. Minneapolis: University of Minnesota Press.

Sontag, Susan (1996) 'The Decay of Cinema', *New York Times Magazine*, 25 February, 60–1.

Strauven, Wanda (ed.) (2007) *The Cinema of Attractions Reloaded*. Amsterdam: Amsterdam University Press.

Tashiro, Charles Shiro (1991) 'Videophilia: What Happens When You Wait for It on Video', *Film Quarterly*, 45, 1, 7–17.

Willemen, Paul (1994a [1982]) '*Photogénie* and Epstein', in *Looks and Frictions: Essays in Cultural Studies and Film Theory*. London: British Film Institute, 124–33.

____ (1994b) 'Through the Glass Darkly: Cinephilia Reconsidered', in *Looks and Frictions: Essays in Cultural Studies and Film Theory*. London: British Film Institute, 223–57.

Wollen, Peter (2001) 'An Alphabet of Cinema', *New Left Review*, 12, 115–34.

CHAPTER ONE
BEYOND THE FRAGMENTS OF CINEPHILIA: TOWARDS A SYNTHETIC ANALYSIS
Adrian Martin

Over two decades ago I remarked, in the course of an essay on the international history of cinephilia: 'There is an aspect of cinephilia which resides intractably within the pleasures of the privileged moment or sublime fragment. This is a phenomenon which I believe calls out for a higher level of discussion and theorisation' (1988: 127). At that time, such theorisation seemed stranded between two extremes. On the one hand, there was a relatively classical approach to film analysis, fed by literary methods – associated with then unfashionable but since re-evaluated critic/scholars of *Movie* and *Cineaction* magazines such as V. F. Perkins, Robin Wood and Andrew Britton – which stressed the coherent, organic action of *whole* texts, and called upon privileged moments (as writing or teaching, within their various time and space constraints, must inevitably do) as the best rhetorical way to condense or pinpoint the experience of the totality. On the other hand, we had what seemed to me in 1987

> a somewhat philistine, wilfully empty-headed tendency within cinephilia that aligns the camp enjoyment of privileged moments with an encyclopedic recitation of release dates, behind-the-scenes trivia, bit-players' names, and the like; similar in constitution to [Jean-André] Fieschi's bête noire of 'that cinephile's aberration of only seeing in a film that wonderful moment when Jack Elam crushes his cigarette butt into the left eye of a one-legged Apache chief while whistling the Marseillaise'. Ibid.[1]

Throughout the 1970s and 1980s, however, something rather more powerful than the camp gesture had been brewing within film studies. Much of the criticism and analysis influenced by poststructuralist methods such as semiotics took it as given – without really bothering to define why – that one must seize, break open, transgress, fragment a text, precisely in opposition to the organic/ classical approach (Stephen Heath's 1970s work in *Screen* is a classic example). But this *parti pris*, in its heyday, did not fly under the banner of cinephilia; quite the contrary, it usually explicitly or implicitly opposed itself to cinephilia – whether of the cultish kind that Fieschi targeted or the more sophisticated cinephilia of

Movie – which was all smeared with the tag of *fetishisation*. It was Christian Metz who, in a highly influential 1975 meditation, *The Imaginary Signifier: Psychoanalysis and the Cinema*, set this tone of abuse, although in his case it was a richly ambivalent diagnosis: the intellectual task, as he saw it, was to lay to rest the cinephile within, while recalling (without nostalgia) the kind of fascination one felt in that younger, more naïve state (see Metz 1986: 14–16).

Today, however, the study of film finds itself in a very different historical situation. The theorisation of the 'pleasures of the privileged moment or sublime fragment' which I called for has indeed arrived, with a vengeance – and this time as a revamped, positively valued cinephilia. In recent works, scholars including Leo Charney (1998), Greg Taylor (1999), Christian Keathley (2006), Rashna Wadia Richards (2006) and various contributors to the collection *Cinephilia: Movies, Love and Memory* (de Valck and Hagener 2005) seize on the aspect of cinephilia which is hooked into the magical moment or special fragment of a film – detachable lines, gestures, camera movements – and frequently linked to the kind of spectator *epiphany* or revelation that is associated with *involuntary memory*.[2] This is a very different notion of epiphany to the classical one which, for instance, Vladimir Nabokov gestured to in his 1950s classroom discussion of Marcel Proust's *In Search of Lost Time*:

> It is only at the last party, in the final volume of the whole work, that the narrator, by then an old man of fifty, received in rapid succession three shocks, three revelations (what present-day critics would call an *epiphany*) – the combined sensations of the present and recollections of the past – the uneven cobbles, the tingle of a spoon, the stiffness of a napkin. And for the first time he realises the *artistic importance* of this experience. (1982: 222; emphasis in original)

The artistic epiphany for Nabokov is not involuntary, but precisely *constructed* as a dramatic effect by the work. But once fragmented according to contemporary sensibility, cinema is yoked to the influential wave of cultural studies associated with the legacy of, among others, Walter Benjamin and Siegfried Kracauer (it was the latter who said of the former: 'knowledge arises out of ruins'; see 1995: 264). The experience of cinema becomes a matter of negotiating and combining pieces, ruins, sensorial memories of elements disconnected from the initial textual logic or system that contained them. The figure of the cinephile is almost mythologically inflated by being associated with, on the one hand, the Artist (creatively remembering and rewriting the fragments of culture) and, on the other hand, the supposedly ordinary, average spectator (whose experience of the cinema is quotidian and mundane, a sentimental thread in an entire social existence, not a technical or specialist engagement). Furthermore, this particular way of using cinema is given a persuasive, and until recently fairly overlooked, genealogy including Manny Farber, Parker Tyler (a pioneer of camp/queer film analysis), Jairo Ferreira (flamboyant champion of the Brazilian underground), and Susan Sontag in her occasional pronouncements on the state of the art of cinema and its discourse (hers is a *belles lettres* style of criticism, based more on passionate assertion about the surface mood or *gestalt* of a film, than on its close textual analysis).

Paul Willemen and Noel King, in a 1992 dialogue, were the first to crystallise some of the recently circulating ideas around cinephilia, bringing to it a number of scattered historical associations: surrealism, Jean Epstein's writings, and so on. King suggests:

> Across the apparent diversity of cinephilic practice one finds a regularity of critical description. There is *always* the fetishising of a particular moment, the isolating of a crystallisingly expressive detail. (In Willemen 1994: 227; emphasis added)

Willemen calls such details 'fleeting, evanescent moments' (1994: 232), and describes cinephilic viewing as the 'serialisation of moments of revelation' (1994: 233). Evoking the notion of excess, he argues that cinephilia involves:

> an aspect of cinema that is not strictly programmable in terms of aesthetic strategies. What is being looked for is a moment or, given that a moment is too unitary, a dimension of a moment which triggers for the viewer either the realisation or the illusion of a realisation that what is being seen is in excess of what is shown. (1994: 237)

Willemen approaches the point here of removing cinephilia altogether from the created object onscreen – beyond 'aesthetic strategies' – and locating it entirely within the subjective phantasms or illusions of the spectator. I would rather choose the route of taking certain striking phenomena endemic to spectatorship and cinephilia – such as that dimension of *affective excess* noted by Willemen, or the experience of epiphany – and converting them into aesthetic *questions* that beg to be unravelled.

Willemen's speculative account of cinephilia at least has the virtue (little practiced since 1992) of refusing to reduce 'love of cinema' to an unproblematic homily, and of using psychoanalysis (among other critical tools) to explore the murkier aspects of a concept that 'may well be ... a displacement, a smokescreen for something else' (1994: 226). All the same, Willemen's fighting predisposition against standard classical approaches (a polemical thrust of his work since the early-1970s), and his eagerness to consider the essence of cinema as its detachable fetish-fragments, powerfully fuel the assumptions underlying today's neo-cinephilia; virtually all contemporary discussions of cinephilia (at least in the English language) adopt and elaborate the terms sketched by Willemen and King. But one can begin discussion from several, quite different conceptualisations of cinephilia – something that will be implied in much of what follows.

There are many ways to discuss and contextualise cinephilia: as a cultural-political phenomenon, as a mode of psychic fantasy, as a literary genre, even as a lifestyle. In this essay, I choose to look at cinephilia within the broad history of debates within aesthetics – specifically, cinema aesthetics: how to critically evaluate, from an aesthetic standpoint, the contemporary penchant for a cinephilia based on privileged moments.

The level at which cinephilia and aesthetics (uneasily) meet can be pinpointed as the *relation of the part to the whole* – of the fragment (or ruin) to the totality (see Henderson 1980: 16–31). And this issue crystallises the differences between what I will call the two major *economies* of film analysis: the *classical* tradition and the *poststructural* tradition. Neither tradition constitutes a rigid, formalised school, and both develop in an uneven, international, frequently overlapping way. But the essential difference in method and sensibility is clear enough: where the classical tradition grows from *Movie*, *Positif* and *Cineaction* – and, more recently, reaches a summit in the work of Deborah Thomas (2001) or Andrew Klevan (2005) – the poststructural tradition (linked to broader developments in modernist and postmodernist culture) is associated with *Cahiers du cinéma* in the 1960s, *Screen* in the 1970s and 1980s, *Camera Obscura*, and many academic journals in the field – its most prevalent current form being a deconstructive philosophical investigation of cinema exemplified by Leo Bersani and Ulysse Dutoit's *Forms of Being* (2004).

My aim here is not to take sides with any one of these schools over any other. Rather, I seek (eventually) a *synthesis* of methods and insights from the two broad tendencies in the field of film analysis – in an effort to take the measure of the richness and complexity of the cinematic medium itself. However, laying out the history of these tendencies and setting out the possible conditions for their fruitful encounter will require a lengthy detour before we can return to the intriguing place of cinephilia in the current film culture scene.

Within the classical model of aesthetics, the part is usually posed as the microcosm of the whole (at least in fully achieved works) – giving rise to such useful precepts as 'the structure/logic of the entire film will be found mirrored in each of its parts'. Scene analysis within the classical tradition thus tries to fix on the richest part of a film, the part where the greatest number of motifs, stylistic devices, and so on, can be observed at their peak of artistic action. This also creates a problem for global analysis: to work through an entire film in this fashion risks unearthing a great deal of repetition in the analysis, thus revealing that the classical work, in its particular economy, rests on a large degree of *redundancy* (how often can one say, for instance, that within a single film the standard shot/

reverse-shot cutting opposes or unites the characters?). On the other hand, the poststructuralist sensibility, as we have seen, has no problem approaching the cinematic moment as precisely a fragment or a ruin; the genealogy of this sensibility runs from the testimonies of surrealist artists in the 1920s who would walk in and out of movies at will, grabbing random fragments, and – forty years later – Jean-Luc Godard, who would do the same, through to the ritualistic practices of DVD connoisseurs fetishising their favourite audiovisual chapter, and Godard weaving his epic video piece *Histoire(s) du cinéma* (1988–98) from small and large clips wrenched from their original filmic context and completely reworked or rewritten.

Although the description of exactly what classical cinema might once have been or is today is the subject of ongoing debate, there is no doubt that a classical aesthetics looks for and favours films that can be construed as organic, coherent, expressive, controlled art. (I make no distinction here between so-called art cinema and commercial/entertainment cinema.) And world cinema, it seems, has no shortage of films that can be profitably approached in this classical way, from the highly professionalised studio films made in America during the 1940s and 1950s, through to the lush, big-budget, costume drama productions made in mainland China since the 1980s (indeed, two adaptations of Stefan Zweig's novella *Letter from an Unknown Woman*, directed first by Max Ophüls in 1948 and then in China by Xu Jinglei in 2004, could serve as rhetorical markers of this tradition and its endurance).

What is an *economy* in aesthetic/textual terms? The stylistic elements of cinema can be uncontroversially listed: properties of image (*mise-en-scène* or staging, including the pictorial elements of camera framing and production design); properties of the soundtrack; acting performance; and editing. More difficult is to decide on the *economy* of these elements in relation to each other, as well as in relation to their narrative and thematic contexts, and in relation to their intended or actual *effect* on the cinema spectator.

A classical aesthetics of cinema rests upon a particular proposition (explicit or implicit) about the ideal economy or interrelationship between the various elements of filmic style – and, even more determiningly, the relation of style to subject or story.[3] In essence, according to classicism, style exists to *serve* the subject or story. This is an *expressive* economy: style expresses subject. As Roland Barthes once put it, where the classical artist proceeds from *signified* to *signifier* in order to find the best touch to convey an idea, feeling or situation – going from 'content to form, from idea to text, from passion to expression' (1974: 174) – the critic/analyst proceeds from the signifier back to the signified, tracking the intended or achieved meaning. (Barthes drolly added that this makes the artist a god, and the critic a priest deciphering the writing of the god.)

Crucial to this process within the classical system is each film's creation of its own fictional world, its particular reality (however stylised or surreal) which acts as a mirror (reassuring or critical) of our own. Dramatic illusion matters not so much for itself (it is not a matter of fooling or hypnotising the spectator into accepting a piece of trickery) as for – following the theory of Paul Ricoeur – the *mimetic metaphor* it can offer viewers.[4] The fictional world becomes a dramatisation and embodiment of a perspective (the perspective of the storyteller, however we wish to construe that narrative agent – as the individual auteur/director or something more collective or abstract) particular to each film. This *symbolic world* activates 'that possibility which is open to mimesis of constructing critical metaphorical models of reality' (Britton 1982: 99).

With a world in place, a story in train, and characters evolving, the classical film then gets down to its most intricate work – precisely, its moment-to-moment style. What does classical style serve? Above all, it expresses a *theme* or thematic structure. It is facile (although a widespread reflex) to reduce themes in film to banal proverbs, truisms or messages (like 'war is hell' or 'overcome your fear to become yourself'). But theme is what gives richness – and symbolic weight – to the basic building blocks of story, character and fictional world. I stress the *moment-to-moment* action of style in cinema because, just as a theme is not a mere statement, style (in the best classical cases) is not a mere coating (comprised of such strategies as a certain colour scheme, a moody score, fast editing and so forth), laid over the story. The style is what *articulates*, *modulates* and *develops* the thematic structure. And a theme – precisely as a living, mobile structure rather than an inert, reducible 'thing' or token – is more like a question (I think of it as the *semantic question*) than a statement; it is a structure which generates multi-layered contrasts, comparisons, ongoing considerations that get weighed up in the course of the film. Hence the centrality, within classical aesthetics, of the devices of *motif* and *rhyme* – those tropes which shape the articulation, modulation and development of a thematic structure; as well as, correspondingly, the elaboration of a method of *interpretation* that uncovers, collects, compares, contrasts and builds up these tropes into a gradual and finally overall reading.

The uncovering of thematic meaning in a film is sometimes mistaken (particularly by those either new or hostile to it) as a superficial trawling operation devoted to spotting *symbols*. Indeed, the notion that the classical film can be arbitrarily drilled into and that the selected elements are then affixed with meaning-tags is central to David Bordwell's disapproving account of the procedure of thematic reading in *Making Meaning* (1989). However, a brief sketch of the interpretation of a rich classical work can be offered.

David Cronenberg's *A History of Violence* (2005) shows that, instead of taking recourse to pasted-on symbolism to signal its theme, a classically-structured work more often cannily *systematises* into a meaningful pattern what are ordinary, everyday gestures and actions: walking, eating, driving and so forth; indeed, one way of gauging a director's skill and inventiveness is to see how they are able to illuminate such seemingly invisible items. This notion is central to Shigehiko Hasumi's remarkable body of critical analysis (see 2004; 2005); to V. F. Perkins' assumption that classical directors work within the verisimilitude of their given fictional worlds, rather than breaking it and imposing or heavily underlining significance (see 1972: 75–115); and to Alain Masson's assertion that the challenge for any inventive filmmaker (his example is Billy Wilder) is – via the twin processes of *motivation* (in the strict sense of creating narrative *motifs*) and *thematisation* – to bring 'renewal and change' to the 'familiar and the unoriginal' elements in that 'heavy residue of material existence' which constitutes 'the phenomenal world' (1992: 168).

A History of Violence could be described, in broad terms, as a dramatic investigation – a dramatic essay, in a sense – into *thresholds* in daily, social and domestic life, and their flimsiness: the thin line between civilisation and savagery, between law and order and criminality, between the present, clean masquerade that people maintain and their past sins, between an adopted identity and a repressed or discarded one. This way of stating the theme was not something I imposed on the film from the outset but which came to me gradually after I began to notice, during a first viewing, an unobtrusive detail which gently insists: the use of doorways within the staging of many key scenes (further viewings confirmed this pattern in the film). The doorway is, of course, a literal threshold, ubiquitous in daily life, and Cronenberg cleverly places it at the centre of every turning point of the film: it is within and around doorways that murders occur, that a wife mistakes her husband for a home-invader, that strangers enter the domestic space, and so forth.

Two inaugural structures of this extremely rigorous narrative film can also be mentioned here. The movie begins with what appears to be an allusion to, and condensation of, the first minutes of John Ford's classic western *The Searchers* (1955): two men exit the door of a cabin-like motel room, the camera tracking backwards to (as it were) draw them out (see Gibson 2005). At the end of a long take in which the men (two criminals) drive a short distance, talk and argue, one of them heads back into the motel's main office: here we find a similar trauma to that which drives *The Searchers*, a massacred family (in the case of Ford's film, a white settler family killed by native Americans).

This opening of *A History of Violence* inaugurates two types of narrative *folds*, to use a concept elaborated by Nicole Brenez in her book about filmmaker Abel Ferrara (see 2007). The first is a large-scale *anamorphosis*, whereby the final scene does not merely reiterate (in terms of motif) or answer the first in a neat rhyme but, in a deeper sense, *unfolds* its meaning in an ultimate, dramatic way: the two consecutive doors of a demolished domestic space in the opening scene correspond to the two consecutive doors at which the husband, Tom Stall (Viggo Mortensen), halts on his way to the family dinner table, where what is staged, with unsettling ambiguity, is the supposed reintegration or repair of the home, rather than its devastation at the hands of a violent, criminal male. (This exactly inverts the typical anamorphic fold which structures several films by Abel Ferrara, where the story leads us from a banal, domestic scene in which the husband/father heads off to work, to a final spectacle of total ruination.) The second type of fold accomplished at the start of *A History of Violence* is local, in that, via a strong transition-linkage, it establishes a meaningful alternation of, and comparison between, two narrative threads or worlds that seem, initially, unconnected: from the murder of a little girl at the motel we pass to the scream of another girl, in her bed, awaking from a nightmare.

This creates a thematic structure with several levels: not only are we being asked to superimpose the girls and begin a comparison of two worlds, but the hint that the first scene might have been a gruesome dream imagined within the domestic sphere sets up a central theme of identity disturbance in the story: as the anti-hero's gangster brother Richie Cusack (William Hurt) later asks him, when he dreams, is he his old self or his new self? Something characteristic of Cronenberg as an auteur, working in the tradition of Luis Buñuel's narrative films, can be noted here: the way in which, without overtly violating the rules or conventions of surface verisimilitude, he is able to insinuate the surrealist dimension of a dream world, in which aspects of the story come to represent unconscious phantasms and drives belonging to the social and cultural context as much as to individual characters.

Even in this sketch, the analysis of *A History of Violence* offers an example of a closed, finite reading – finite in the sense that it promises to capture all of the meaningful elements in the film and exhaustively interrelate them within a framework of artistic system, order and coherence. The degree of *openness* in a thematic structure has, however, long been a point of debate among critics. Those classically-minded critics who diligently follow the tracks of a film's unfolding see their task of interpretation as intuiting and explicating where the film takes us, and what balance of thematic propositions it ultimately leaves us with; Barthes noted (again drolly) that, in the classical narrative text, 'semic space' (i.e., thematic meaning) is 'always glued to hermeneutic space' (i.e., narrative unfolding), where 'the point is always to locate in the perspective of the classic text a profound or final truth (the profound is what is discovered *at the end*)' (1974: 171–2; emphasis in original). For classical critics, such effects of profundity would, by definition, constitute that aforementioned force of emotional epiphany afforded by the great movies (*Letter from an Unknown Woman*, in either of its versions, provides a canonical example in its final minutes – as does, indeed, *A History of Violence*) – precisely the effect in literature described above by Nabokov. Within this tradition, Perkins has suggested that 'interpretation is not an attempt to clarify what the picture has obscured' but rather an act of presenting and explicating what there is in the film 'for all to see, and to see the sense of ... a meaning presented is a meaning made overt within the chosen medium' (1990a: 4).

In the history of film criticism, the classical aesthetic finds one of its principal and most influential statements in Perkins' 1972 *Film as Film*, but it can be traced back to much earlier in the century, at least to Louis Delluc circa 1920. According to André S. Labarthe, it was Delluc who first differentiated, in order to then relate within a particular aesthetic economy, the subject of a film from its 'rendering'. And 'ever since Delluc, to evaluate a film is *always* to evaluate the performance of the actors, the quality of the dialogue, the beauty of the photography, the efficacy of the editing...' (1967: 66; my translation; emphasis in original).

The poststructuralist revolution overturned this economy of style to subject posited by classical aesthetics. Indeed, Jean-André Fieschi, an influential critic who was involved in both *Cahiers du cinéma* (writing perhaps the first Lacanian critiques of films) in the early 1960s and the burgeoning area of university-based semiological studies in the early 1970s, retrospectively heralded F. W. Murnau's *Nosferatu* (1922) – 'with this film the modern cinema was born' – with a decisive gesture of *economic rearrangement*: '*Nosferatu* marks the advent of a total cinema in which the plastic, rhythmic and narrative elements are no longer graded in importance, but in strict interdependence upon each other' (1980: 710; translation amended).

Poststructuralist thought, taking its cue from Barthes' 1971 essay, 'From Work to Text', made a division between a film as a *work* (meaning that it obeyed the precepts of classical aesthetics) and a film as a *text*:

> The Text can be approached, experienced in reaction to the sign. The work closes on a signified ... The generation of the perpetual signifier ... in the field of the text ... is realised not according to an organic process of maturation or a hermeneutic course of deepening investigation, but, rather, according to a serial movement of disconnections, overlappings, variations. The logic regulating the Text is not comprehensive ... but metonymic; the activity of associations, contiguities, carryings-over coincides with a liberation of symbolic energy ...; the work – in the best of cases – is *moderately* symbolic; the Text is *radically* symbolic: *a work conceived, perceived and received in its integrally symbolic nature is a text.* (1977: 158–9; emphasis in original)

Clearly, the sense which Barthes here gives to the term *symbolic* is very different to that which informs Ricoeur's notion of symbolic or metaphoric fictional worlds. Barthes does not pose classical meaning against avant-garde non-meaning (or meaninglessness), but rather puts the stress on what he considers the *contain-*

ment of meaning (and of the interpretative act) which is constitutive of the classical ethos. In classicism, meaning rides along the clear tracks laid down for it by the central elements of the fictional world: stable, three-dimensional characters, a coherent plot, and a systematically ordered thematic development. Classicists, of course, would not see this as something lamentable, or as an error of method; Perkins, for example, speaks of grasping the 'structure of understandings the film has built' (1990b: 59). In Barthes' vision of the Text, however, meanings proliferate, free-associating from the confines of the work and beyond it; he provided a model of such analysis – *textual analysis*, as it came to be known – in his celebrated *S/Z* (1974). Textual analysis offers a freer mode of interpretation than that elaborated by classical aesthetics.

Where the text is (in Barthes' terms) *polysemic*, the classical work offers a kind of policing of meaning or (to pick a less inflammatory metaphor) an orchestration of it. Where the film-work tries to present itself (as much as it possibly can) as a homogenous, seamless, unified artistic object, the film-text declares its inherently heterogeneous, polyphonic, splintered character (hence its proclivity for the fragment-ruin). Where classical work is contained and unostentatious, aiming to stay in control of its elements, the modern or postmodern work is exhibitionistic and performative, a work 'in pieces' that flaunts its shifts in texture, tone, mood, topic, direction, address, courting waywardness, unruliness and excess. Indeed, if classicism is the school of the expressive, one could even speak of poststructuralism as the school of the excessive.[5]

A striking comparison between two films was offered by Sam Rohdie in 2000: while Luchino Visconti's *Ossessione* (1943) displays a classical-realist 'way of filming' that is depressingly 'interpretative, closed, complete' (2000: 122), Roberto Rossellini's *India* (1959) offers 'reality' as 'not a thing or essence to be defined, but a relationship of levels, and of different types of reality, which come into conflict or open out to each other … It is the separation, the difference that is disrupting, even scandalous' (2000: 120). The aesthetic evaluation that accompanies this comparative description by Rohdie is quite clear: 'interpretative' is bad, 'scandalous' is good.

Let us sketch, as for *A History of Violence*, how a clearly excessive film calls forth an analysis in this same spirit. *Vivre sa vie* (1962) is, like many films by Jean-Luc Godard, a virtual manifesto of modernist anti-coherence – sometimes teasing in its elusiveness, sometimes outrageous in its provocations against viewers and critics alike. Even in this more seemingly minimalist and controlled film (which borrows its mood and look from an amalgam of canonical art-movie greats: Robert Bresson, Michelangelo Antonioni, Carl Dreyer, Roberto Rossellini), Godard holds true to the impulsiveness that has characterised much of his career: it is a *collage* (this was the favoured art-derived term used to describe his work in the 1960s) full of digressions, cameos, joke insertions, various blunt interventions on the director's part (such as violent jump-cut editing to match the firing of a machine gun) and, especially, quotations of all kinds (anecdotes and parables told, passages from books recited, films watched). Indeed, much of the plot seems like a pastiche of the B movies to which it is dedicated. The story sometimes stops dead for tableaux that function either as cool demonstrations (a documentary-like montage of the workaday life of a prostitute; a café discourse from language philosopher Brice Parain) or comedic turns (a crook incongruously launches into a stand-up routine, mimicking how a child blows up a balloon). *Vivre sa vie* is a paradoxical object: although explicitly divided into twelve tableaux and following a complex novelistic trail in its depiction of the decline and fall of a desperate woman, Nana Klein (Anna Karina), much of the film refuses to add up to anything conventionally satisfying or meaningful in terms of character, theme or fictional world. In fact, Perkins wrote a lengthy essay in which he tried, but failed, to get to grips with the film within his own classical critical system; he can only conclude the following (despite points of local interest and even the richness of isolated moments, moods, realised situations and ideas):

> In suggesting these interpretations, I am conscious of choosing the least unlikely connections rather than of elucidating meanings developed convincingly in the film's structure ... Perhaps the basic fault is Godard's unwillingness to allow the movie the *degree of anonymity* that a fully coherent work assumes ... the context is severely limiting. (1969: 39; emphasis added)

Aesthetic anonymity is, of course, the last thing on Godard's modernist mind. For a poststructuralist critic, one path into the analysis of *Vivre sa vie* would be through a detail of Godard's unique working process: he commissioned from composer Michel Legrand a theme and eleven variations – 'because that's the way the film is constructed', as Legrand recalls the director's brief (in Brown 1994: 189) – but, in the final edit and mix, characteristically opted to use only three constantly repeated fragments from one of the variations. The film as a whole can also be considered as a suite of truncated variations that are missing their dominant theme, the key or core from which they are derived. As Perkins discovered, it is hard to pinpoint what this film is centrally about, as it raises and drops so many subjects: prostitution (as sociological reality and social or existential metaphor), non-communication in the modern world, language and thought, existence and essence, the world as outward appearance or inner mental processes and so on. But what if we refuse the facile, once-fashionable recourse to declaring that the film is thus about everything that passed through Godard's mind during filming, or that it is a documentary/diary of Paris in 1962, while still wishing to analyse its modernism? A filmic collage, yes; but is there anything to be *made* of this collage, beyond the brute fact of its dazzling heterogeneity of textures, moods and elements?

Perkins inadvertently stumbled upon one of the central formal or stylistic principles underlying this collage when he mused that the film seems to offer 'a string of suggestions as to how one *might* film a conversation' (1969: 33; emphasis in original). Put differently and more pointedly, Godard's film explores *a question of how to represent* – not in completely universal or general terms (how to film the world? how to tell a story?), but in terms of specific items of representation that become, in a complex, non-literary sense, the subjects of the film. One can only sense what this film is addressing (or questioning) by looking and listening to it closely, moment by moment and shot by shot. Each new shot seems to ask, from the camera position of Godard, the enunciator: how am I to frame or *regard* (in the double sense of that word) what I am seeing before me? What position am I to take up in relation to it?

The film begins, during its credit sequence, with three views of Nana/Karina, almost completely in the dark: left profile, right profile, head-on. The shots evoke at least three social practices of image-making: police mug-shots of criminals (later, Nana will indeed be interrogated by cops); portraiture in art (Godard noted at the time that painterly tableaux are frequently portraits); and the test shots that are routinely made on a film set to test lights and make-up, as well as to try out key poses of the actors. All of these image-practices are forms of documentation or *description*: they seek to nail down the subject-as-object, and posit another subject, out of frame, who is attempting this task of circumscription. So there is already a multiple relation, three parallel (and not necessarily intersecting) tracks set up by the film: society tries to fix a woman in her place inside or outside the law; Godard tries to fix Karina (his wife at the time), his muse, on celluloid; the history of art and representation supply icons of Woman. In the subsequent, nominally more realistic scene, Nana is only ever viewed from the back (Godardian provocation), and speaks, in character, of her desire to become an actress. Immediately, this onscreen person is an intriguing, complex amalgam: at once an actor (Karina); a three-dimensional, psychological individual with needs and wants (Nana); and a figure that is unformed (Alain Masson notes that the film's first three portrait shots could imaginably be of three different people; see 1994: 18), hard to catch (the back view sunders her voice from her lips, the standard guarantee of a film character's reality), without clear identity, without selfhood or definition, except in the gazes of others (producers, clients, pimps, spectators, Godard the director). Swiftly in the course of the film, she also becomes a sign (of iconic, movie-made glamour and femininity), as well as a subject for metaphoric speculation, a kind of philosophical emblem: she is repeatedly aligned with one fable or another about the nature and fate of the human being, having or lacking a heart, a soul, free will...

Where a classical critic such as Perkins finds this all-over-the-place quality, this proliferation of levels on which the character signifies, to be a problem for coherence, the filmmaker Harun Farocki and theorist Kaja Silverman, in their book *Speaking About Godard*, celebrate this constant shifting and lack of definition as the very subject of the film: 'the film accommodates relationships between the most divergent of terms, since it does not predicate those relationships on the basis of identity' (1998: 6) – where identity does not mean personal identity, but rather the philosophic notion of exact likeness, being identical, *identicality*. In cinematic terms, they are referring to the non-alignment of Karina, Nana, the unformed female figure, the iconic image and so on: at no point do these various avatars of a character add up to a single, whole, unified creature, and hence Nana never becomes identical with herself. She is always in excess. An analysis of *Vivre sa vie*, then, would seek to retrace the action, movement and shifting contours of the question 'how to represent this woman?' as they unfold across the film.

So, after my contrasting accounts of *A History of Violence* and *Vivre sa vie*, we are faced – as has often been the case since the 1960s – with the yawning gap of a seeming incommensurability between classical and post-classical critical methods. What ground is there on which a synthesis can be attempted?

In relation to the specific field of cinema aesthetics there is indeed one crucial point, somewhat obscured by the polemical divides in the critical literature, at which classical and poststructural methods overlap. An indication of it can be found in Barthes' evocation, cited above, of 'the logic regulating the Text', and in Willemen's mention of 'a system or a logic' that can be found productively at work in the oeuvres of certain directors, such as Douglas Sirk (1994: 246). The attempt to describe the *logic* of a film cuts across the received division between strict narrative coherence (the organic ideal) on the one hand, and rampant textual heterogeneity (the fragment as king) on the other. One might say, in this light, that what classicism can teach poststructuralism is a sense of the productive ordering of filmic elements, while what poststructuralism can teach classicism is that the *range* of these elements needs to be expanded from what is normally included in the style/subject economy of illusionistic drama. A sufficiently expanded concept of textual logic promises to be a powerful bridge upon which to propose a synthetic analysis of film.

In this regard, one of the most important developments in the study of film since the mid-1990s, still little-known or practised beyond France, has been the rise of *figural analysis*. This exists in an intriguing relation to the various schools and methods already surveyed here. Although it pays close attention to narrative structure and motif (the fertile idea of the *fold* used above is drawn from the protocol of figural analysis), it has virtually no interest in three-dimensional character psychology, and eschews all conventional engagement with the inner motivations and implied feelings of fictional beings (and the moral judgement we are to make of them), the sort of engagement that structures most workaday movie journalism. Figural analysis shares with poststructuralism a strong, primal sense of the heterogeneity of any film, the materiality of its signifiers (which it refers to as the *plastic* dimension of cinema). Unlike classicism, it can accept a formalistic attitude – colour, rhythm, light and so on, can exist in the foreground of a work, especially as experimental cinema is such a dominant reference in its conception of cinema history – and, like poststructuralism, it places an essential importance on intimations or revelations of the underlying cinematic apparatus in all its physical, psychic and industrial dimensions. But figural analysis is rigorously committed to the discovery of a dynamic *system* or *logic* to all these elements.

The most novel element of the figural approach is its treatment of cinematic representations in general. Figural analysis treats all elements of plot, character and setting as secondhand or 'second degree' – as relating, in the first place, not to a direct, identifiable, corresponding reality outside the film (as in the classical theory of mimesis) but to other, previous instances of the same semiotic signs.[6] Laura Mulvey's analysis of *Imitation of Life* (1959), for example, heads in this direction in her treatment of the characters less as psychological individuals than archetypes or stereotypes of femininity (see 2006: 151–4). However, figurality goes much further in regards to the *work* that a film does (or can do) with those signs and their socio-cultural history, beyond simple parody or subversion (such as characterises much camp comedy) or even finger-pointing critique. *Figures*, in this conceptual framework, are precisely *constellations* or *ensembles* that cluster around elements of content and form over time; and each figure itself poses, explicitly or implicitly, a *question of how to represent* a certain referent, phenomenon, state, emotion, perception or idea. The process of questioning does not, of course, remain static. Each filmmaker has the possibility of radically renewing a historic figural question by rearranging its elements, inverting them, posing them in a new way, in a new relationship. This, for figural analysis, is where the politics of cinema, its capacity for intervention in belief, experience and social affect, is to be sought.

Vivre sa vie, as my discussion already indicated, gives itself readily to figural analysis (and, indeed, Godard has already been the subject of much work in this area),[7] because of its unfolding inquiry into woman-as-sign. But what of *A History of Violence* – can figural analysis tell us something more about this film not discernible or accessible through the classical interpretative route? Another level of the film indeed emerges under figural inspection, and it is precisely the level that bothered many otherwise admiring critics: so many elements of the film seem like generic quotes taken from movie lore – criminal heavies, happy family around the dinner table, the friendly small-town cop, the quaint main street with its modest businesses and so forth. In truth, the film is an extraordinary excavation of a certain iconography of Americana – from the evocation of John Ford's westerns right down to the echoes of Charles Ives in Howard Shore's sparsely used musical score – which it links to an entire social sensibility or ideology: the belief in second chances for the sovereign US individual, the possibility of start-ing over or being born again. And it is this very conversion – the possibility of it, the fervent belief in it, the implications of it – that the film poses, at the heart of its figural logic, as an agonising question.

Some figures may find their obvious repetitions in particular genres (for example, the figuration of power in gangster cinema) but, by positing the need for an expanded *history of forms* that crosses all genres and types of cinema, this method of analysis proceeds by often surprising connective leaps between apparently very dissimilar films. Any figural analysis of a given film has, almost by definition, to begin elsewhere, with another film, a prior instance of a pertinent ensemble of figurative elements. It is useful to summarise the argumentative structure of a brief piece of figural analysis: the discussion by Nicole Brenez (1997) (a pioneer in this field of analysis) of Michael Haneke's original version of *Funny Games* (1997 – the film has since been remade by Haneke in the US (2008)).[8] This analysis begins with a precursor, Elia Kazan's *The Visitors* (1971) – inspired by the same true-life incident from the Vietnam War that later served Brian De Palma in *Casualties of War* (1990) – in order to define a figural ensem-ble: isolated house within a wilderness, typical middle-class nuclear family unit (complete with pet dog), the sadistic menace brought into this setting by several thuggish strangers who may hold a secret that problematises reigning bourgeois complacency, and a 'prolonged death ritual'. There is a formal link between the two films: both play on the edge of the frame as the best site, in terms of a cinematic ethics, for the indirect (non-exploitative or anti-sensationalist) repre-sentation of obscenely violent acts, completely different to how they would be depicted in conventional cinematic or television action-dramas; and both seek to confront viewers, to the extent of compelling them to identify themselves, through every interpellative means inherent to the cinematic apparatus, with the naked face of evil. But, across these two films, everything else is different: 'Bar-barism, torture, truth – none of these signify the same thing in both films, and they evoke neither the same figurative economy nor the same conception of humanity' (Brenez 1997: 41). The 'conception of humanity' brings in a consid-eration (as often in figural analysis) of major politico-philosophical frameworks and their history: where, for Kazan, evil (allied with the human propensity for violence) is like a terrible curse that erupts within the everyday, for Haneke it is the veritable foundation of a society in which 'hatred nourishes all connections', thus reviving for our time Thomas Hobbes' pitiless vision of social relations as a constant, gladiatorial war.

On the level of figurative economy, *Funny Games* 'no longer offers a succes-sion of actions and reactions, strong and weak moments [as in Kazan], but forms of insistence and persistence, manifesting themselves best in simple plastic trajectories, such as those associated with the colour white, the white of the eggs and the toy games, which end up being concentrated, horribly, in the golf ball that rolls all the way up to the father, announcing the unremitting return of the torturers' (Brenez 1997: 42). This function of white is neither a textual excess for its own sake, nor a conventional motif in the service of an expressive narrative structure; rather it is a systematisation of an almost primal cinematic force (the bright light that alternates with darkness, in a ceaselessly flickering pulsation, in the *défilement* of any celluloid strip), and the 'forms of insistence and persistence' in which it is elaborated also have a drive-based, psychoanalytic energy. After all – and this is what the figural approach can teach poststructuralism – even explosions of excess can, within the philosophical framework first suggested by Georges Bataille (1985), have a decisive logic.

It is important to hold on to a sense of how films can *formalise* themselves – that is, insist, logically and systematically, on their own formal structures. This is something which I find lacking from the expressive school, and which I derive from those loosely labelled formalist approaches (of Noël Burch (1973), Fieschi (1980) and others) that slightly predate both the rise of poststructuralism and the more narrowly defined neoformalism practised by David Bordwell (2007) and Kristin Thompson (1988). The formalised side of a film can often be appreciated for its abstractness rather than its point-by-point relationship to either a thematic structure or a figural commentary. Yet, for all that, abstractness does not have to be thought of as free-floating, amorphous or overall in its effect. *Textures* (of and within the image, in conjunction with the sound design) partly or wholly disengaged from a plot structure, can enter into a parallel, autonomous aesthetic structure, as in Masson's account of the multiple, simultaneous paths along which narrative cinema proceeds (see 1994: 51–60). While, for Fred Camper (2006), 'there is an "abstract" level to the style of what are for me great films that goes beyond articulating, translating, or interpreting the story' – a highly logical system of relations tying together depictions of space, place, environment, human and animal figures, objects, sensations, moods, and so on. This could be thought of as a more rigorous extension of Farber's motion of termite art, that is, the subterranean aesthetic structures that work in and through a narrative; like Farber, Camper rates Raoul Walsh high in his pantheon as one who offers 'a great example of a style that is not really involved in articulating the narrative in a scene to scene way'.[9]

I return once more to *Vivre sa vie* as an example of how the factors of formalisation, human presence (considered without the entire ontological 'world viewed' baggage proposed by André Bazin (1978) or Stanley Cavell (1979)) and abstract texture work as dimensions that can enrich a film. That this film is stunningly formalised is evident from the first moments of the credit sequence already cited, where large patches of silence alternate with the precisely snipped and isolated phrases of Legrand's score, and these phrases are then mapped onto the three inaugural head-shots of Karina. Yet the unique brand of formal systematicity in Godard rests in the fact that, if he is systematic about anything, it is in breaking his own systems! (For example, what initially appear to be certain formal parameters of the film – no music or sound during the tableaux' chapter titles, tableaux that are perfectly self-contained in narrative terms – are blithely broken at some late point.) That is to say, Godard plays obsessively with what we might call a *combinatory* or *permutational* logic, one that can become absorbing for the spectator alert to this level of materiality in Godard's command of the filmic medium, but which does not correspond easily to the modulations of an expressive aesthetic. As his collaborator/assistant Suzanne Schiffman was in the best position to observe in the mid-1960s, Godard always began with a solid sense of a formal structure, even before it was filled with specific content:

> He says ahead of time: 'Sequence 1 will last two minutes; sequence 5 will last thirty seconds; and sequence 4 has to last three minutes; I don't know what will happen – people will talk, we'll see...'. He works out a sketch for the rhythm; he invents successive blocks of time. (In Cournot 1972: 46; translation amended)

Schiffman's account testifies to the capital role that *rhythm* plays in Godard's work – and the often purely formal pleasure that it can bring to spectators. Texture works in the same way. In *Vivre sa vie*, Godard deliberately chooses for his locations a string of bars and cafés that strongly resemble each other, so that, within this overall pattern of sameness, striking differences of design, brightness or shade can emerge – and so that the varied, successive experiments in *representing* such a social and architectural space (side or frontal angles, the amount of 'head room' in the placing of figures, the gradual or immediate revealing or mapping of the space and so o) can co-occupy the foreground of a scene alongside its nominal, conventional content.

As for human presence, it can scarcely be absent from a film in which the physical reality and nature of the lead actress is never subsumed into her fictional role, and in which – as is Godard's practice with many actors, central or peripheral – directing performers amounts to the process of arranging it 'so that the spectator might have the desire to watch them and be interested' (Godard in Blue 1968: 247). Yet there is much in *Vivre sa vie* that goes beyond what Gilberto Perez (1998: 345–52) wonderfully evokes as a 'song' of lyrical celebration centred on Karina. As Godard uses a semi-improvised or *impulsivist* process, drawing on whatever inspiration comes to hand in his quest for the 'definitive by chance' (Godard 1972: 185), a high degree of psycho-sexual melodrama enters into his depiction of Karina, a subterranean but intense thread of real-life intrigue in which – as Silverman has remarked in relation to the same director's *Weekend*

(1968) – 'Godard seems to be working through something personal here. What is interesting is that he consistently problematises what seems to obsess him most sexually' (in Silverman & Farocki 1998: 236). From a sociological or political viewpoint, *Vivre sa vie* offers the first illustration of what Godard would, in 1966, call 'one of his pet theories':

> in order to live in society in Paris today, on no matter what social level, one is forced
> to prostitute oneself in one way or another – or to put it another way, to live under
> conditions resembling those of prostitution. (1968: 278)

This keys us to what is, today, indeed a striking aspect of the film: from the first moment of seeing a bored Nana working in a record store (tableau number two), she is suffering 'conditions resembling those of prostitution' – and hence her slide into literally that profession seems like a natural or at least inevitable movement. But there is a buried detail, of a novelistic density unusual in Godard, noticed by few commentators, preceding even the shop scene. During a throwaway moment with Paul (André S. Labarthe) on the street, looking at photos of their children, Nana is stared at by a passerby: it is the character of Raoul the pimp (Saddy Rebbot) whom we will not properly meet until tableau six. In the way that Raoul later recalls this moment, it is clear that, in the gaze of a pimp, Nana is already marked as a whore – and suddenly, the opening portraits of Karina under the credits retrospectively take on a further signification: a whore is precisely somebody who (according to what we see in the highly stylised vignettes of daily prostitution in tableaux eight and ten) poses for and 'takes direction' from a client. But there is more to this branding of woman-as-prostitute: in the murkiest depths of the film, one can sense a disquieting misogyny that equates female neurosis with a constant need to be desired and flattered (exactly as Nana, with her dreams of being an actress, wishes to be admired as 'special'), and hence a willingness to be always open to offers from wealthy or influential men, eternally available. This is the unsettling significance that, after many viewings, comes to rest on the film's documentary-style glimpses of street life taken from a moving car: all women, in their everyday postures and gestures of waiting or pausing, suddenly look exactly like streetwalkers and hustlers, on the lookout for a trick.

Long after *Vivre sa vie* and his marital split from Karina, Godard mused on the intimate relationship between a male director and his female star, referring to himself, rather bitterly, as his wife's 'client' (1980: 67) – and, tellingly, not as her pimp! Even at the time, he made clear that he preyed on Karina's uncertainties about who her character was meant to be and how she was meant to play her, saying that 'an actor likes to feel he's in control of his character, even if it isn't true, and with me they rarely do' (1972: 180) – creating an aura of anxiety, and a vacillating sense of self, that work to the film's aesthetic advantage within the interpretive terms already proposed. Godard later claimed – as hard as this is to believe – that Karina thought the film made her look ugly and that it harmed her career in movies, hence sowing the first seeds of their 'rupture' (1980: 67). All this drama is far from being 'behind the scenes', as it mostly would be in a conventional film: it is woven, like an open secret, into the moment-by-moment unfolding of *Vivre sa vie*'s textures, figurations and attractions. Intriguingly, Barthélemy Amengual (the prolific French critic and scholar who died in 2005) concludes his brilliant book-length analysis of Godard's *Bande à part* (1964) with a biographical revelation ('true or false, it doesn't matter') which, he argues, casts all of the Godard/Karina films in a revealing light: the filmmaker is alleged to have literally bought his star (for four thousand francs!) from her previous lover (see Amengual 1993: 64). Amengual titles this conclusion: 'Le cinéma, la vie' ('cinema, life').

The heady conjunction of cinema and life: this brings us forcibly back to the issue of cinephilia today. In the current celebration of a neo-cinephilia, what I have identified as a central question of any aesthetics – the relation of the part to the whole – is brutally, summarily decided in massive favour of the part, without the question itself even being acknowledged or interrogated. The fragment becomes the essence and truth of cinema, while any regard (classical or otherwise) for the work as a totality (however conceived) goes to hell. I do not believe such semi-conscious bandwagon-jumping can do the cause of cinematic aesthetics much good – as Bob Dylan once sang, 'A change in the weather can be extreme/But it ain't like changing horses in midstream.'[10] However, cinephilia severed from rigorous aesthetic investigation – scarcely distinguishable from the fandom celebrated by a certain strain of cultural studies – seems to me a bloodless pursuit, easily co-opted by mainstream capitalist interests. Such a tendency is, indeed, already evident in the number and intensity of cinephile texts devoted solely to mainstream American blockbusters in the most formulaic genres.

A closely associated issue is the current, intense temptation to relate the neo-cinephile conception of cinema to the enormous developments in viewing technology and consumption patterns since the 1980s – especially via the rise of DVD and personal computers. Mulvey is explicit in linking the most novel aspects of the DVD viewing experience – selecting chapters, freezing and downloading the frame, exploring the film through the commentaries and informational options provided – with the resurgence of a kind of democratic-popular poststructural attitude. In terms deliberately reminiscent of *Screen*-speak of the 1970s, she writes:

> extra-diegetic elements have broken through the barrier that has traditionally protected the diegetic world of narrative film and its linear structure. Furthermore, as a DVD indexes a film into chapters, the heterogeneity of add-ons is taken a step

further by non-linear access to its story … new modes of spectatorship illuminate aspects of cinema that, like the still frame, have been hidden from view …
digital spectatorship also affects the internal pattern of narrative: sequences can
be easily skipped or repeated, overturning hierarchies of privilege, and setting up
unexpected links that displace the chain of meaning invested in cause and effect.
This kind of interactive spectatorship brings with it pleasures reminiscent of the
processes of textual analysis that open up understanding and unexpected emotion
while also attacking the text's original cohesion. (2006: 27–8)

Mulvey's own analyses give flesh to this dream, but one can doubt – as with much
rhetoric that accompanies the current period of digital technological advance-
ment – whether films, not to mention modes of viewing, experiencing and writing about them, are really changing all that rapidly, pervasively or profoundly. It is
too easy to mistake the virtual *possibilities* of a new technology (with the implications for a progressive political practice that Mulvey is all too ready to impute to
them) for an already-adopted, widespread reality.

The editorial of the first issue of *Monogram* magazine in 1971 – situated
strategically and cannily midway between the then-mounting quarrel between
the *Movie* and *Screen* camps in the UK – boldly stated: 'We are not persuaded
that a particular political commitment will necessarily dispose of, or resolve, certain fundamental aesthetic problems … concerning evaluation and meaning, we
will take a film on its own terms and respect its particular frame of reference'
(Elsaesser 1971: ii). In a similar spirit, I question whether the mere invocation of
that tremendous 'love of cinema' constitutive of cinephilia – and the merry will to
pull films apart, Barthes in one hand and a DVD remote in the other – can banish
these problems either. In this move, we risk selling short the complexity of films
as objects and as experiences, and of cinema as a multi-faceted, multi-layered
history and tradition – the history of its critical discourse included.

I end on something which has just come to hand: the 'coffee table' book
Defining Moments in Movies (retitled for the UK as *The Little Black Book: Movies*) edited by Chris Fujiwara (2007). Its format and concept is striking: on each
page, two brief (250-word) appreciations of what the author judges to be a significant or key moment in cinema history – a pure expression of contemporary
cinephilia. Normally, one could entirely predict the content and tone of such a
project: predominantly Hollywood classics and stars, with a few enshrined international art-house masterpieces and icons appended, and (for the 'broader view')
celebrations of this or that technological breakthrough. But *Defining Moments*
is an unlikely, almost impossible object: its superficial 'market niche' is contra-
dicted on virtually every page by the intellectual intensity of its texts, the status
of its contributors (including Paolo Cherchi Usai, Jonathan Rosenbaum, Bérénice
Reynaud and Miguel Marías), and the truly international span of its examples and

obsessions (Asian cinemas, the avant-garde, 'extreme' genres, for instance).[11] For me, the book is a happy sign of a truly synthetic future in film studies. As its title – conjuring both a state ('defining' as an adjective) and a process ('defining' as a verb) – indicates, it offers an open-ended and open-minded approach to the very notion of the *moment* in cinema. In fact, every imaginable approach to the filmic fragment is on show here: the moment as ruin; as epiphany; as classical condensation of the whole; as a purely subjective appropriation; as a political *move* within a specific cultural or historical field.

Among my favourite passages in *Defining Moments* is an appreciation, by the young Austrian cinephile/critic Christoph Huber, of the great 'turning point' in George Romero's *Land of the Dead* (2005): the moment when the fireworks in the sky, once effective as a means of distracting the horde of mindless zombies, no longer holds their attention – they lower their eyes after a few seconds and keep on marching towards the metropolis they hope to seize (see Huber 2007: 768).[12] It is, in the context of the film, a brilliantly conceived sign that the zombies have, in fact, evolved – and that they will constitute the basis of a new civilisation. On a quite different and more modest allegorical level, I also take the scene as a metaphor for cinephilia – or, at least, the type of contemporary cinephilia I am willing to embrace: able to blissfully immerse itself in the seductions of the spectacle, but equally able to snap to attention when the cultural war is raging all around.

NOTES

1   Fieschi's statement is from Jean-Louis Comolli, Jean-André Fieschi, Gérard Guégan, Michel Mardore, Claude Ollier and André Téchiné (1986: 203).

2   Two significant discussions of the work of involuntary memory in cinema are Lesley Stern (1995) and Felicity Collins & Therese Davis (2004).

3   An earlier formulation of some of these ideas appears in Martin (1992).

4   See Andrew Britton (1982). Britton makes use of Paul Ricoeur (1977).

5   On the notion of cinematic excess, see Kristin Thompson (1981: 287–302).

6   See, for the best introduction in English to figural analysis, William D. Routt (2000).

7   See Jacques Aumont (2000: 97–112); Nicole Brenez (1998: 339–60).

8   This is a German version; I am translating from the author's original French manuscript.

9   These quotes are taken from postings by Fred Camper (2006) to Yahoo group *A Film By*.

10 Bob Dylan (1975) 'You're a Big Girl Now', *Blood on the Tracks* (Sony Records).

11 Necessary disclosure: I am the author of 38 entries in the book.

12 For more on this scene and the film as a whole, see Martin (2007: 28–32).

REFERENCES

Amengual, Barthélemy (1993) *Bande à part*. Crisnée: Editions Yellow Now.

Aumont, Jacques (2000) 'Mortal Beauty', in Michael Temple & James S. Williams (eds) *The Cinema Alone: Essays on the Work of Jean-Luc Godard 1985–2000*. Amsterdam: Amsterdam University Press, 97–112.

Barthes, Roland (1974) *S/Z*. New York: Hill and Wang.

____ (1977) 'From Work to Text', trans. S. Heath, in *Image-Music-Text*. London: Fontana, 155–64.

Bataille, Georges (1985) *Visions of Excess: Selected Writings 1927–1939*. Minneapolis: University of Minnesota Press.

Bazin, André (1967) *What is Cinema?* Volume 1, trans. Hugh Gray. Berkeley: University of California Press.

Bersani, Leo and Ulysse Dutoit (2004) *Forms of Being: Cinema, Aesthetics, Subjectivity*. London: British Film Institute.

Blue, James (1968) 'Excerpt from an Interview with Richard Grenier and Jean-Luc Godard', in Toby Mussman (ed.) *Jean-Luc Godard*. New York: E. P. Dutton, 245–53.

Bordwell, David (1989) *Making Meaning: Inference and Rhetoric in the Interpretation of Cinema*. Cambridge, MA: Harvard University Press.

____ (2007) *Poetics of Cinema*. London: Routledge.

Brenez, Nicole (1997) 'Replay', *Meteor*, 11, 40–3.

____ (1998) *De la figure en général et du corps en particulier. L'invention figurative au cinéma*. Bruxelles: De Boeck.

____ (2007) *Abel Ferrara*. Illinois: Illinois University Press.

Britton, Andrew (1982) 'Metaphor and Mimesis: *Madame de …*', *Movie*, 29/30, 90–107.

Brown, Royal S. (1994) *Overtones and Undertones: Reading Film Music*. Berkeley: University of California Press.

Burch, Noël (1973) *Theory of Film Practice*. London: Secker and Warburg.

Camper, Fred (2006) *A Film By*, 28 February 2006. Online. Available at: www.groups.yahoo.com. Accessed 28 February 2006.

Cavell, Stanley (1979) *The World Viewed, Enlarged Edition: Reflections on the Ontology of Film*. Cambridge: Harvard University Press.

Charney, Leo (1998) *Empty Moments: Cinema, Modernity, and Drift*. Durham, NC: Duke University Press.

Collins, Felicity and Therese Davis (2004) *Australian Cinema After Mabo*. Cambridge: Cambridge University Press.

Comolli, Jean-Louis, Jean-André Fieschi, Gérard Guégan, Michel Mardore, Claude Ollier and André Téchiné (1986) 'Twenty Years On: A Discussion about American Cinema and the *politique des auteurs*', in Jim Hillier (ed.) *Cahiers du cinéma 1960–1968: New Wave, New Cinema, Re-Evaluating Hollywood*. Harvard: Harvard University Press, 196–209.

Cournot, Michel (1972) 'A Leap into Emptiness: Interview with Suzanne Schiffman, Continuity Girl for *Alphaville*', in Royal S. Brown (ed.) *Focus on Godard*. New Jersey: Prentice-Hall, 46–9.

de Valck, Marijke and Malte Hagener (eds) (2005) *Cinephilia: Movies, Love and Memory*. Amsterdam: Amsterdam University Press.

Elsaesser, Thomas (1971) 'Editorial', *Monogram*, 1, April, i–iii.

Farber, Manny (1998) *Negative Space*. New York: Da Capo.

Silverman, Kaja and Harun Farocki (1998) *Speaking about Godard*. New York and London: New York University Press.

Ferreira, Jairo (1985) 'Brazil – Post Cinema Novo', Special Issue of *Framework*.

Fieschi, Jean-André (1980) 'F.W. Murnau', in Richard Roud (ed.) *Cinema: A Critical Dictionary*. London: Secker & Warburg, 704–20.

Gibson, Ross (2005) '*The Searchers* – Dismantled', *Rouge*, 7. Online. Available at: www.rouge.com.au. Accessed 20 February 2008.

Godard, Jean-Luc (1968) 'One or Two Things', in Toby Mussman (ed.) *Jean-Luc Godard*. New York: E. P. Dutton, 274–83.

____ (1972) *Godard on Godard*, trans. T. Milne. London: Secker & Warburg.

____ (1980) *Introduction à une véritable histoire du cinéma*. Paris: Albatros.

Hasumi, Shigehiko (2004) 'Ozu's Angry Women', *Rouge*, 4. Online. Available at: http://rouge.com.au/4/ozu_women.html. Accessed 20 February 2008.

____ (2005) 'John Ford, or the Eloquence of Gesture', *Rouge*, 7. Online. Available at: http://rouge.com.au/7/ford.html. Accessed 20 February 2008.

Henderson, Brian (1980) *A Critique of Film Theory*. New York: E. P. Dutton.

Huber, Christoph (2007) 'Key Scene: The Fireworks No Longer Work', in Chris Fujiwara (ed.) *Defining Moments in Movies*. New York: Cassell, 768.

Keathley, Christian (2005) *Cinephilia and History, or The Wind in the Trees*. Bloomington: Indiana University Press.

Klevan, Andrew (2005) *Film Performance: From Achievement to Appreciation*. London: Wallflower Press.

Kracauer, Siegfried (1995 [1928]) 'On the Writings of Walter Benjamin', *The Mass Ornament: Weimar Essays*. Harvard: Harvard University Press, 259–64.

Labarthe, André S. (1967) 'Mort d'un mot', *Cahiers du cinéma*, 195, 66.

Martin, Adrian (1988) 'No Flowers for the Cinephile: The Fates of Cultural Populism 1960–1988', in Paul Foss (ed.) *Island in the Stream: Myths of Place in Australian Culture*. Sydney: Pluto Press, 117–38, 221–25.

____ (1992) '*Mise en scène* is Dead: The Expressive, the Excessive, the Technical and the Stylish', *Continuum*, 5, 2, 87–140.

____ (2007) 'The Turning Point', *Ray*, June, 28–32.

Masson, Alain (1992) 'A Sequence from *Avanti!*', *Continuum*, 5, 2, 167–78.

____ (1994) *Le Récit au cinéma*. Paris: Cahiers du cinéma.

Metz, Christian (1986) *The Imaginary Signifier: Psychoanalysis and the Cinema*. Bloomington: Indiana University Press.

Mulvey, Laura (2006) *Death 24x a Second*. London: Reaktion.

Nabokov, Vladimir (1982) 'The Walk By *Swann's Way* (1913)', *Lectures on Literature*. San
Diego: Harcourt, 205–49.

Perez, Gilberto (1998) 'The Signifiers of Tenderness', *The Material Ghost: Films and Their
Medium*. Baltimore: Johns Hopkins University Press, 336–66.

Perkins, V. F. (1969) '*Vivre sa vie*', in Ian Cameron (ed.) *The Films of Jean-Luc Godard*.
Revised edition. London: Studio Vista, 32–9.

____ (1972) *Film as Film: Understanding and Judging Movies*. London: Penguin.

____ (1990a) 'Must We Say What They Mean? Film Criticism and Interpretation', *Movie*,
34/35, 1–6.

____ (1990b) 'Film Authorship: The Premature Burial', *CineAction!*, 21/22, 57–64.

Richards, Rashna Wadia (2006) 'Re-Viewing Cinephilia: The Movement and the Moment',
Politics and Culture, 1. Online. Available at: http://aspen.conncoll.edu/politicsandcul-
ture. Accessed 20 February 2008.

Ricoeur, Paul (1977) *The Rule of Metaphor*. Toronto: University of Toronto Press.

Rohdie, Sam (2000) '*India*', in David Forgacs, Sarah Lutton and Geoffrey Nowell-Smith (eds)
Roberto Rossellini: Magician of the Real. London: British Film Institute, 122, 112–25.

Routt, William D. (2000) 'For Criticism', *Screening the Past*, 9, March. Online. Available
at: http://www.latrobe.edu.au/screeningthepast/shorts/reviews/rev0300/wr1br9a.htm.
Accessed 20 February 2008.

Sontag, Susan (1970) *Against Interpretation and Other Essays*. New York: Dell.

Stern, Lesley (1995) *The Scorsese Connection*. London: British Film Institute.

Taylor, Greg (1999) *Artists in the Audience: Cults, Camp, and American Film Criticism*. New
Jersey: Princeton University Press.

Thomas, Deborah (2001) *Reading Hollywood: Spaces and Meanings in American Film*. London: Wallflower Press.

Thompson, Kristin (1981) *Eisenstein's Ivan the Terrible: A Neoformalist Analysis*. New Jersey: Princeton University Press.

____ (1988) *Breaking the Glass Armor: Neoformalist Film Analysis*. Princeton: Princeton
University Press.

Tyler, Parker (1971) *Magic and Myth of the Movies*. London: Secker & Warburg.

Willemen, Paul (1994) 'Through the Glass Darkly: Cinephilia Reconsidered', in *Looks and
Frictions: Essays in Cultural Studies and Film Theory*. London: British Film Institute,
223–57.

CHAPTER TWO

THE DIGITAL CINE-CLUB: LETTERS ON BLOGGING, CINEPHILIA AND THE INTERNET

Girish Shambu, Zach Campbell (eds),
with Brian Darr, Dan Sallitt, Andy Horbal

The online proliferation of film- and media-related blogs has introduced to screen studies yet another self-reflexive form: blogs can be studied as objects unto them-selves, or they can choose any number of objects in which to join the discourse. The following letters were written in the spirit of conversational self-appraisal. Five film bloggers engage here on topics concerning the Internet, writing and cinephilia. The epistolary format facilitates and echoes the loose, interpersonal practice of blogging.

Buffalo. 9 July 2007

Dear Zach, Brian, Andy and Dan,

I think it's safe to say that there are at least two things we have in common: (1) we regard each other as cinephile-blogger comrades; and (2) we have all found inspiration in the *Movie Mutations* letters (Rosenbaum and Martin 2003).[1] So, I write these words to you to put in motion a conversation among us. I'm eager to hear your thoughts on cinephilia, the Internet and cinephile blogging practices. In this letter, I thought I'd try to open up some potential spaces for our exchange and invite you to either step into one or more of them, expand them, or create new ones entirely. Before I do that, perhaps I should begin by speaking a bit about my own personal cinephilia and its history, and how it might colour and inflect my perspective on these matters.

As someone who feels passionately about film culture and film thought, I nevertheless consider myself a cinema *amateur*. I'm a chemical engineer by education; my PhD is in manufacturing systems, and I'm an academic whose field is quantitative analysis. When I was growing up, my parents noticed that math and science came relatively easily to me, and they guided me strongly to a career in keeping with my aptitudes. But from those teenage years in Calcutta, my most exciting experiences and memories feature neither math nor science but instead powerful formative encounters I had with art and culture: cinema (Guru Dutt, Mrinal Sen, Hitchcock); music (R. D. Burman, the Beatles); and literature (Tagore, Nabokov).

In college, I was put through a rigorous technical curriculum that included not one course in the humanities. If this was some sort of conspiracy to exorcise my love for the arts, it didn't work; in fact, it had the opposite effect. I found myself setting a parallel course of self-education. Every new film, album, book or essay that stimulated me or taught me something, anything, became a precious discovery, a fruit of hard autodidactic work. I became a hungry, driven amateur with a lifelong appetite and love for the arts, especially cinema. Art and culture, this amateur came to believe, didn't just belong to a few professionals and experts (artists, scholars, critics): its doors were open, equally, to everyone.

Now, let me turn to the history of cinephilia for a moment. *Movie Mutations* makes a distinction between an older cinephilia and a cinephilia of the present. The 'first-generation cinephilia', as Thomas Elsaesser calls it in *Cinephilia: Movies, Love and Memory* (2005: 36), was formed in the crucible of the French scene in the 1950s that included *Cahiers du cinéma* and the soon-to-be *nouvelle vague* filmmakers. Its impact was felt in America in the 1960s. At that time, film culture (large numbers of cinephiles, access to a wide variety of films, home base for film journals and magazines) was generally concentrated in a few big cities worldwide (New York, Paris, London, etc). What's more, writing about cinema was produced by a relatively small number of 'professionals' who were 'sanctioned experts', working either in the journalistic sphere or, less commonly, in academia. This made for a small number of (active) writers and a large number of (passive) readers.

The present-generation, 'mutated' cinephilia belongs to the age of the Internet and DVD, both of which have impacted film culture by breaking up its geographic concentration and dispersing it. Both access to films and the production of writing about film are no longer confined to a few centres. But even within the era of the Internet, we can identify two distinct periods. Until a few years ago, in the age of Web 1.0, a good deal of the writing on film occurred largely on websites that were relatively static and only occasionally updated. With some exceptions, Web 1.0 still reflected the reader/writer relationship and proportions that were found in earlier film culture.

But Web 2.0 technologies of the present day (blogging, YouTube and so forth) have radically reconfigured those relationships. User-generated content and extensive, real-time social networking have allowed a large number of erstwhile readers to now become (for better or for worse) active content-producers rather than remain passive content-consumers. Technology has rendered easy the formation of communities, and the activities of collaboration and sharing.

Suddenly, we've been presented with opportunities to help create a new kind of film culture. I'm curious to hear from you: what might be, in your mind, some characteristics of such a film culture?

Let me offer a couple of thoughts. In the aftermath of May '68, the Project 16 group (which included figures like Resnais, Rivette, Comolli and so on) proposed reforms in the film production, dissemination and (importantly) reception systems in France. Sylvia Harvey writes:

> A living film culture could not grow simply out of the watching of movies, rather it would grow out of the relationship between the act of watching and a critical awareness of the techniques of the cinema [which will] make possible a more active role for the spectator: the role of challenging, analyzing and criticising the spectacle, not simply consuming it. (1978: 24)

My own conviction is that we need a film culture driven by constant, churning *critical thought* about cinema, fed not just by models of journalistic writing (as it is in the film blogosphere today) but also by ideas and tools from academic writing about film. Most film bloggers are not specialised professionals in the fields of cinema studies or filmmaking; and they don't blog for economic reasons. This has an advantage. Their amateur status allows them freedom to roam and the opportunity to operate in certain 'gaps' or 'in-between spaces', in a way that is influenced and informed by multiple modes of writing and thought. Unconstrained by the demands of specialisation in a particular discipline, they can become border-crossers (Serge Daney's *passeurs*), moving between disparate areas both within cinema and across the arts, letting their viewing, reading and conversing flow into communal streams and cross-streams of thought in a daily, ongoing, process-oriented fashion.

All this, of course, threatens to unleash a dilettantism run wild. So, as readers, how do we manage this deluge of words and thought, of great variability in quality, which inundates our already-busy reading lives? One tool, RSS software, can help lighten our load. (It notifies the reader of any blogs that have been updated, making it unnecessary to repeatedly check to see if a new post has appeared at any blog.) I subscribe to about 125 film blogs. This sounds like a lot, but all told, I spend less than an hour each day in the film blogosphere, reading new posts and commenting on them. RSS makes such efficiencies possible.

Finally, I believe we need an outward-looking, communally aware, *generous* cinephilia on the Internet. By this, I don't mean an undiscriminating boosterism but instead a collective vigilance that seeks out quality film thought, highlights it (by means of spreading the word through linking), and actively encourages these writers to continue and deepen their work. The entry and exit barriers to the blogosphere are famously low; it takes ten minutes (and costs nothing) to set up a fully-functioning blog. Since film blogging is often a labor of love, commenting on a good post and linking to it can often provide positive reinforcement for a writer that can make all the difference between life and death for a blog. And even if good blogs die (and many of them do), their work doesn't die with them; it stays in the blog archives as part of the Wayback Machine that is the Internet. Future work can continue to build upon it.

Before I close, I think it's critical to note that the five cinephile bloggers who are part of this letter exchange are notable in many ways for their *lack* of diversity. We are all American, male, ranging in age from the early twenties to early fifties; we all write in English. We cannot claim to be a representative demographic sampling of film blogging on the web. In addition, the hegemony of American cinema and culture that one finds worldwide will no doubt also unconsciously emerge from this group, its concerns and its discourse. It is important to keep this in mind.

I have spent this letter dreaming a bit, living in a utopia not yet here but one that seems (at least in my fantasy) visible on the horizon, as visible, anyway, as a mirage. Perhaps, dear friends, you will help reconcile the dream to reality in your letters, and also continue the dreaming.

In comradeship, and affectionately,

Girish
http://www.girishshambu.com/blog

Pittsburgh. 19 July 2007

Dear 'cinephile-blogger comrades',

Girish tantalisingly suggests in his letter that this exchange of ideas is an 'opportunity to help create a new kind of film culture'. While it is tempting to imagine us as participants in a cinephiliac Congress of Vienna, though, this isn't a conversation that I feel equipped to have. I am fairly young (25) and, like Girish, I am (adamantly) a cinema amateur; I left college with a degree in film studies and plans to study that discipline in graduate school, but then I got a job at my alma mater's library and now, three years later, I'm working on a Masters in Library and Information Science so that I can become a professional librarian. Because I'm young, I lack experience with life and with the cinema; because I have a full-time job and go to school half-time, I have a finite amount of time available to gain that experience.

My guiding light as a blogger, cinephile and critic, therefore, is a question that I ask myself constantly: 'What can I do in the meantime?' In order to write the context-rich, historically engaged criticism that I aspire to, I first need to do a lot of reading and watch a lot of films; but what can I do in the meantime? In order to properly consider the question of what a new film culture should look like, I first need to learn a lot more about the kinds of film culture that existed in the past; but what can I talk about right now in this letter?

My answer to the question of what to write about when 'good' film criticism (by my own, admittedly severe, standards) is out of my reach has been to focus on the subjective experience of watching movies and of being a film lover. It's as essential to talk about movies as it is to watch them, and this approach allows me to kill that bird and a few more (I'm learning how to write, I'm producing something that is at least original, I'm 'keeping in touch' with my Internet film friends) with one stone while I direct the bulk of my energies to my grand project of cinephile self-improvement. Similarly, I'll spend the rest of this letter talking about what inspires me and worries me about our corner of the Internet cinephile universe (it should be pointed out that we all belong to more or less the same online 'set') and what I hope to see more of in the future. Perhaps if we revisit this project in five years I'll have something more objective to offer!

What inspires me is easy: far and away the most exciting development in film criticism is what Adrian Martin (in the conversation between him and *Miradas de Cine* that Girish indirectly referenced by using Martin's wonderfully evocative phrase 'generous cinephilia') called criticism 'moving a little closer to its object, cinema, and sharing its language (of image and sound) a little more' (2007). Martin talks about DVD frame-captures and graphic design, which some of us already use to good effect; what I have in mind, though, is even more radical. I look at some of Mike Russell's *CulturePulp* comic strips (especially his interview from 2006 with Richard Linklater upon the occasion of the release of *A Scanner Darkly* (2006)), the video 'mashups' that no less a personage than Dave Kehr has called 'the best criticism on the Internet', and at blogger/critic/filmmakers like David Lowery and Peet Gelderblom (who also draws comics!) who publish their films and their criticism side-by-side on the same blog, and I can imagine a future in which the barriers between film and film criticism, between *cineaste* and cinephile, have been torn down completely.

It's a bit trickier to distill my worries about cinephile/blogger film culture, but I think a lot of my concerns boil down to a fear that we are chronically disinterested in criticising ourselves. Girish notes, for instance, that 'Web 2.0' (I'm still wary of this phrase) technologies have 'rendered easy the formation of communities'. I wonder, though, if the feeling of fellowship that comes from being part of a far-flung group of cinephiles (a *granfalloon*[2] if ever there was one) isn't lulling us into a complacent willingness to accept the absence or deterioration of a local film culture that would introduce us to (flesh and blood) kindred spirits in our geographic communities. And about those geographic communities: a localised film culture is at least aware of its isolation. Internet cinephile communities are often more insular than they look; the illusion of diversity prevents us from actively seeking new voices from other countries and cultures, while the illusion of the 'unified Internet' prevents us from looking for other cinephile communities. For everything beneficial about cinephilia's shift to the Internet, there must be something correspondingly detrimental, and to ignore these negatives is to profoundly disrespect the cinema.

What I'd like to see more of is, in a word, *responsibility*. I want to see cinephiles taking responsibility for their film culture (local, national and international) by taking an active part in the processes of filmmaking, distribution and exhibition. I want to see cinephiles *seeking* 'gaps' and 'in-between spaces' to fill in by researching understudied subjects, looking for necessary services that they can perform for their communities, and by experimenting with new ways of conceptualising, talking about and experiencing cinema. I'd like to see a cinephilia that isn't just *generous*, but that is also *grateful* – a cinephilia that tries to give something back to the cinema that has given us so much. I don't know what a 'new film culture' would look like, and whether it's still far away or 'visible on the horizon', this is merely what I'd like to see 'in the meantime'.

Cheers,

Andy H.
http://truespies.org/mirror-stage

San Francisco. 29 July 2007

Dear Andy, Dan, Girish and Zach,

After reading Girish on the subject of his own amateurism, and Andy's comment about being 'adamantly' amateur, I too feel compelled to announce my amateurism when it comes to film writing. Suddenly it occurs to me that using *Movie Mutations* as a model for this group might be enormously hubristic. The participants in that set of letters and essays were all, as I understand it, 'in the trenches' of film criticism: globetrotting to film festivals, serving on juries, publishing pieces in books and widely-circulated periodicals, teaching cinema in classroom settings, etc. Their perspectives on the mutating course of cinema carried a certain weight due to their positions in the profession of film criticism.

But we are in another set of trenches: those dug by the proliferation of online tools allowing anybody with more than the barest computer literacy to publish a relatively attractive personal website on any topic they desire. We're bloggers, each a tiny piece of the so-called 'Web 2.0' whether we intend to be or not. Though we may not publish a new post every day, I'd wager we are still thinking daily about our posts new and old, and the comments they may be attracting.

Before I file a report from my furrow in the cine-blogosphere, though, I think I should outline how I got here in the first place. Like most active participants in modern culture, I've held a fascination for movies from a young age, when my mother took me to see *Snow White and the Seven Dwarfs* (1937), or else when my father took me to *Star Wars* (1977). But truly my cinephilia was born online.

My teenage obsession was music and my appreciation for movies was long focused largely on my interest in their scores and soundtracks. While an undergraduate, I began to explore Internet resources such as Usenet discussion groups. I zeroed in on the rec.music hierarchy, where I observed and eventually began to participate in discussions of musical topics from across the spectrum of relatively unpopular musical genres. I didn't see much point in discussing popular acts and styles online – for that I could find plenty of real-life conversations to participate in. So, as I began to discover my online writing 'voice' I was also becoming accustomed to using it mostly to talk about off-the-beaten-path subjects.

After graduating from college in 1996, I started drifting from music discussion groups to film music discussion groups, to film discussion groups. I stumbled upon a particularly lively message board that brought together lifelong film buffs from several continents, authors of film books and young cinephiles-in-the-making. To keep up with the discussions there, I found it was no longer enough for me to have an opinion on a film and express it. I now wanted to work on the development of my own 'idea of cinema', and to expand my understanding of the historical, geographic, political and other contexts in which a film at hand might be examined. I started watching films that previously would never have attracted my interest, either in order to participate in the community discussions, or else because of a recommendation from one of the online voices I was increasingly coming to trust. Though I'd lived in San Francisco for most of my life, I'd rarely taken advantage of the overwhelming number of rare filmgoing opportunities here before. But now, thanks to the Internet, I had help in navigating the calendars of local venues like the Castro Theatre or the Pacific Film Archive. I soon found myself structuring a great deal of time around attending repertory and festival films, and I haven't really looked back since.

There are a few still-thriving film message boards that I follow and occasionally contribute to, but I spend far more time maintaining my own blog and reading others' these days. I share Andy's concern that we bloggers may be 'chronically disinterested in criticising ourselves'. There's no doubt that the comparatively 'neutral' space of a message board tends to welcome more open disagreement, and more expression of different, often contradictory 'ideas of cinema' (I still haven't settled on mine, by the way). But the seemingly inevitable domination of many such spaces by anonymous conflict-hounds surely has driven me to prefer a venue of expression that's less of a strife-magnet. In the blogosphere, the preferred way to express dissatisfaction with another's point of view is to write your own blog about it.

One of the main reasons I chose to focus my blog on my local filmgoing scene from the outset was my dissatisfaction that such a gaping niche existed in the first place. I was troubled that so much of the film writing I was finding on the web was fixated on the DVD fetish-object, a wonderful invention for film scholars and pack rats. It's been a lovely ride. I'm sure I've learned as much about film programming, filmmaking and film criticism in the past two years or so than I had in the previous 32 combined. And I've formed bonds with cinephiles from around the world and in my own backyard.

I don't, however, share Andy's concern about what to do 'in the meantime' because my own cinephilia is all about enjoying the cinematic experience as it's happening, and doing my best to record it along the way. I've come to realise that the day I graduate from being a searching, probing, grasping, failing film watcher, the day I finally do settle down with my 'idea of cinema', and consider myself now fully qualified to pass it down, is probably the day I completely lose interest in doing so. And I'm very glad that I currently have a corner of cyberspace to continue my learning and growing process.

Peace,

Brian
http://hellonfriscobay.blogspot.com/

New York. 5 August 2007

Dear Girish, Zach, Brian and Andy,

One of Girish's assumptions about this group of correspondents was incorrect in my case: I've never read *Movie Mutations*, and didn't even know about it until Zach mentioned it to me recently. I think I'm much older than the rest of you (I'm 52), so I guess the impact of those letters must have fallen into some generational hole between you and me.

Elsaesser's 'first generation' could itself be broken down into a number of waves of cinephiles, each reacting to what came before. I became a film buff in 1972, almost ten years after Andrew Sarris's *Film Culture* article (1963) that got the American auteurist movement off to a running start. At the time I thought of my peers and me as a second wave of auteurists, and our canon eventually diverged slightly from the one we learned. I once playfully categorised film buffs according to which Welles film was their favorite: *Citizen Kane* (1941) for the old guard, *The Magnificent Ambersons* (1942) for the first generation auteurists, *Chimes at Midnight* (1965) for the second generation, *Touch of Evil* (1958) for the film-school crowd who filled the gap between my generation and yours. Maybe there's a new Welles film for the Web 2.0 generation: *The Immortal Story* (1968)? *F for Fake* (1974)?

The Internet came along to rescue me from the decline that awaits all cinephiles who attempt to 'have a life'. Around the time I hit 30, my movie intake began to diminish, and I spent more than a decade in a maintenance pattern, checking out new works by directors I already knew, catching titles with critical buzz and mostly leaving exploration to the newcomers. In 1999, two things happened that reversed my slide: I joined my first Internet movie mailing list; and, influenced by the people I met there, I began traveling to the Toronto Film Festival. That first list (to which I still belong) wasn't by any means a perfect fit for me. I had very little in common with the prevailing tastes of the group, and even the style of socialising there made me feel like a bit of a fuddy-duddy. But here was the first evidence I'd seen in ages that cinephilia was still alive and kicking, Susan Sontag's gloomy prognosis notwithstanding (see 1996). Even if I had trouble relating to the listers' tastes, they followed the festival scene closely, kept track of new film movements at home and abroad, and went to Toronto in packs every September. I was inspired to take a new interest in contemporary filmmaking around the world and eventually decided that the 00s were actually quite a good decade for international cinema.

Interestingly, I noticed that the people on that list with whom I had the most in common were the youngest, the kids in their teens and twenties. (Zach was one of them.) The youngsters didn't necessarily identify themselves as auteurists, the way that my generation did. But they seemed to want auteurism as one of the arrows in their quiver, as an outlook they could learn from and could deploy when it was useful. I began to think that my brand of cinephilia had skipped a generation and was coming back into vogue. Was *Movie Mutations* behind it all?

As for Web 2.0, it's a recent development for me. I stuck with the mailing-list model for years – there was something I liked about the immediate sense of community that it gave, and the way that one's ideas were triggered by input from others. But we all know about the fate that befalls mailing lists, which Brian alluded to: the phases of expansion and contraction that they inevitably undergo; the cycle of enthusiasm, disappointment and resignation. Blogging used to strike me as a bit egocentric, but I came to want an Internet environment where I had a chance of controlling the tone. And, thanks to all of you, I discovered that the blogosphere is not an abstraction, but an active connection that bloggers forge among themselves. If the sense of community on a mailing list is something like that of a kibbutz, then the blogosphere is akin to a frontier territory where the nearest neighbors are miles away, but come around to help you raise a barn.

Girish asked what might be the characteristics of a new, Internet-based film culture. I know what I'm in it for, and it was summed up perfectly by Andrew Sarris, in a phrase that I tried to put into the masthead of my blog (I lost the first battle against Blogger's programming interface, but I mean to have another go at it): 'Eventually we must talk of everything if there is enough time and space and printer's ink.' Blogging gives us infinite flexibility of format. We can write as much or as little as we want about a subject; we don't have to throw away ideas that aren't book-length or article-length. If I have a paragraph to add to a decades-long debate about an idea or a film, I can put it out there and hope that someone else will build on it, now or later. This is my vision of Internet film culture: people feeding small or large ideas into each other's views of cinema, chipping away at the huge task of 'talking about everything'.

Andy talked about his interest in cultivating local, flesh-and-blood film cultures. From my relatively elderly perspective, I hope that even those of you lucky enough to enjoy, or diligent enough to foster, a thriving, corporeal film scene in our own communities will invest in the future by creating as rich an Internet film environment for yourselves as possible. Even if you now sit around coffeehouses having spirited debates with your film friends, you won't be at those tables forever! Film communities are fragile, notoriously subject to attrition. But those of us who are cinephiles for the long haul will be able to take the Internet with us into our nursing homes.

A parting word to those of you who think of yourselves as 'amateurs': the professionals really haven't done that immaculate a job of landscaping the grounds for critical thought in our medium. As I see it, the field is wide open. There are a billion important things to do, and the competition is far from fierce. Just help yourself!

Best wishes,

Dan
http://www.panix.com/~sallitt/blog/

New York. 17 August 2007

Dear Cine-comrades,

As I see it there are three general themes in your four letters. First, the existence and importance of 'Web 2.0' and other digital technologies (interactivity is key). Second, the overlapping lines of amateurism, dilettantism and fragmentation. Third, a few reflections, some oblique, on the history of taste.

On the presence of the Internet in forging online communities: Girish pointed to the static nature of earlier web publishing. The interactive possibilities of blogs and everything a little like them have, I think, proven to be a special impetus on the information superhighway. What matters – what is new – is not so much that the information can be put out by a few suppliers for a large audience, but that this large audience can communicate amongst itself in conjunction with the more static approach. Listservs, message boards, blogs, file sharing, video sites and other dynamic fora give the lie to the stereotype of the cinephile as the myopic, sunless, *solitary* creature. People who love films clearly want to interact, and are doing so in a number of capacities. Plus – as Andy points out – witness the presence of video mash-ups and clips, the use of frame captures (thanks to DVDs, those mixed blessings and 'fetish-objects', as per Brian's perfect label). People don't *only* want to engage with each other; they want to engage with the material in a few new ways as well. At any event, I have tried to think about film blogging *qua* film blogging here, but discussing it as a larger practice now makes little sense unless we couch it in all of its Web 2.0 corollaries. The same crisscrossing network of desires and tendencies fuels so much of it.

On amateurism (and the threat of dilettantism): the question of our amateur status seems to loom for some of us, even at our most optimistic, precisely because of our lapses in knowledge of the objects at our disposal – filmic, or altogether cultural in any sense. It's a vicious cycle. But, as Dan points out, the pros haven't done the best 'landscaping' job on the cinema. Nor are they often allowed to try, if they are critics and reviewers. The most well-meaning and omnivorous film reviewer will still have to answer to her editor, to the interests of advertisers and to demands of currency and cachet. The independent blogger, who answers to no one but herself, possesses more potential freedom – the freedom to jot a few lines or write a string of posts worthy of an entire book; to write at irregular intervals; to hyperlink at her own discretion. Blogging need not be automatic or immediate: it's important for non-bloggers to understand that you can save a post, edit it, refine it for an indefinite length of time before posting it. (Some blogs can be casual in tone and yet indicate a great deal of work and polish – like the one shared by scholarly superstars David Bordwell and Kristin Thompson.)[3] The fragmented approach has a flexibility that is laudable. It may allow for bad or undisciplined writing – sometimes – but this in no way invalidates the great work done in its format. Just perhaps, 'dilettantism run wild' is the price we pay for a smaller handful of great bloggers. I have no problems with this proposition. To me the question that Andy raises – 'what do I do in the meantime?' – is perhaps best left to answer itself. Thus far we have seen that blogging is most accurately defined *by* its proliferation of activities, its generally nonstandardised practices. Among other activities film bloggers fill in gaps, act as gadflies, blaze new trails: that's a start, no?

On the history of taste: like Dan, I came out of a certain auteurist background – mine different from his, but leeching off of his and others' tastes and assumptions in order to better form my own. And this still constitutes a certain important connotation of the word 'cinephilia': as I think I half-joked to Andy once, to me a cinephile is someone who takes Joseph H. Lewis very, very seriously. This has nothing to do with movie love in general, it has everything to do with *what* movies you love, *whose* movies you love. Lines drawn in the sand (for example, the films of Frank Tashlin and Jerry Lewis, which deserve respect even if they elicit no love). In one sense, *that* is what cinephilia means to me. It's intensely personal, a bit solipsistic in fact, and I've tied the meaning to the *content* and *politics* of taste more than to the intensity of filmic devotion (which would be assumed rather than measured). But it is the intensity that brings us together. I would remind Brian, who contrasts our *amateurism* with the 'trench' activities of the *Movie Mutations* writers, that those writers themselves differentiated between someone like Nicole Brenez (an academic who could spend a long period of time analyzing a single film) versus someone like Rosenbaum (who reviews films regularly and goes to many festivals). For the purposes of the letters' content, what united them was not so much the prestige of their employment as the devotion of their activity.

One of the most enjoyable and informative parts of discovering and meeting ('meeting'?) new people online through blogs is finding how people feel and express their feelings on art; how they categorise and when they refuse to categorise; where they draw their own lines in the sand. Look at Girish's pairing of major figures of Bengali culture (Dutt, Sen, R. D. Burman, Tagore) with European talents who came to America and sent shockwaves through its culture (Hitchcock, Nabokov, the Beatles) – just seven names thrown out *sans* commentary, but even that a sketched aspect of Girish's tastes and history, which tells a story about who, in part, Girish is and has been. The sharing of tastes can, too, devolve into a mere listing and trading of 'fetish-objects'. Look at the 'About Me' sections on social utility networks like Facebook or MySpace (or Blogspot), where profiles actively encourage one to list facts about oneself in terms of what music, films, books, etc. one enjoys – that is, code for what products one buys and endorses. This is the pitfall to be mindful of when we discuss tastes, but the proliferation and conversation of all these varying individual tastes is otherwise exciting.

I think the less structured nature of blogging can quite easily amplify these personal configurations. This is a good thing provided we keep our balance with several questions in mind – including a sense of self-criticism (*pace* Andy) that will allow bloggers to set their own parameters and informally *referee* each other in the proper circumstances (if that's the proper term): to correct misinformation, challenge lazy thinking, identify and outline hazy areas in terms of our understanding. This is a huge, hydra-headed project with tremendous potential. And this in particular is a question whose resonance has little to do with film discussion per se, film discussion as itself, and everything to do with politics, ethics and society. I should say that I am not entirely optimistic of this development's well-being because of my distrust of the political institutions and interests which own and guide the technology and products that make all this talk possible. *But* – there is a world of possibility here, and if a culture can ever be remade through the will of the people, let us hope that these kinds of new networks of communication, new paths of commentary, play their modest part. Blogging cinephiles can and should act as Daney-like *passeurs*, and with this job comes the prospect of a vital ethical application – to question the sources of images as well as their meanings, to evaluate function as well as beauty, and to always draw connections between the seen and the unseen. Let's hope that whatever freedoms we've been able to latch onto allow us to do just that.

Sincerely,

Zach
http://elusivelucidity.blogspot.com/

NOTES

1   These letters, first published in the French magazine *Trafic* in 1997, were initiated by Jonathan Rosenbaum. He noticed a commonality of tastes among a group of globally dispersed cinephiles – Adrian Martin in Melbourne, Kent Jones in New York, Alexander Horwath in Vienna and Nicole Brenez in Paris – all of whom were born around the year 1960. Rosenbaum's curiosity about 'the generational conditions of this unconscious bond between strangers that traversed so many national linguistic borders' formed the starting point for this letter relay on changes in world cinephilia.

2   A *granfalloon* is 'a seeming team that was meaningless in terms of the ways God gets things done'; see Vonnegut (1963: 67).

3 See Bordwell and Thompson's ongoing blog: 'Observations on film art and FILM ART'. Online. Available at: http://www.davidbordwell.net/blog/. Accessed 23 August 2007.

REFERENCES

Bordwell, David and Kristin Thompson (n. d.) 'Observations on film art and FILM ART'. Online. Available at: http://www.davidbordwell.net/blog/. Accessed 23 August 2007.

Elsaesser, Thomas (2005) 'Cinephilia or the Uses of Disenchantment', in Marijke de Valck and Malte Hagener (eds) *Cinephilia: Movies, Love and Memory*. Amsterdam: Amsterdam University Press, 27–43.

Gelderblom, Peet (n. d.) 'Lost In Negative Space'. Online. Available at: http://peet.wordpress.com/. Accessed 23 August 2007.

Harvey, Sylvia (1978) *May '68 and Film Culture*. London: British Film Institute.

Kehr, Dave (n. d.) 'The Real Web Critics'. Online. Available at: http://davekehr.com/?p=84. Accessed 23 August 2007.

Lowery, David (n. d.) 'Drifting: A Director's Log'. Online. Available at: http://www.road-dog-productions.com/weblog. Accessed 23 August 2007.

Martin, Adrian (2007) 'Responsibility and Criticism', *Cinemascope*, 7, Jan–Apr. Online. Available at: http://www.cinemascope.it/Issue%207/Articoli_n7/Articoli_n7_05/Adrian_Martin.pdf. Accessed 23 August 2007.

Rosenbaum, Jonathan and Adrian Martin (eds) (2003) *Movie Mutations*. London: British Film Institute.

Russell, Mike (2006) 'The Richard Linklater Interview', *CulturePulp*, 54. Online. Available at: http://homepage.mac.com/merussell/iblog/B835531044/C1162162177/E20060717001411/index.html. Accessed 23 August 2007.

Sarris, Andrew (1963) 'Special Issue: American Directors', *Film Culture*, 28.

Sontag, Susan (1996) 'The Decay of Cinema', *New York Times Magazine*, 25 February, 6–10.

Vonnegut, Kurt (1963) *Cat's Cradle*. New York: Dell.

AFFECTS

CHAPTER THREE

A POINT OF LIGHT: EPIPHANIC CINEPHILIA IN MAMORU OSHII'S *AVALON* (2001)
Jenna Ng

> The instant flashed forth like a point of light and now from cloud on cloud of vague circumstance confused form was veiling softly its afterglow.
>
> — James Joyce, *A Portrait of the Artist as a Young Man*[1]

> I didn't choose film ... Film chose me. I saw a film at 15 that lifted me out of my seat, turned me upside down, shook the change out of my pants, and dropped me with a thud on the floor. It, and some others that followed, cleaned out my sensorium and changed the whole way I see the world. They brought me to the same kind of rapturous ecstasy, and seemed to convey the same kind of powerful 'meanings', that I was just starting to find in Beethoven and Bach. As I explored more, I found that each filmmaker I loved defined cinema differently, and that part of the pleasure and meaning of film for me was discovering a huge variety of ways of seeing that are different from my own. These discoveries took me out of the narrowness of my self, and expanded my sense of what was possible in seeing and in thought.
>
> — Fred Camper, *Frameworks*[2]

INTRODUCTION

Fred Camper's experience of cinema might well mirror every cinephile's story, when the lights go down and our faces turn, transfixed, towards a glowing screen, the darkness heralding joy – 'as if the whole darkening world were dimming its lights for a party' (Pastan 1998: 39). In the ensuing flickers, we laugh and cry, are thrilled and pacified, lost and found; we stumble out of the room, our worlds and ideas of possibilities transformed.

In that vein, we might note the recurrent associations between cinema (and the viewing of cinema) and powers of revelation, our wonder of which runs as a dominant thread through the history and theory of film. A sprinkling of examples suffice: the early French theorists, for instance, enthuse about the 'wondrous' reality presented by cinema, even of a 'soul', where the crucial, if mysterious, element of *photogénie* metamorphises an object's ordinariness into marvel once beheld in image.[3] René Clair declares: 'There is no detail of reality which is not immediately extended here [in cinema] into the domain of the wondrous' (in Willemen 1994a: 125). Antonin Artaud similarly writes of the 'unpredictable' and 'mysterious' element of cinema, whereby 'even the driest and most banal is transformed on the screen' (1978: 49–50). And, to Franz Werfel, cinema is a medium which reveals magic and marvel, asserting the 'true meaning' and 'real possibilities' of film as those which 'consist in its unique faculty to express by natural means and with incomparable persuasiveness all that is fairylike, marvellous, supernatural' (in Benjamin 1970: 221).[4]

It is in this context of cinema's transfigurative mystique that Paul Willemen, in an interview with Noel King, pulls together his ideas on cinephilia, revelation and ontology. Transcribed as a chapter titled 'Through the Glass Darkly: Cinephilia Reconsidered' in his book, *Looks and Frictions*, Willemen suggests, *inter alia*, that cinephilia – the love of cinema[5] – is itself a condition of revelation: it is a mode of excess, a status of a beyond, by which the cinephile sees more than she is shown – the quintessence of revelation. Love, therefore, is not blind; on the contrary, it sees more than before. To Willemen, this additional vision, and/or the capability of it, forms the basis of cinephilia:

> There is something that persists, which is the moment of revelation ... What is being looked for [in selecting a cinephiliac moment] is a moment or ... a dimension of a moment which triggers for the viewer either the realisation or the illusion of a realisation that *what is being seen is in excess of what is being shown. Consequently you see something that is revelatory.* It reveals an aspect of a dimension of a person ... which is not choreographed for you to see. It is produced *en plus*, in excess or in addition, almost involuntarily. There is a moment of potential dislocation, *of seeing something beyond what is given to you to see.* (1994b: 236–7; emphasis added)

Willemen thus defines the cinephiliac mode by the revelatory properties of these 'moments of excess', 'fished up by particular people in order to designate their relationship of pleasure to a particular film' (1994b: 230). But he takes his thesis a step further by deliberately linking cinephilia (in the revelatory sense) to the ontology of the image. Presenting the two concepts 'in solidarity' (further declaring it to be 'a contradiction' should one reject one and not the other), Willemen asserts that 'one of the presuppositions of cinephilia is what André Bazin theorised in terms of an ontology of cinema' (1994b: 243). This, of course, refers to Bazin's famous essay, 'The Ontology of the Photographic Image' (1945), in which he argues that a privileged relation exists between the film image and reality due to the mechanical production of the image (see Bazin 1967). To Bazin, the image is thus revelatory in the exposition of its embedded reality, made possible by the image's ontological properties via the unique relationship between object and photographic image. Willemen seizes on this connection: ontology predicates revelation and, hence, cinephilia. Tagging onto the Bazinian argument of the unique relationship between image and object, Willemen pursues the reality in the image, if only to 'fetishise the dimension of the real which shines through' (1994b: 243). The only difference lies in their mission, in which Willemen reads revelation rather than reality, and which he ultimately derives, as did Bazin, from the recording process of the camera:

> The fact that [the neo-realists] shot on location, without much rehearsal, in difficult conditions, meant that *something shone through into the film*. There again, these are mystical notions of revelation. That aesthetic can be talked about, polemicised about, in a hundred different ways. *The ontology argument underpins them all.* (Ibid.; emphasis added)

Without engaging in any extended criticism or review of the Bazinian argument here (of which much has already been said[6]), my essay, rather, will concentrate on developing Willemen's notion of cinephilia as revelation and, in particular, re-examining its relationship to reality via the recording process. For Willemen, the two are melded such that one cannot be without the other; as he insists, that would be 'a contradiction':

> The cinephile shares the notion of an ontology of cinema. And the *less* the image has a Bazinian ontological relation to the real (the death-mask notion of the real), the *more* the image gets electronified, with each pixel becoming programmable in its own terms, *the less appropriate cinephilia becomes.* (ibid.; emphasis added)

To be precise, Willemen's reference to the electronic image is made in the context of television, but his conclusions might well apply to the computer-generated image, similarly divorced from reality in the Bazinian framework. Created from polygons and axis-based shapes and its nature comprising of bytes and binary code, Computer-Generated Imagery (CGI) possesses the same ontological disconnection from reality: images created not from light reflected off objects and locations but graphically in a computer with photo-editing programs and image-rendering software. In the absence of a 'real' which shines through a camera, do these computer-generated images lose the capacity for cinephilic revelation, the excess of the moment, as Willemen maintains?[7] How fundamental is the link between ontology and cinephilia?

In these respects, I will argue in this essay for a cinephilia which is revelatory in nature, yet appropriate precisely for CGI. Rather than reject Willemen's thesis, my intention is to expand on his ideas of revelatory cinephilia, to take cinephilia beyond the emphases on ontological differences so as to account for CGI, now cramming our screens in such profusion. I will argue, instead, that the aesthetics and motivations of CGI, while phenomenologically disconnected from reality, nonetheless interweave with the real in manifold ways so as to give rise to a singular ruptured response, not in terms, as conceived by Willemen, of a revelation in the sense of seeing (and being shown) *more*, but in terms of a reaction so highly self-conscious, reflexive and affected to be rendered an atypical, even extraordinary, moment of cinema, a reaction which I term 'epiphanic cinephilia'. In the rest of this essay, I will develop and elaborate on this, first by exploring the notion of epiphany and surveying some theoretical approaches which might underpin its concepts of revelation, before applying the idea to my own cinephiliac experience in viewing Mamoru Oshii's *Avalon* (2001).

PLEASURES OLD AND NEW: NEGOTIATING THE FAMILIAR AND THE UNFAMILIAR

> Behind all literary talk about what a poem means or how it comes to have meaning or whether it means anything lies the simple fact that certain experiences in life rise to a position of psychic prominence.
>
> – Ashton Nichols, *The Poetics of Epiphany*[8]

The most salient element of epiphany is that of a manifestation, in which respect it is similar to a revelation: both are gifts of privileged insight. The idea of a showing, a revealing, may be seen in the origins of the word 'epiphany', which the Oxford English Dictionary traces to the Greek terms *epiphainein* and *epiphaneia*, respectively 'to manifest, formed as' and 'manifestation'. In Plato's account of the 'moment of *exaiphnes*', he also refers to 'the sudden achievement of full cognition', in which 'the ideas of the Good, the True and the Beautiful supposedly coincide' (see Wägenbaur 1993: 16–17). The OED's primary definition of 'epiphany' is also that of 'a manifestation of some divine or superhuman being', or 'any sudden and important manifestation or realisation'.[9]

Of significance is that the critical treatment of epiphany, particularly 'the new literary epiphany' (Nichols 1987: 28). in modern literature, emphasises the *content* of its manifestation as one which is internal, psychological and self-conscious – a deliberate departure from the literal and original meaning of the term, which records the epiphanic manifestation as one of divinity or culmination of knowledge (the latter now termed 'theophany' in order to differentiate it from its more modern derivation). Epiphany in this sense thus moves away from the strictness of applying meaning to insight, focusing, rather, on the heightened psychological, perceptual and emotional intensity of the moment, as Ashton Nichols elaborates:

The Romantics and their followers are not looking for a single, blinding, all encom-
passing insight into the nature of reality and the self's place in the world. Instead
*they are building up a self defined by its relations, a self created out of its own
awareness of its responses to experience.* Epiphany becomes a key to this achievement by imaginatively describing moments when the perceiving self sees its own
imaginative and associative powers helping to create the world. (Ibid.; emphasis
added)

It is this sense of epiphany on which I want to build my argument: a response
which is highly self-conscious, eliciting a new way of immediately apprehending
and perceiving the world, alternatively engaging with past experience and being
implicated by affective memory, from which meaning is derived to build up 'a self
created out of its own awareness of its responses to experience' (ibid.).[10]

To that extent, the recorded film image is arguably the diametrical opposite
of such an experience. The ontology of the photographic-based image is connected so persistently to its reality because of the unique process of its capture
– light pressed upon chemical film to warrant the existence of the object at that
moment in time. Indeed, Roland Barthes writes of this connection as one which
is more than a photochemical process, but also an emotional relationship, an
exposition of demise and love: 'It is as if the Photograph always carries its referent with itself, both affected by the same amorous or funereal immobility, at
the very heart of the moving world' (2000: 6).[11] Returning to Willemen's thesis
of cinephiliac revelation, the very reason we receive any privileged insight in the
image is *precisely* because of this relationship – to 'fetishise the dimension of the
real which shines through' (1994b: 243) – around which his argument revolves.
There is no place or role for a psychological response in the eliciting of that revelation, no emphasis on a subjective receptivity which might generate insight
from its own intense and vivid viewing, for everything is ontologically related to
the objective world and the objective capture of it in the chemical-based image.

Other scholars, taking up Willemen's thesis of cinephilia, similarly identify and
emphasise the question of ontology as its touchstone, albeit framed in varying
terms. Christian Keathley, for example, expanding on what he calls 'the revelatory potential of cinema', describes cinephiliac potential by linking Bazinian theory
to surrealism as well as via the aesthetics of realism – yet at all times centering
his analysis on the Bazinian theory of the image and the ensuing relationship
between image and object, which in turn entrenches the latter in the former
(see 2006: 54–81). Similarly, Mary Ann Doane discusses cinephilia with respect
to its relationship to reality, albeit expressed in terms of the image's registration of indexicality. Citing Willemen and Miriam Hansen, she posits cinephilia as
the 'predilection' of the contingent, a momentary access to insight sustained by
photographic indexicality: 'What is at stake here, as in Willemen's description of

cinephilia, is a *relation* between spectator and image, but it is the photographic base which acts as the condition of such a possibility for such a relation' (2002: 227–8; emphasis in original). Bazin himself predicates the recorded reality of the film in explicit opposition to its psychological apprehension – the unique ontology of the photographic image and its relation to reality directly contrasts with any subjective response to it. Describing the film *Annapurna* (1953) by Marcel Ichac, Bazin expressly extols, to the extent of imbuing it with religious awe, the indexical nature of the image, the *imprint* of the object on film: 'This time the camera is there like the veil of Veronica pressed to the face of human suffering' (1967: 163). Tellingly, against this lies subjective memory as its antithesis: 'Memory is the most faithful of films … but who can fail to see the difference between memory and that objective image that gives it eternal substance?' (ibid.).[12]

It follows that the most common position of the ontology of CGI is its divorce from reality, reducing CGI to a mere copy, a simulacra which invariably calls up the dystopic Baudrillardian hyperreal, 'the generation by models of a real without origin or reality' (Baudrillard 1983: 2). Without the recorded imprint of light which entrenches the reliability of the film image, the relation between CGI and reality is instead deemed to be a graphic, painterly representation, iconic rather than indexical: 'No longer strictly locked in the photographic, cinema opens itself toward the painterly' (Manovich 2001: 304). Lev Manovich concludes: 'Cinema becomes a particular branch of painting – painting in time. No longer a kino eye, but a kino-brush' (2001: 308). His implication is clear: as a kino-brush, CGI's connection with reality is only as graphic likeness and avatar. It is on this premise that Willemen writes of the inappropriateness of cinephilia for the electronic image: it cannot exist in the absence of the indexical imprint of reality, for cinephilia revolves around the revelation of a real shining through.

However, I think it is precisely in this element of simulation that CGI retains a distinct connection to reality, one which, while not phenomenologically involved, nonetheless taps so chronically into reality that the image sometimes invokes, even demands, a different engagement with it. Reality and CGI interface in diverse ways, if not ontologically, and numerous scholars have already noted the different interchanges between CGI and live action, such that *one taps into the other in channels of triggered recognition*. Stephen Prince, for instance, calls for such an alternative connection in his proposition of 'a correspondence-based model of cinematic representation' (1999: 399). Attributing the photorealism of 'referentially fictional' imagery, such as the ping-pong ball in *Forrest Gump* (1994), to built-in 'perceptual correspondences' made in relation to a viewer's extra filmic audiovisual, social and physical experience, Prince describes a model of engagement whereby the 'unreal images' of CGI, while not necessarily grounded indexically to a referent, are nonetheless still connected to the real world because of their myriad correspondences with our perceptual realities. Warren Buckland also highlights the combinations of digital and live-action imagery in Steven Spielberg's *Jurassic Park* (1993), where the digitally created dinosaurs, through sophisticated techniques of compositing as well as suture, interact flawlessly with the human actors, so that digital and analogue merge into 'a single coherent image' inhabiting 'a unified diegetic space' (1999: 187). The photorealism of CGI reality is, thus, not merely simulacra, but a complex engagement between real and digital worlds in their seamless composition. Michele Pierson, in her analysis of CGI special effects in science fiction films, notes the dual oppositions of 'photographic realism' and 'synthetic hyperrealism' which she argues occupied the aesthetics of early to mid-1990s CGI cinema. Yet, even what she argues to be a hyperreal, synthetic aesthetic of CGI cinema retains an element of the familiar. The debate she outlines on the CGI effects of *The Last Starfighter* (1984) is telling, where fans proclaimed its imagery 'looks more real than real', even as critics decried its surreal look as 'a defect of the technique' (1999: 172; see also Pierson 2002). Yet, the point remains: notwithstanding the wizardry of a synthetic, hyperreal aesthetic, some recognition of an element of the real world is displayed, be it for acceptance or rejection. We find the familiar within the unfamiliar; we recognise our real world in fictional worlds.[13]

What is involved in this exercise is thus not merely connecting image and reality in simulation per se, but in the building of what I call an 'impulse' within the image: an element in the form of technique or aesthetic which excites a response in terms of recognition or empathy with our experiences from the real world. I use the word 'impulse' as analogised to its meaning in physiology, where an impulse is the electrochemical transmission of a signal along a nerve fibre that produces an excitatory or inhibitory response at a target tissue, such as a muscle or another nerve. Taking its key ideas of signal, recognition and target, my argument is that, in the same way, CGI builds into its effects and imagery details or cues of the real world which act as signals to trigger an excited response of recognition and identification or, perhaps, more than that, a response of recognition which may return to the viewer in such strength and intensity that it vaults into something a little more extraordinary – not simply an acknowledgement but a reverberation both experiential and affective, and which ultimately commits the moment into memorable encounter.[14] Akin to the epiphany of the Proustian *'memoire involuntaire'*, where Marcel Proust's memories of Combray arise as epiphanic visions upon the familiar taste of the madeleine, his childhood treat,[15] triggers of *familiarity* may invoke in one a response so profound and intense that it fosters an extraordinarily acute consciousness, a heightened dimension of awareness.

Lesley Stern, writing of body and movement in Ridley Scott's *Blade Runner* (1982), describes a key moment in the film where Pris (Daryl Hannah) suddenly somersaults towards the viewer. It is 'a cinematic moment – a moving image' which affected and haunted her deeply (1997: 361). She is astonished by the 'breathtaking' way in which Pris moves through the air, the speed of the astounding somersault – 'this transformation of a body in space and time' – and how foreign it is to her own physical capabilities 'that my bodily response lags behind' (ibid.). Yet, crucially, the strange experience triggers in her reaction a familiarity in the unfamiliarity: 'It's like what happens when you are in a lift and suddenly without warning it drops – instantaneously the movement of the lift is *in you*' (ibid.; emphasis in original). Her confrontation with the fantastic somersault is inextricably tied up with the engagement of her own structurally corresponding experience; her inspired reaction – her exhilarated consciousness of her body and bodily sensations – stems from the contraposed yet consonant interweaving of the strangeness and the accustomed.

In the context of CGI cinema, we are similarly struck by the same impulses and triggers of recognitions and intensities. Vivian Sobchack, for example, notes the same concurrence of unfamiliarity and familiarity in her account of her reaction to the T1000 'metal-morph' in *Terminator 2: Judgment Day* (1991) describing how she feels the 'human impossibility and strangeness' of the morphing process even as she simultaneously identifies with it: 'My own body quickens to its effortless transformations at some deep molecular level and *I recognise the morph as strangely familiar*' (2000: 132; emphasis added). In her essay, 'Cutting to the Quick', she advances recognition to re-cognition (though is not the latter also a precedent function of the former?) via a breathtaking analysis of Zhang Yimou's *Hero* (2002). Using Samuel Weber's '*anagnoresis as peripeteia*' – 'a formula for the uncanny recognition of something that, in being the same, reveals itself to be different' – she lays out the raindrops, falling in hyper-slow motion in the battle scene between Nameless (Jet Li) and Sky (Donnie Yen), as sheer, extraordinary revelation: 'an astonished and awe-full recognition ... a profound (even tragic) "re cognition" that dramatically reverses our orientation' (2007: 350). The re( )cognitions which Sobchack so remarkably identifies thus triple-plays the consciousness: the unfamiliar (hyper-slow raindrops) which triggers the familiar (falling raindrops '*of* and *in* that physical world') in turn eliciting yet another unfamiliar (that these movements 'are not "for us"' (ibid.; emphasis in original)). We cannot grasp their strangeness (and thus wonder) without first perceiving their familiarity, and it is their interplay which enraptures and enchants us, thrillingly, sublimely, and which is also epiphanic, if only for that one moment it makes us all too conscious of our reactions, our selves, our world and that *not* of our world.

To that extent, what transpires in CGI cinema is not merely a rejection of the inappropriateness, or unrealistic-ness, of the real, but, rather, a more complex interweaving of double sensations, familiarity and unfamiliarity, pleasures old and new, accustomed and strange. This slide between the familiar and the unfamiliar inevitably conjures up the '*unheimlich*', the concept that Sigmund Freud develops from Ernst Jentsch's 1906 essay, 'On the Psychology of the Uncanny', in his own work, 'The Uncanny' (1919), which Freud invokes with respect to the return of 'something which is secretly familiar, which has undergone repression' (1955: 224). Freud's emphasis, predictably, is on the psychological ramifications arising from this return of the repressed, yet the point remains that this is a sensation which does not go unnoticed; it marks our memories, sears our senses. To that extent, the reactive engagements between CGI and reality are always more complicated than pure simulacra: there are cues, impulses and triggers withal to which we respond in deep, affected ways, ways which heighten our consciousness of and provoke extraordinary acuteness in our reactions – reactions of epiphanic cinephilia – to the images. We know those moments; we feel them, we respond to them, we write about them. Ashton Nichols speaks of the existence of these exceptional experiences and reactions – '[risen] to a position of psychic prominence' – as 'simple fact', one whose actuality undermines everything else, including meaning itself. That seems a little blasé (should wonder be reduced to a bald fact?), yet true.

'WELCOME TO CLASS REAL': PLEASURE AND EPIPHANY IN *AVALON*

Tell me about Special A.

– Ash[16]

There is one more twist. If the unfamiliarity of CGI may provoke in us a deep response due to its complex meshing with the triggers of real-world familiarity, the equation may also be inverted: familiarity of CGI may interplay with real-world unfamiliarity, so the result is a double consciousness, not only of the strangeness of CGI, but also of a new-found alien eye on customary, real-world sights.

But how may CGI, so often used to create imagery of the impossible and the wondrous, become more familiar than the familiarity of our real world? This would require a different visual paradigm, one which applies CGI as the state of default, the norm rather than the exception. To this end, I wish, in this penultimate section, to examine Mamoru Oshii's *Avalon*, a film which not only invokes but deliberately reverses the poles of familiarity, such that the CGI special effects become what we are accustomed to, whereas live-action imagery rattles us from established content. Familiarity, in this case, breeds not contempt but convention.

A Japanese/Polish production, *Avalon* was shot mostly in Poland with a Polish cast and crew, but directed by a Japanese director and post-produced in Japan. Set in 'the near future', the disillusioned youths of *Avalon* seek escapism by playing Avalon, 'an illegal virtual reality war game', which has the occupational hazard of leaving a player brain-dead if he/she were to get lost in the virtual reality of the game. Our protagonist is Ash (Malgorzata Foremniak), an expert Class A player, cold and bitter after having let down her teammates, with disastrous consequences, in a past game, and who now plays Avalon purely for financial reasons (as a character notes, 'there are lots of ways to make a living in Avalon').

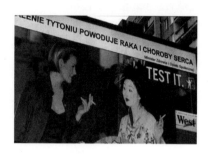

Gradually, however, Ash is drawn to playing Special A, the highest level of Avalon, not only to discover the truth about the game, but also to look for Murphy (Jerzy Gudejko), her previous team leader now lost in Avalon after himself attempting to play Special A.

The film is, not unexpectedly, replete with CGI work, particularly in the virtual reality game world, where armoured CGI monsters advance, explosions freeze and characters, when shot, flatten into two-dimensional projections before they disintegrate and disappear. *Avalon* is ruled by a monochrome, sepia-toned aesthetic; even the non-game world is colourless, tinted over by a singular wash of unvaryingly dull brown. Nothing prepares us for the game world of Special A, however, until we read its game screen: 'Welcome to Class Real'. As Ash enters this highest level of Avalon, whose building 'has taken huge amounts of very sophisticated data', she pushes past a door from a darkened room only to find herself looking out at, of all places, modern-day Warsaw. As she peers past the edge of the door, the sepia-toned image gradually grows lighter as Ash and the screen gain colour – a literal dawning upon both character and viewer. Suddenly, the screen is awash with colour as we cut to shots of ubiquitous city-life: rumbling ad-bearing trams, a Coca-Cola sign in its instantly recognisable cursive, another sign advertising cigarettes, depicting a Western woman facing a Japanese geisha, their differences accentuated in their superficial cultural make-up (a modern suit for the former; traditional dress for the latter), even as their commonality is affirmed in their balancing the same-brand cigarette between their fingers.

This image is particularly significant. On one level, it is, of course, a nuanced statement on the cultural commingling of the co-production, which is marked as much by its commonality in terms of achieving a mutual goal (to make the film) as the cultural differences in the project (apparent if only by the number of translators necessarily running around the set). On a more pertinent level, however, this is also a telling de-delineation of familiarity and unfamiliarity, where the latter is ostensibly occupied by the Otherness of the Oriental feminine,[17] unfathomable in her chalk white mask of make-up, exotic in her bizarre hair style, yet with the boundaries of strangeness deliberately merged in explicit connection in their holding (and presumably smoking) the same brand of cigarette. One who should look, sound and seem so strange and unfamiliar to the other suddenly no longer does, bonded as they are to the common causes of cancerous ills and capitalist gains.

In the same way, our axes of familiarity with the imagery in the film are correspondingly obscured. For one instant, the ordinarily familiar real-world reality suddenly appears startlingly unfamiliar, radically inverted as it is from the CGI imagery of the game-world to which we have become accustomed, while the ostensibly unfamiliar, sepia-toned virtual reality of monsters and projections seems ordinary instead. The boundaries between the strange and the accustomed, demarcating the real/unreal/SFX poles of the image, are effectively now inverted, such that CGI is now reality, while contemporary Warsaw is exposed as special effect. More than that, they are also indistinguishable, as shock quickly subsides into recognition, so that the real world is familiar again, even if still lingeringly unfamiliar. Yet, that instant is sufficient to jolt me: how can something as inordinately pervasive as the Coca-Cola logo, something I have seen a million times before, strike me as being so unfamiliar? What binds my poles of strangeness and recognition at that moment is not seeing *the familiar within the unfamiliar*, as with the cases of the reactions in the previous section, but the unfamiliar within the familiar. In reconciling that newness within the old, I see the latter afresh and with startling clarity, as if I am seeing it as a strange object and for the first time. Yet, I am struck not because I have not seen it before, but precisely because I have. This, then, is the continuation of Proust's epiphanic visions – beyond the returning memories triggered by the recognised sensations of the madeleine, there is also the sense that they, unfamiliar even as they are familiar, are encountered anew, an event so profound and affected as to constitute epiphany, an experience 'so highly conscious':

> Yes: if … the returning memory can throw no bridge, form no connecting link between itself and the present minute, if it remains in the context of its own place and date, if it keeps its distance … for this very reason it causes us suddenly to breathe a new air, *an air which is new precisely because we have breathed it in the past*, that purer air which the poets have vainly tried to situate in paradise and which could induce so profound a sensation of renewal *only if it had been breathed before*, since the true paradises are the paradises that we have lost. (Proust 1992: 182; emphasis added)

In seeing the familiar as the unfamiliar and, further, in paradoxically realising its unfamiliarity as the core of its familiarity, vision is doubly enriched in its seeing something that is both new and old *at the same time*.

But what more can be achieved out of this extraordinary instant of vision? I return to the original point of epiphany: to manifest, to achieve insight, to create a greater awareness of our self and consciousness. Sometimes, I think our eyes get too tired of seeing the same familiar things and we simply *stop* – we become blind. Indeed, we are often blinder than we think. James Elkins, in his book on vision, *The Object Stares Back*, writes eloquently of how much we do *not* see:

> There are things we do not see and things we cannot see and things we refuse to see, and there are also things we can't make out, puzzling things and sickening things that make us wince. There are things too boring to see, too normal or unremarkable to ever catch the eye, things that fall through the cracks of vision, things so odd we never figure them out ... There are things emptied of meaning because they have no use, they answer to no desire ... There are flickering things we can't quite catch in the corner of our eye, movements that are gone when we turn our head ... The field of vision appears to be seamless, but it is shot through with holes. (1996: 205)

In the same way, there are also things we do not see simply because we see them too much, because they have become too familiar. CGI has created wondrous images of fantasy and imagination for the screen, yet we can still find in ourselves a deep reaction in seeing the ubiquitous and the mundane, simply by seeing them again. In that sense, we are not that much different from the 1890s audiences of the Lumière brothers' *L'Arroseur arrosé* (1895), who were reportedly 'delighted less by the scene being staged for their amusement than by the fact that, in the background, the leaves were fluttering in the wind' (Keathley n. d.). Yet, more than delight, more than wonder, the sense of insight, of the culminated heightened awareness of my consciousness, of epiphany, lies purely in its existence, its sheer fact of Cartesian simplicity: *I see*. I see, not because of any kind of extraordinary illumination, nor even the early novelties of cinema in representing the world, but because the use of CGI and technologies have inverted our poles of vision so that, engulfed in that wondrous unfamiliar, we have literally lost sight of the familiar, until in such moments, when we see it again. The wonder of post-CGI cinema is simply in the seeing of pre-CGI cinema again. Our visual re-apprehension is thus more than just in seeing, but also *re*-seeing – the seeing of seeing, and the seeing that we have forgotten to see. And sometimes what we have forgotten is more important than what we have remembered.

Undoubtedly, this notion of re-seeing as electric epiphany has been discussed before (albeit only in relation to photographic-based cinema). Anäis Nin, for example, describes a similar phenomenon of blinding familiarity in her 1963 lecture at the University of Chicago: 'The motion picture is capable of revealing objects and people as they are when you peel off the crust of indifference, of habit, of familiarity which blinds us' (1963–64: 13). But, for Nin, redemption lies in the poetics of the image, and its transfiguration is dramatic: 'And when, as in these films [such as *Venice Etude One* (1963/71)], it is done by poetic distillation it establishes direct, intimate contact with the reality concealed by clichés, and it is then that for a moment we can attain what the poets call inner illumination' (ibid.). Elkins, too, writes of epiphany in vision: 'Once in a great while there may be a flash of lightning and we see everything, but then the darkness returns' (1996: 206). But they are both writing of seeing the extraordinary, that which punctures everyday tedium with a clap of thunder. My point, rather, is the extraordinary in seeing the ordinary: the simplicity of merely seeing. Not everything requires trumpets, or poetry, or lightning, and occasionally, revelation lies simply in just seeing, nothing more or less. One little spot may do no more than quietly flash forth a little more unexpectedly – 'a point of light' – simply to allow us to again see something very ordinary, if only for a little while.

CONCLUSION

I have two final tasks to complete in my conclusion. The first is to connect epiph-any to love, which, I believe, linked etymologically or otherwise, is the core of cinephilia; I have argued elsewhere that cinephilia must encompass love, no mat-ter how subjective, personal or uncontainable in objective theory (see 2005). This platform of cinephiliac love easily applies to general epiphany: we love the cinema not least because, in every cinephile's experience, it has altered our lives (some more radically than others), and brought to us some form of transfiguration. Fred Camper's personal anecdote is, thus, really a collective one: how those lights and shadows have transformed our lives, changed the way we live, love and laugh.

However, with respect to the specific cinephiliac epiphany I have endeavoured to analyse here, in which a highly self-conscious and deeply affected moment is experienced in the interplay between familiar and unfamiliar sights, love may be a little more subtle. I suppose one could love insight, but insight could also be *of* love, and here I return to Willemen's basis of cinephilia, addressed in my intro-duction, whereby he refers to love as the function of revelation. On that same premise, I have posited an alternative vision which specifically relies on interplay between familiar and unfamiliar, so that old and new are not that remote from each other, and at times may even be of each other. The specific quest to engage CGI and digital technologies in my elaboration of these experiences is, thus, not motivated by trying to explicate a way of loving the new, but of loving the old in a way which engages and involves the new.

My second task, then, is to locate my thoughts in the broader contexts, to place where they might lie in furthering the discussion. In this lies my deliberate focus on the intermeshing of recorded and CGI visual regimes, in which I have hoped my discussion in this essay might offer another angle of address in two contexts. The first is that of discourse on the digital image, which mostly contin-ues to emphasise its differences from imagery of analogue inscription, in some cases rendering the two visual regimes not merely distinct but in bitter divorce.[18]

Yet, old and new media can also be seen to be interwoven in myriad and complex ways. Philip Rosen (2001b) offers one excellent example, elucidating the interfusion between analogue and digital imagery by drawing on the historicity of both media in order to suggest what he calls 'hybridity' in the interaction of their registers.[19] These added takes benefit the discussion in their provision of alternative perspectives; in that respect, I also hope that my essay, in proffering an argument on a cinephilia which includes an aspect of this interaction between film and digital, will provide similar nuance and contrast to the discussion of the digital image.

The second context is simply that of cinephilia itself. So long wrapped in nostalgia and regret for a certain era of love too closely connected to the 'old' regime of film images,[20] one obvious goal of this essay is to deliberately move out of that wistfulness and develop the discussion of cinephilia by extending it to new technologies, an ambition which, needless to say, dovetails with the general objective of the present collection: theorising cinephilia in the age of digital reproduction. To that extent, in this essay of a cinephilia which interweaves old and new, I hope not only to amplify cinephilia to contain CGI but also to echo that past age which so readily took in the wonders of the immediacy of the recorded image, its perfect reproduction of the reality in our world. In that sense, it is not only a small tribute to that sliver of history but also, perhaps, a reminder to ourselves that we had never left that wonder behind.

NOTES

1   See Joyce (2000: 182).

2   See Camper (2006).

3   See, in general, Epstein (1974); Abel (1988). See, in particular, Epstein (1978: 24–5; 1978: 26–30). See also Willemen (1994a: 124–133), which sets out to explicate *photogénie*.

4   The original source of this quote is in Wefel (1935) cited in *Lu* (November 1935).

5   See, generally, de Valck and Hagener (2005), for a varied and excellent exposition of cinephilia as a relation of love.

6   See, for instance, Jarvie (1960: 60–1); MacCabe (1976: 17–27); and Wollen (1976: 7–23).

7   See also Doane (2002: 225–32). Notably, Doane reframes Willemen's cinephilia in terms of indexicality: 'the indexical trace as filmic inscription of contingency is indissociable from affect. In the case of Willemen, that affect takes the precise form of cinephilia' (2002: 225). She similarly concludes that ontological questions spell the same end for

cinephilia *vis-à-vis* digital technologies: 'It is no accident that cinephilia and the conse-quent return to ontology should now emerge as the bearer of such high theoretical stakes ... One doesn't – and can't – love the televisual or the digital in quite the same way' (2002: 228).

8   See Nichols (1987: 206).

9   To this end, also note that the most formal use of 'epiphany' is the denotation of the Feast of Epiphany, a festival observed on the Christian calendar to commemorate the baptism of Jesus and, more significantly, the manifestation of him to the Gentiles, spe-cifically the Magi. The notion of revelation, needless to say, is also conspicuous here.

10   In the context of cinema, the revelatory wonder of the moment – the contingency – has also been discussed in film studies in different ways and contexts: see Doane (2002); Keathley (2006); and Charney (1995). See also Charney (1998).

11   On the other hand, also take note that discourse on this uncanny realism in the moving image may be counterpointed by the penchant for the equally uncanny *un*-real in the image, the ghostliness of replica, relic, shadow, apparition. Jean Epstein, whose con-cept of *photogénie* encapsulates perfectly the amorphous nature of this un-reality in cinema, writes: 'All this drama, all this love are but light and shadow ... *I see what is not and I see this unreal thing exactly*' (1984: 192; emphasis added). Stanley Cavell takes a similar position. Although first appearing to endorse reality in the image ('a photograph does not present us with "likenesses" of things; it presents us, we want to say, with the things themselves'), he immediately expresses his doubt and ambivalence: 'But wanting to say that may well make us ontologically restless. "Photographs present us with things themselves" sounds, and ought to sound, false or paradoxical' (1979: 17). See also Moore (2000: 84–95).

12   However, in this respect, note Philip Rosen's reading of Bazin's theory, to which he accredits precisely such a subjective, 'variable manifestation of human imagination' to fill what he describes as 'a gap between referent and signifier' (2001a: 23).

13   Vivian Sobchack writes of a similar 'the alien and the familiar' aesthetic in relation to sci-ence fiction films, albeit not in the context of digital technologies (see 1987: 107–45). See also Tom Gunning, who writes of regaining unfamiliarity with old technologies through twin strategies of 'de-familiarisation' and 'renewal' via Shklovsky and Heide-gger respectively (2003: 39–56).

14   Of course, not all CGI will or can possess this capacity to produce such impact; CGI is also often created and intended to be invisible for ease of post-production or other purposes, and most CGI will probably be encountered by the viewer with little or no effect. Cinephilia, after all, is about selectivity – the dredging up of specific moments held in significance. To that extent, it should be understood that my references to CGI cannot be all-inclusive, just as a film cinephile, talking about cinema, will not refer to all films, but only to those which have had a memorable impact on him/her.

15   See Proust: 'à l'instant meme où la gorgée mêlée de miettes de gateau toucha mon palais, je tressaillis, attentive à ce qui se passait d'extraordinaire en moi' (1992: 45).

16 Dialogue from *Avalon*.

17 For the classic thesis on orientalism as the Other, see Said (1985).

18 See, for example, Mitchell (1992). Cf Philip Rosen's excellent thesis, where he percep-
tively blends the historicity of old and new; unsurprisingly, Rosen also warns against
constructing narrow discourses: 'By associating representation in modernity more or
less "purely" with the wide diffusion of visual discourses, cultural theorists run the
danger of repressing the material, sensory and technical hybridity of modern life and
culture' (2001b: 303). Elsewhere, I have also argued that the two regimes of digital and
film are not as clear cut as they may be made out to be: see Ng (2007: 172–80).

19 See also Bolter and Grusin (2000).

20 See Sontag (2001: 117–22), for an essay on what has probably become the *locus clas-
sicus* for cinephilia as nostalgia. See also de Valck and Hagener (2005) as an express
project against such cinephilia.

REFERENCES

Abel, Richard (1988) *French Film Theory and Criticism, A History/Anthology 1907–1939*.
Princeton: Princeton University Press.

Artaud, Antonin (1978 [1927]) 'Sorcery and the Cinema', in P. Adams Sitney (ed.) *The Avant-
Garde Film: A Reader of Theory and Criticism*. New York: New York University Press,
49–50.

Barthes, Roland (2000) *Camera Lucida: Reflections on Photography*, trans. Richard Howard. London: Vintage.

Baudrillard, Jean (1983) *Simulations*, trans. Paul Foss, Paul Patton and Philip Beitchman.
New York: Semiotext(e), 2.

Bazin, André (1967 [1945]) 'The Ontology of the Photographic Image', in *What is Cinema?*
Volume 1, trans. Hugh Gray. Berkeley: University of California Press, 9–16.

Benjamin, Walter (1970 [1936]) 'The Work of Art in the Age of Mechanical Reproduction',
trans. Harry Zohn, in Hannah Arendt (ed.) *Illuminations*. London: Cape, 217–52.

Bolter, Jay David and Richard Grusin (2000) *Remediation: Understanding New Media*. Cambridge, MA: The MIT Press.

Buckland, Warren (1999) 'Between Science Fact and Science Fiction: Spielberg's Digital
Dinosaurs, Possible Worlds, and the New Aesthetic Realism', *Screen*, 40, 2, 177–92.

Camper, Fred (2006) *Frameworks* listserv. Online. Available at: http://www.hi-beam.net/fw/
fw31/0465.html. Accessed 8 February 2006.

Cavell, Stanley (1979) *The World Viewed*. Cambridge, MA: Harvard University Press.

Charney, Leo (1998) *Empty Moments: Cinema, Modernity and Drift*. Durham, NC: Duke
University Press.

_____ (1995) 'In a Moment: Film and the Philosophy of Modernity', in Leo Charney and Van-
essa R. Schwartz (eds.) *Cinema and the Invention of Modern Life*. Berkeley: University
of California Press, 279–96.

de Valck, Marijke and Malte Hagener (eds) (2005) *Cinephilia: Movies, Love and Memory*. Amsterdam: Amsterdam University Press.

Doane, Mary Ann (2002) *The Emergence of Cinematic Time: Modernity, Contingency, The Archive*. Cambridge, MA: Harvard University Press.

Elkins, James (1996) *The Object Stares Back: On the Nature of Seeing*. New York: Harvest.

Epstein, Jean (1974) *Écrits sur le cinema, 1921–1953*. Paris: Seghers.

_____ (1978a [1923]) 'The Essence of Cinema', trans. Stuart Liebman, in P. Adams Sitney (ed.) *The Avant-Garde Film: A Reader of Theory and Criticism*. New York: New York University Press, 24–5.

_____ (1978b [1924]) 'For A New Avant-Garde', trans. Stuart Liebman, in P. Adams Sitney (ed.) *The Avant-Garde Film: A Reader of Theory and Criticism*. New York: New York University Press, 26–30.

_____ (1981/82) 'Cine-Mystique', trans. Stuart Liebman, *Millennium Film Journal*, 10–11, 192–3.

Freud, Sigmund (1955 [1919]) 'The "Uncanny"', *Standard Edition*, vol. 17, trans. James Strachey. London: Hogath Press, 217–52.

Gunning, Tom (2003) 'Re-Newing Old Technologies: Astonishment, Second Nature, and the Uncanny in Technology from the Previous Turn-of-the-Century', in David Thornburn and Henry Jenkins (eds) *Rethinking Media Change: The Aesthetics of Transition*. Cambridge, MA: The MIT Press, 39–56.

Jarvie, Ian (1960) 'Bazin's Ontology', *Film Quarterly*, 14, 1, 60–1.

Joyce, James (2000) *A Portrait of the Artist as a Young Man*. Oxford: Oxford University Press.

Keathley, Christian (2006) *Cinephilia and History, or The Wind in the Trees*. Bloomington: Indiana University Press.

_____ (n. d.) 'The Cinephiliac Moment', *Framework: The Journal of Cinema and Media*. Online. Available at: http://www.frameworkonline.com/42ck.htm. Accessed 7 July 2007.

MacCabe, Colin (1976) 'Theory and Film: Principles of Realism and Pleasure', *Screen*, 17, 3, 17–27.

Manovich, Lev (2001) *The Language of New Media*. Cambridge, MA: The MIT Press.

Mitchell, William J. (1992) *The Reconfigured Eye: Visual Truth in the Post-Photographic Era*. Cambridge, MA: The MIT Press.

Moore, Rachel O. (2000) *Savage Theory: Cinema as Modern Magic*. Durham, NC: Duke University Press.

Ng, Jenna (2005) 'Love in the Time of Transcultural Fusion: Cinephilia, Homage and *Kill Bill*', in Marijke de Valck and Malte Hagener (eds) *Cinephilia: Movies, Love and Memory*. Amsterdam: Amsterdam University Press: 65–79.

_____ (2007) 'Virtual Cinematography and the Digital Real: (dis)placing the Moving Image Between Reality and Simulacra', in Damian Sutton, Susan Brind, Ray McKenzie (eds) *The State of the Real: Aesthetics in the Digital Age*. London: I. B. Tauris, 172–80.

Nichols, Ashton (1987) *The Poetics of Epiphany: Nineteenth-Century Origins of the Modern Literary Movement*. Tuscaloosa and London: University of Alabama Press.

Nin, Anaïs (1963–64) 'Poetics of the Film', *Film Culture*, 31, 12–13.

Pastan, Linda (1998) 'Carnival Evening', in *Carnival Evening: New and Selected Poems 1968–1998*. New York: W. W. Norton, 39.

Pierson, Michele (1999) 'CGI Effects in Hollywood Science-Fiction Cinema 1989–95: the Wonder Years', *Screen* 40, 2, 158–76.

____ (2002) *Special Effects: Still In Search of Wonder*. New York: Columbia University Press.

Prince, Stephen (1999 [1996]) 'True Lies: Perceptual Realism, Digital Images, and Film Theory', in Brian Henderson and Ann Martin (eds.) *Film Quarterly: Forty Years – A Selection*. Berkeley: University of California Press, 392–412.

Proust, Marcel (1992) *Á la recheche du temps perdu*. Paris: Gallimard.

Rosen, Philip (2001a) 'Subject, Ontology, and Historicity in Bazin', in *Change Mummified: Cinema, Historicity, Theory*. Minneapolis: University of Minnesota Press, 3–41.

____ (2001b) 'Old and New: Image, Indexicality, and Historicity in the Digital Utopia', in *Change Mummified: Cinema, Historicity, Theory*. Minneapolis: University of Minnesota Press, 301–49.

Said, Edward (1985) *Orientalism*. Harmondsworth: Penguin.

Sobchack, Vivian (1987) *Screening Space: The American Science Fiction Film*. New York: Ungar.

____ (ed.) (2000) *Meta-Morphing: Visual Transformation and the Culture of Quick-Change*. Minneapolis: University of Minnesota Press.

____ (2007) '"Cutting to the Quick": *Techne*, *Physis*, and *Poiesis* and the Attractions of Slow Motion', in Wanda Strauven (ed.) (2007) *The Cinema of Attractions Reloaded*. Amsterdam: Amsterdam University Press, 337–54.

Sontag, Susan (2001 [1996]) 'A Century of Cinema', in *Where the Stress Falls*. New York: Farrar, Straus and Giroux, 117–22.

Stern, Lesley (1997) 'I Think, Sebastian, Therefore … I Somersault: Film and the Uncanny', *Paradoxa*, 3, 3–4, 348–66.

Wägenbaur, Thomas (1993) *The Moment: A History, Typology and Theory of the Moment in Philosophy and Literature*. Frankfurt: Peter Lang.

Wefel, Franz (1935) 'Ein Sommernachtstraum, Ein Film von Shakespeare und Reinhardt', *Neues Wiener Journal*.

Willemen, Paul (1994a [1982]) '*Photogénie* and Epstein', in *Looks and Frictions: Essays in Cultural Studies and Film Theory*. London: British Film Institute, 124–33.

____ (1994b) 'Through the Glass Darkly: Cinephilia Reconsidered', in *Looks and Frictions: Essays in Cultural Studies and Film Theory*. London: British Film Institute, 223–57.

Wollen, Peter (1976) 'Ontology and Materialism in Film', *Screen*, 17, 1, 7–23.

CHAPTER FOUR
FLOATING HATS: A MERE DIVERSION?
Zach Campbell

Thursday, 6 July 2006

Floating Hats: A Mere Diversion?

While I still haven't reinstalled a DVD driver in my computer yet, I *have* figured out how to capture images playing in media players (a hint for those who were clueless like I was: in the 'tools-options-performance' menu, click 'advanced' and then de-check 'use overlays' under 'video acceleration'). So

this post will partly be an exercise in screen captures! [This post was originally illustrated with frames from MPEG videos–ZC.]

Hans Richter's *Vormittagsspuk* (*Ghosts Before Breakfast*, 1927–28) is regarded as either one of the last Dada films or one of the first surrealist films:

> The story ... was originally intended to follow Werner Gräff's film script about the rebellion of revolvers. Richter opposed this idea, reasoning that revolvers that rebel do not shoot; therefore, not shooting is not an action. Richter settled on a story about benign objects that rebel instead. 'We all had bourgeois bowler hats on.' The hats were attached to black strings on long poles and were swung from the top of a garage in front of the camera. (Foster 1998: 131–2)

A title at the beginning of the film reads, 'The Nazis destroyed the sound version of this film as degenerate art. It shows that even objects revolt against regimentation.' Richter infused his film with semiotic nuance; as Stephen Foster writes:

> The flying hat is another potent metaphor ... For a period of 100 years beginning

in 1827 the hat was commonly used as a symbol in German literature … In the German culture of the nineteenth century, hats that fly from people's heads were a sign of existential danger looming in the near future. The hat was the quintessence of the bourgeois citizen and a symbol of the status quo. Pictures and words indicating that hats no longer fitted well, and were threatening to slip off heads, indicated that society's stability was in danger. A more familiar twentieth-century image is cited by Walter Benjamin about Charlie Chaplin's trademark bowler hat: 'His derby wobbles for a lack of a secure place on his head, giving away the fact that the reign of the bourgeoisie is wobbling too.' (1998: 133)

By the end of the film, the hats of course come back to rest on the cipher-characters' bourgeois heads.

And one could draw the further conclusion that non-regimentation brings harmony (while strict regimentation sows the seeds of confusion and chaos). I don't know that Richter would have liked that reading: it's almost a Deleuzian buggery of his worldview. Still, the underlying principle is that *things get weird*, and hopefully *we get unsettled*.

But if we're unsettled, are we guaranteed to be unsettled out of our (perceived) sociopolitical complacency? When do anti-bourgeois art tactics shock the privileged targets? When do they simply give us something new and unusual to look at? For I have MPEG files of both Richter's *Ghosts Before Breakfast* and also the infamous 'Tara Reid tit slip' on my hard drive, and I find (celebrity gossip whore that I am) that since I have paid for neither of these, I don't know what the concrete difference is – aside from the fact that one is a digital reproduction of a work of art, and the other a digital showcase for, um, a work of plastic surgery.

They both fascinate me. And … might the supreme and carefree stupidity of a Hollywood party-starlet achieve the greater political good, though, galvanising me into disgust for the star system and the culture it sits atop, blinding us to more important things? The fact that I rarely pay for multiplex entertainment – that I went through the calendar year 2005 giving truly *almost nothing* to this monstrous establishment (or even its art-house peripheries) – should stand for *something*, right? Then again, I find that even as I happily skip the films, television shows and music of the celebrities I love to hate, I still spend my time reading, repeating and discussing gossip about them. Is meta-entertainment a new form of entertainment, a new articulation of the culture industry?! It is this possibility that makes me think that something like a Hans Richter film has a renewed cultural viability: its *straightforward* attack on convention, which for a postmodern moment might have seemed achingly quaint, may actually be as *true* as it is *easy*. Sincerity rests at our feet, maybe a valuable tool, and I wonder if we (like the American national soccer team) will fumble with this object at our feet though we are so close to the goal…

(Posted by Zach Campbell)

REFERENCE

Foster, Stephen C. (1998) *Hans Richter: Activism, Modernism and the Avant-Garde.* Cambridge, MA: The MIT Press.

CHAPTER FIVE
SENSING AN INTELLECTUAL *NEMESIS*
Jason Sperb

> The period of grand theory, which saw film studies secure its position as an academic discipline, was marked by a cinephobia that resulted in film academics seeing as their responsibility the systematic undermining and exposure of virtually all of the most basic cinematic pleasures – this in spite of the fact that the majority of these academics were devout cinephiles.
>
> – Christian Keathley, *Cinephilia and History*[1]

The dynamic incision of pleasure, its disruptions and its openings, is a central, though seldom foregrounded, issue within the immense body of critical film studies. And the lingering visibility of pleasure's discursive scar, cinephilia, has not been masked with the emergence of digital visual effects, but rather has become intensified, throbbing, in tandem with the rising awareness of its mutating and liberatory possibilities. Thus, I have a sense that something, in a wave of digital cinephobia, has been missed thus far – a gap in thinking about the unthought, and about cinephilia in the contemporary historical period. This chapter argues that there is generous room within, and in excess of, a visual effects cinema, for addressing the lingering question of cinephilia.

Let me start with what has been called a 'cinephiliac anecdote'[2]: a few years back, I went with a friend to see *Star Trek: Nemesis* (2002) at the Carmike 10 in Stillwater, Oklahoma. The Carmike is an old, run-down multiplex on the outskirts of a small town and, therefore, not the preferred method of seeing a big-screen, special effects spectacle. But, for spectators unwilling to drive fifty minutes to the latest AMC twenty-screen palace outside Oklahoma City, it is the only option for seeing a new release. In spite of the poor audiovisual quality, I loved the film; reviews suggest that I am the only one. Indeed, my friend seemed almost beside herself in confusion as to why I liked it (we had a similar conversation that winter about *Die Another Day* (2002) – quite odd, in retrospect, given that I'm used to being disappointed by such hyped films). It was immediately clear I could not quite account for my response to the film; I could only say that I loved it – loved the experience of watching it. My inability to provide an objective or logical reason for this love is a hallmark of the cinephiliac moment. As Christian Keathley explains, 'Because cinephiliac moments are themselves intensely subjective, bound up perhaps with personal value of some unrecoverable meaning, writing about such moments will often mobilise personal information' (2006: 145). Thus, somehow, *Nemesis* awoke the cinephiliac within me. There were several things that intrigued me about *Nemesis* (both plot twists and technical wizardry featuring scale models and Computer-Generated Imagery (CGI)), yet when I tried to explain to my friend why I liked the film, I could only boil it down to one moment in the narrative.

Halfway through the film, the Starship Enterprise collides head-on with the Reman battleship, the Scimitar, in a striking sequence featuring effective model work, sensual digital imagery and hauntingly sparse sounds. The score drops off the soundtrack, leaving only the boom of the collision, followed by the awkward silence of space. When I tried to explain the impact this moment had on me, however, I could only say, 'I just really liked the scene where the ships collided. It felt real.' This was hardly an intellectually satisfying account of a moment which had produced such pleasure, especially given that we were two aspiring academics. Perhaps, in retrospect, my inability to reinscribe it with much meaning or cognitive value was inversely a testament to the intense pleasures the film aroused within me. Indeed, Keathley writes, 'If a moment … produces a flush of intense pleasure, its explanation is always a bit of a disappointment, for it inevitably deflates the number of imagined potential readings, settling comfortably and unambiguously on just one' (2006: 137).[3] The overwhelming pleasure perhaps explains my own ineffective explanation.

Yet I had no idea then that I had devolved (or evolved) into a cinephile in that moment. I had only enjoyed myself. Keathley argues that 'not only do these encounters exist as quasi-memories, but often times, cinephiliac moments are not identified except upon reflection' (2006: 145). And so, looking back at that scene again, returning to and reflecting upon that first moment of irretrievable bliss[4] several years later, I realise that indeed much was there to arouse such pleasures – I loved the prolonged digital images of the two collided ships as one, meshed together, the front of the Enterprise penetrating deeply into the hull of the Reman vessel to the point where they look almost indistinguishable. And I loved the moments when the two ships pulled back apart – slowly, awkwardly, painfully, before re-engaging in battle – as much as I had loved the initial moment of impact. And watching it again, I realised that what still provokes a great deal of love from me for the film is not just the astonishing spectacle of the collision. It is more specific than that. I look closely and see the fragments of the two ships' hulls, dispersing randomly into space after that first moment of collision. Tiny particles of metal float up into space, first upon the devastating, tortured invasion of the one ship into the other, and then again as the Reman ship pulls back. It is not the overall spectacle of these moments as much as it is the details – the particle animation of floating metal.

There is little doubt here that this sequence – *something* in the sequence – provoked a *cinephiliac moment* for me. One of the most noted recent critics on cinephilia, Paul Willemen, has dubbed '"the cinephiliac moment" [as] the fetishising of fragments of a film, either individual shots or marginal (often unintentional) details in the image, especially those that appear only for a moment' (in Keathley 2006: 7). Willemen also says, 'when a cinephile selects a fragment, a net is cast over the film which trawls up particular moments' (1994: 237). Although Willemen is not referring to digital effects, *Nemesis* is especially useful in this instance because it provokes the fetishising of fragments (in this case, literally); *Nemesis* arouses joy in me. And, co-presently, it provokes thought, provokes the obligation to 'make our intuition intelligible' (Keathley 2006: 145). It compels me to look closer, at the specific production details of that particular shot. As detailed in *Cinefex* (see Norton 2003: 107), the collision itself was first done with 1/45-scale models and then in post-production they 'were lined up and blended with the full CG versions of both ships' (2003: 108). As I learned later, the fragments themselves were both model shards and reconstituted computer-generated particles. According to associate visual effects supervisor Kelly Port, 'it was really tricky because there was just so much minute debris' and the designers merged the debris from the original model crash with 'additional CG debris' to the point that they were all indistinguishable (in Norton 2003: 109). And, by looking at the production of that shot, one begins to sense the larger, though perhaps unheralded, significance of cinephiliac fragments to visual effects films.

There is a sense in which this 'fetishising of fragments' – if we define it a little more broadly than Willemen does – speaks to the larger discussion of cinephilia's relationship to digital effects in contemporary films of this nature. For example, many films featuring overt digital work rely on the lingering effect of small moments and images within the larger film, and within the larger frame, both to promote significant opening weekends at the box office, and to attract repeat business. In the course of making a film, technicians will spend months on a single sequence, or even a single shot, with the anticipation that it is the fragments (embedded within the more celebrated spectacle of the overall effects images) that will cement the film's appeal. Moreover, it is often the affective jolt of fragments (debris, rubble, scraps, particles), more so than the intended central object of the image (spaceships, say), which add to the sense of realism in these shots, giving them a defamiliarising effect – just when one might be inclined to say that 'of course, the shot is fake', a fragment, or two, or a hundred, scatter across the screen, which then disrupt that conscious assumption. There is, as another example, a shot in *Terminator 3: Rise of the Machines* (2003), which achieves a similar effect to that in *Nemesis*. As the back of a crane truck slowly rises into the air and prepares to flip over during a crash, digitised fragments of the truck can be seen falling from the vehicle's underbelly in the background. Here, it is as much the parts of the crane truck coming loose as it is the flipping vehicle itself which makes the shot so effective. Likewise, there is a largely digital shot in *Final Destination 2* (2003) of logs falling off a trailer at high speeds on the highway, an image that works in no small part because of the added debris – the bits of bark flying off the wood as it hits the open road. In each of the three cases, there was a conscious effort (as the respective DVD special features all make a point to highlight) to insert fragments of various sorts into the shot, to enhance the existing image with additional debris, to make it more memorable for audiences. Specifically, they were added by the computer designers to heighten the effect of realism within and in excess of the overall digital shots. It is this Bazinian *effect* of realism (to which I will return later) that is often crucial to current theories of cinephilia. And, it is important to note, this is what cinephilia has become today – not a historical moment or cultural movement alone, but a theory.

Likewise, I am not writing this with the intention of positing an intellectual argument for *Nemesis*'s cultural or historical value; rather, I am trying to articulate its *affect*, the sense I get from it and that it makes for me. Some may not consciously think of the fragments when watching these films, but it is the particles that contribute immensely to how the image disturbs the spectator, and it may in retrospect be the fragments that the viewer holds onto – fetishises – on subsequent viewings and within acts of reflection. Prior to an exploration of a film's production, or of its kinship to other films of that nature, I am articulating a first moment of intuition, which I believe can be there for any number of people experiencing an overtly digital cinema:

> Intuition does come with a demand, however; namely, that we make our intuition intelligible, to ourselves and to others. We can only do that by following our intuition to the point of tuition – to the point where our intuition teaches us something. The goal of the cinephile is, similarly, to bring our interest in (or our intuition about) a particular filmic moment to the point where we can learn from it, or with it. (Keathley 2006: 134)

I write here about *Nemesis* precisely because it instils in me that which I cannot quite grasp, but which also causes me to believe that we can make an intelligible argument about something – namely, the virtual pleasures of effects such as CGI. This essay follows Keathley's notion of an intuitive approach to digital effects and digital cinema, and thus remains open to the possibility of cinephilia within this new milieu. For what is this concept of love if not a feeling? And, in a way, *Nemesis*'s marginal status – on a parallel track – makes it all the more perfect for the cinephile. The possibility that its critical and box office failure may well have helped to kill *The Next Generation* film franchise makes it that ideal object of such obscurity, novelty and rarity which serves – in part – to help define the cinephile's tendencies. *Nemesis* does not, of course, occupy the same space that *Star Wars* or *Lord of the Rings* does, or even other *Star Trek* films. While recent scholars such as Thomas Elsaesser theorise cinephilia in relation to more mainstream films, older ways of thinking about cinephilia seem rooted in the pursuit of hard-to-find, elusive films as well as in particular reception practices. Implicit in traditional cinephilia is the cult value of things not yet seen by many.

Perhaps the new generation of cinephiles will find joy where others have refused to go (or even to acknowledge) – special effects films. Perhaps, what is today secret is the love of (mainstream) films most present. But to inject the affect of CGI into a discussion of cinephilia is to risk creating a temporal paradox – can we reconcile the nostalgia of cinephilia with the advances of digital imagery? Can the pastness of one continue to reinvigorate the newness of the other? In a recent article, Drehli Robnik argues that 'the isolated, fetishised "key image" that achieves paradigmatic status in digital cinema can be seen as the mass cultural aggregate of cinephilia's fascinating, revelatory moment' (2005: 59). And we can break that image and that moment down further, so that – as in *Nemesis* – the 'key image' contains different 'revelatory' moments for different people. I think we can begin more explicitly to think of cinephilia for its affective qualities – what it inspires in the viewer, within but also beyond fascination. According to Peter Wollen, cinephilia means an 'obsessive infatuation with film, to the point of letting it dominate your life' (2001: 133). Even though *Nemesis* is a movie I hadn't thought of in years, it has provoked within me the present project – studying this material and recording this moment, even though I can barely understand what it was that I experienced. Revealing the cinephile that sustains the scholar, I can say I've not based too many essays on just one cinematic moment.

As Scott Bukatman notes in what may be the first cinephiliac reading of contemporary visual effects, *'there is no getting rid of me in the following pages* – my initial or ongoing fascination guides my writing, and I write primarily out of respect for that fascination' (2003: 6; emphasis added). To argue for *Nemesis* and the spectacular pleasures provided by CGI, as well as mainstream cinephilia, implies working against established academic models of thinking. This essay attempts to sense and give sense to that which rational intellect tells me does not exist – cinephilia (except maybe as a historical movement in the past). It is a relatively short trek back through the more recent discussions of cinephilia, with the hopes of modestly raising the possibilities of such for some of the pleasures of digital cinema – a sense of joy, in spite of the intellectual tendency to dismiss feeling and pleasure. Keathley notes how writing about cinephilia is 'a discursive echo, a simulation through research and writing of the initial filmic experience' (2006: 151). Academics and critics often use cinephilia to echo what we originally heard and saw. And thus academia cannot but help to privilege the echoes. Indeed, as one character says in *Nemesis*, there is always the possibility of the 'victory of the echo over the voice'. But, conversely, this essay is not an attempt to justify or explain what happened that cold November night in Oklahoma (for that moment is forever lost to time, trapped in an unformed blur of nostalgia and memory), but is an attempt to show how such moments could have happened (and will one day again).

THE PRESENCE OF CINEPHILIA PAST

If nothing else, it is difficult to deny the *potential* of digital visual effects, and with it new cinematic possibilities. And, crucially, it is that potential which one cannot help but celebrate. Adrian Martin writes: 'the cinema of highly technological artifice, of special effects, digitalisation and morphing, leads us to contemplate a radically different kind of cinematic body' (in Rosenbaum *et al.* 2003: 7). And yet, some remain unconvinced. David Mamet laments the spectacle of films today. Not surprisingly, he – an accomplished playwright and screenwriter – focuses on the insignificance of the screenwriter today: 'It does not require a dramatist to "script" a film based on thrills. The requirements of such films are not more elaborate than and, in effect, are fairly identical to those of a straight-out pornographic film' (1996: 120).[5] Ironically (because some embrace the very same comparison), Mamet links the mindless films of today with the cinema's original attractions:

> Films have degenerated to their original operation as carnival amusement – they offer not drama, but *thrills* (the early nickelodeon showed a freight train steaming toward the audience, and they, unused to the technology, said, 'how real', and were stunned. Today's computer morphing, bluescreen, et cetera, function similarly). (Ibid.; emphasis in original)

Mamet focuses on how the screenplay no longer needs to be literate. It can vaguely describe that (action sequences, sex scenes) which filmmakers will later develop themselves in the production or post-production process. Mamet criticises the lack of opportunity for screenwriters to show drama, to reveal its subtleties, in favour of a bland description that assumes the reader already knows what's being described. 'The pornographic and the mass market Hollywood film', he bemoans, 'string together titillating instances of sex, violence and emotional exploitativeness – these instances separated by boring bits of nonsense called, in the trade, backstory or narration' (1996: 125). Yet in attacking spectacle and bluescreen, Mamet misses what those who lament the death of cinephilia also miss – that the experience of cinema might be considered beyond language. Though his own work has produced much joy for others (on stage and on screen), Mamet himself is reluctant to find pleasure in the cinema today.

Mamet's cynicism about the state of cinema is hardly unique. The most famous lament remains Susan Sontag's short but highly productive attack on cinephilia in the mid-1990s. In it, Sontag suggests that 'ordinary films, films made purely for entertainment (that is, commercial) purposes, will continue to be astonishingly witless; already the vast majority fail resoundingly to appeal to their cynically targeted audiences' (2001: 117). Sontag does not see future opportunity and possibility in the proliferation of the cinema and its mass distribution, but instead considers that 'the sheer ubiquity of moving images has steadily under-mined the standards people once had for cinema as art ' (2001: 119). Under the guise of a decay of cinema, Sontag is really lamenting cinephilia here: 'perhaps it is not cinema which has ended but only cinephilia – the name of the distinctive kind of love that cinema inspired' (2001: 117). For her, cinephilia was 'born of the conviction that cinema was an art unlike any other: quintessentially modern; distinctively accessible; poetic and mysterious and erotic and moral – all at the same time' (2001: 117–18). It was in the postwar era 'that going to movies, thinking about movies, talking about movies became a passion among university students and other young people' (2001: 119). Certainly, an innocence pervades her article – a nostalgia and a deep sense of history not uncommon in many valu-able discussions of cinephilia.

To read Sontag's utopian description of the experience of moviegoing – 'to surrender to, to be transported by, what was on the screen' (2001: 118) – it is not hard to see how she could have come to such cynical conclusions about its cur-rent state. 'No amount of mourning', she emphasises, 'will revive the vanished rituals – erotic, ruminative – of the darkened theatre' (2001: 119). In the age of this 'mourning', it seems impossible that cinephilia could still hold a place in discussions, for certainly the moments Sontag spoke of are gone. Indeed, at the heart of her essay is a requiem for the death of cinephilia:

> Predictably, the love of cinema has waned. People still like going to the movies, and
> some people still care about and expect something special, necessary from a film
> … But one hardly finds anymore, at least among the young, the distinctive cineph-
> ilic love of movies, which is not simply love of but a certain taste in films (grounded
> in a vast appetite for seeing and reseeing as much as possible of cinema's glorious
> past). Cinephilia itself has come under attack, as something quaint, outmoded,
> snobbish. For cinephilia implies that films are unique, unrepeatable, magic experi-
> ences. (2001: 122)

The affective powers of film may allow, in a way, for any film to continue to be a 'unique, unrepeatable, magic experience', whereby even the cinephile's notori-ous desire for repetition is itself predicated on, and driven by the lack within, the reality of the unrepeatable experience (just as, for instance, this essay is written under the explicit recognition that one cannot return to Oklahoma in the winter of 2002). If cinephilia has waned for spectators of Sontag's generation, it might be because they hold on so tightly to a historically specific mode of cine-philia (described above) that newer, 'young' generations seem unable to grasp (unable to reproduce or proliferate), particularly since exhibition and distribution practices have changed so radically in the past three decades. Paradoxically, cine-philia must embrace the unrepeatable in order to be repeatable – that is, free the fragments of the cinephiliac moment from their social and historical origins. In Sontag's defence, she does hold out hope for change, acknowledging the evolu-tion of generations. 'If cinephilia is dead, then movies are dead ... no matter how many times movies, even very good ones, go on being made', she reiterates, adding though, that, 'if cinema can be resurrected, it will only be through the birth of a new kind of cine-love' (ibid.). So, perhaps, Sontag leaves the door open after all. And, indeed, by working my way through the recent scholarship on cinephilia, I hope to show at once the fixation on the past and, simultaneously, the cracks opening up the possibilities for a new generation of cinephilia, one rooted in the spirit if not in the specifics of the older cinephilia. For if the next generation is to give birth to a new kind of 'cine-love', its roots must first be present in the past.

Sontag's greatest contribution ultimately may not have been the essay itself, but the ways in which her essay provoked others into taking up the issue of cinephilia once again – not to lament the decay of cinema, but to force others to give birth to the next cinephilia, towards which Thomas Elsaesser points us in earnest, acknowledging the need to rethink the temporality of cinephilia:

> Cinephilia take two [the second wave of cinephilia] is therefore painfully aware of the paradox that Cinephilia take one may have lived out in practice, but would not ultimately confront. Namely, that attachment to the unique moment and to that special place [...] is already (as psychoanalysis was at pains to point out) the enact-ment of a search for lost time, and thus the acknowledgement that the singular moment stands under the regime of repetition, of the re-take, of the iterative, the compulsively serial, the fetishistic, the fragmented and the fractal. (2005: 39)

Cinephilia take one collapsed under the weight of this paradox, and thus to talk presently of cinephilia is to see such tension as an antimony – past and pres-ent, the unrepeatable and repetition, co-exist, but are irreducible to each other. Sontag's death of cinephilia is tied exclusively to 'the unique moment and to that special place'. But it is the unrepeatable which provokes the desire for repeti-tion. Her proclamation of the death of cinephilia conversely prolonged its life by bringing cinephilia back into consciousness, forcing people such as Elsaesser to articulate the possibility of a 'Cinephilia take two', which would acknowledge 'the regime of repetition, of the re-take, of the iterative, the compulsively serial, the fetishistic, the fragmented and the fractal' inherent in a love of film, and which both contains and (as Sontag seemed unable to do) rejects, through that containment, the past on which it is built.

'I read recently an article by Susan Sontag in which she argued that cinephilia was dead, even in Paris', writes Peter Wollen. 'I hope not. I am not convinced' (2001: 119). Wollen sees cinema for the cinephile 'as the symptom of a desire to remain within a child's view of the world, always outside, always fascinated by a mysterious parental drama, always seeking to master one's anxiety by compulsive repetition' (ibid.). This certainly contrasts with Sontag's belief that cinephilia was unique and unrepeatable. Yet, as evidenced in part by the metaphor of a child, Wollen too is trapped in the past – 'when these decrepit, run-down cinemas [he visited as a kid] closed, classic cinema ended with them' (ibid.). He retraces the paths of the old ways of cinephilia. 'The first cinephiles gathered in clandestinity, in secret cine-clubs', he writes, 'to watch forbidden films from the prewar days' (2001: 120).

Movie Mutations: The Changing Face of World Cinephilia, too, responds to Sontag's decree, while confronting the question of digital cinema's place in the history of cinephilia. 'The main message someone of my generation (born in 1943) hears almost daily', writes Jonathan Rosenbaum, referencing the laments of figures such as Sontag, 'is that cinephilia as we once knew it is dying' (2003: 1). A collected dialogue of several noted scholars, the book features their cinephilia as rooted in the ability to uncover new and/or unfamiliar international films, and to tap into a growing global community of cinephiles. They also take up, loosely, the issue of CGI cinema, with conflicting and inconclusive results. Adrian Martin notes 'this mysterious thing popularly called "digital cinema", which brings with it a new definition of the filmic image' (in Rosenbaum & Martin 2003: vii). Alexander Horwath is harsher in his views – 'I have to admit that I perceive most pop blockbusters (which pursue a complete dematerialisation and virtualisation) as genuinely inhuman' (in Rosenbaum *et al.* 2003: 17). For Horwath, the use of primitive, low-tech and low-budget effects create a more authentic image and experience than digital effects. He adds, 'if we believe in cinema, we must also believe that it will always find a beautiful antibody for each virus' (ibid.). I, too, do not like every CGI image I see – many seem horribly fake and distracting. That said, the critics of *Movie Mutations* are generally optimistic about the future of film, putting them at odds with Sontag's cynicism, though they do not explicitly endorse digital cinema. When addressing popular cinema, Martin admits that:

> I get a different kind of energy, no less for the soul's survival, from a completely commercial kind of cinema, a cinema of spectacle decried still today by so many of even a slightly Situationist bent. I mean a kind of pop cinema that includes De Palma's *Mission Impossible* (1996), Tim Burton's movies, Joe Dante's *Gremlins*

2 (1990) – kinetic, sometimes cartoonish, extremely artificial and technologically mutated movies with no small claim on the cinematic language of tomorrow … films completely comprised of pop quotes, clichés and stereotypes, but blessed with the will and the inventiveness to animate these tokens, to combine and revive and spin them at a dizzy rate. (In Rosenbaum *et al*. 2003: 6)

Though, like Wollen and Sontag, very much still rooted in the past, *Movie Mutations* shows an appreciation for the present, and for the future. Adds Nicole Brenez: 'the cinema seems to me above all inexhaustibly generous' (in Rosenbaum *et al*. 2003: 27). If there is one thing that both this particular cinephilia and CGI have in common, it is potential – a generous, excessive potential.

In a more recent article in *Michigan Quarterly Review*, James Morrison also discusses cinephilia, responding specifically to Sontag's proclamation. 'All the chatter about the death of cinema was somehow predictable, especially at the onset of new digital media that posed direct challenges to the primacy of film' (2005: 393). Morrison assumes that the death of cinephilia as it was previously articulated extends from the mass distribution and availability of films today. 'The urge of the cinephile was to rescue such works', he argues, 'to restore them to the greatness that was proper to them, while also protecting them, keeping them from the grasp of the uncomprehending masses' (2005: 395). Morrison argues that postwar cinephiles desired the mystique or aura around film, and that film's increasing ubiquity and accessibility in the era of the Internet, DVDs and mass distribution, makes such an aura impossible. As films become more accessible to us, they lose their cinephiliac value to audiences. While valid in so far as it no doubt reflects the prevailing attitudes of many DVD collectors, this argument would also seem to perhaps suggest the disputable assertion that the mass distribution of films somehow makes these experiences any less unique. Just because we can see any number of once-elusive films at any given point does not automatically rob them of their mystique. Each film and each film moment still contains the possibility of a unique affect on a particular viewer, irrespective of circulation.

Indeed, the most famous and oft-quoted response to Sontag is probably Willemen's, which offers a Lacanian approach to cinephilia and emphasises the effects of the Real. Although he does not place emphasis on the word, Willemen nevertheless pushes us towards an affective theory of cinephilia, 'something that escaped rationalised, critical-theoretical discourse' (1994: 233). He also attempts to think what is unthought – in his case, the Real – and works against the belief that 'the desire for cinema is encompassed by a socio-political framework that excludes the very possibility of relating to cinema in any terms other than socio-political productivity manifested in the modification of behaviour' (1994: 224). Willemen raises the possibility of cinephilia as an emphasis on the moment and on the details, though he proceeds cautiously. After acknowledging that 'not everyone would agree with the idea that cinephilia is a fetishising of a particular moment in film', he notes:

> they would think they were just, as the word says, 'loving cinema'. They would not necessarily privilege one aspect of cinema. In a sense that's the problem I'm trying to address through the notion of cinephilia. Cinephilia itself describes simultaneously a particular relationship to cinema (and the question then opens up of what kind of relationship that might be) and it also describes a particular historical period of relating to cinema. (1994: 227)

Willemen goes on to raise the idea of a 'cinephiliac moment', which he notes is 'my preferred description because it has overtones of necrophilia, of relating to something that is dead, past, but alive in memory' (ibid.). Thus Willemen responds to Sontag by acknowledging that while a historically past mode of cinephilia may be dead, it remains alive as a new cinephilia that focuses on memory and in which 'affect, pleasure, intensity, neuroses and their forms of rationalisation, all … go hand-in-hand' (1994: 233).

The historical variability of cinephilia is compounded by the fact that cinephiliac moments are not uniform and are always already passing. This is so because 'what is being revealed is subjective, fleeting, variable, depending on a set of desires and the subjective constitution that is involved in a specific encounter with a specific film' (1994: 236). And yet what is at play here (for me, Willemen, Keathley and others) is not just pleasure – but what pleasure compels us to. 'There are moments which, when encountered in a film, spark something that then produces the energy and the desire to write, to find formulations to convey something about the intensity of that spark … But the rationalisation did not make the sparks go away' (1994: 235). Although Willemen avoids the problem of digital cinema directly, his language pushes us towards the new possibilities of experience, affect and cinephilia in the future, and not just the past:

> What is being looked for is a moment or, given that a moment is too unitary, a dimension of a moment which triggers for the viewer either the realisation or the illusion of a realisation that what is being seen is in excess of what is being shown. Consequently, you see something that is revelatory. It reveals an aspect or a dimension of a person, whether it's the actor or the director, which is not choreographed for you to see. It is produced *en plus*, in excess or in addition, almost involuntarily. (1994: 237)

We have here the surplus of the cinephiliac moment – what is perceived by the cinephile in excess of the representation itself. This moment is neither choreographed nor explicitly planned and generates fascination that may be entirely unique and subjective. What we see compels us to think further about the experience we had and the pleasure it instilled in us. 'In the sense that revelation presupposes surprise or presupposes a moment that is not programmed', he writes, 'then the spark can happen that activates the cinephiliac's pleasures' (ibid.). We have in Willemen's work the first inklings of an affective cinephilia – the emphasis on what is generated in the viewer by the image. There is a *something* that is necessarily elusive and nonverbal, 'that comes through because of the cinema's ontological dimension and because of the nature of attention and the relationship of pleasure which is catered for between the image and the viewer' (1994: 256). Affect is productive here, I think, because it both articulates – however fleetingly – experience, and foregrounds the secondary nature of representation. Representation is relevant in so far as it generates something beyond representation. In Willemen's terms, representation is 'what is being shown', affect is what 'is being seen'. In this sense, it seems difficult for CGI and other digital effects not to have relevance for the cinephiliac, since the cinephiliac moment is itself *outside the narrative* – that is, in the same place where critics of overtly digital cinema place the spectacle. Yet, this is an issue Willemen avoids addressing and in fact specifically rejects, because of his and Keathley's reliance on the legacy of André Bazin, a writer whose work would seem on the surface antithetical to any discussion of digital cinema.

Though there is not sufficient room to develop adequately the extent of his importance, Bazin's presence looms large in cinephilia. I would like in earnest to raise the possibility that Bazin should in time be reconsidered – that is, his own temporal destiny will demand a rethinking both of digital effects and of cinephilia, two debates at whose core his theories of realism rest. The spark of realism in the image, read through Bazin, in part constitutes for Willemen and Keathley the possibilities for the cinephiliac moment. It is my contention, however, that Bazin's theories depend upon a spark which is an affect of realism, and not merely a representation of realism. That is to say, 'realism' *begins* in and in excess of the image, or what Thomas Elsaesser and Warren Buckland have called Bazin's 'surplus of realism' (2002: 211). And yet a tension nevertheless remains. 'Cinema is still perceived as being completely locked into the "before" of the electronification of the image', Willemen writes. 'It doesn't necessarily have to be locked into that moment, but cinephilia is one of the discourses that says cinema is locked into it. And I agree with the cinephiles' (1994: 244). But such a position is simply not historically viable – there is no going 'before' the electronification of the image, nor can anything grow (including cinephilia) in such a Sontagian time freeze. And it perceives Bazin's 'Ontology of the Photographic Image' (1945) as positing a realism through its mimetic qualities, rather than in the image itself. Indeed, it seems difficult – when one examines what Bazin calls the 'myth of total cinema' – to argue that representation is not primary to the constitution of realism, rather than the reverse. Adds Willemen, 'what people like Bazin want you to relate to in their polemic is precisely the dimension of revelation that is obtained by pointing your camera at something that hasn't been staged for the camera' (1994: 243). It is the act of 'revelation' that really preoccupies Bazin. By identifying the 'likeness of the real, with its own temporal destiny' (1967: 10), Bazin implicitly, but clearly, makes a distinction between the real and its reproductions. It is not the creation of the real, but rather of a representation of an ideal world with an ontology separate from the real. Working off the history of perspective and representation, Bazin imagines 'a kind of psychic fourth dimension that could suggest life in the tortured immobility of baroque art' (1967: 11). For Bazin, movement creates life *in* art, as opposed to art reproducing or representing life.

The ontology of the image for Bazin is realism, but I believe it is a realism created *in* the image – not a realism retrieved *through* the image. As he himself admits, 'no one believes any longer in the ontological identity of model and image' (1967: 10). And in this sense, it becomes difficult to argue that Bazin has no relevance when talking about the electronification of the image, if the original model itself is not the primary concern. This isn't to say that Bazin can be directly translated to digital cinema, and as I said above there is not sufficient room to develop fully the possibilities. I am only attempting to suggest that in works such as 'The Ontology of the Photographic Image', Bazin is focused on *what the medium does*, more so than what exists prior to the medium. 'It should be evident', Bukatman writes of the sublime in special effects, 'that spectacular experience – the experience of spectacle – is something more than a virtual, illusory, engagement with a not so real world. Media do not simply (or pretend to) mediate a pre-existent real. Our experience of media is a *real* experience, not just an idea of one' (2003: 4 emphasis added). I would add, too, that Bazin's 'experience of media is a *real* experience, not just an idea of one' – the spark of realism is in the frame, not just the idea (or representation) of that spark.

Christian Keathley's response to Sontag and Willemen is helpful to a discussion of cinephilia and digital cinema. Keathley adopts the 1920s brand of cinephilia that embraced the new modern medium and its creative potential, and uses it to benefit film history and reception studies, expanding Willemen's concept of the cinephiliac moment as 'this fetishisation of marginal, otherwise ordinary details in the motion picture image is as old as the cinema itself' (2006: 8). Keathley's work considers 'an area of spectatorial experience that resists co-optation by meaning; indeed, if the cinephiliac moment is among the most intense of cinematic experiences, it seems to draw its intensity partly from the fact that it cannot be reduced or tamed by interpretation' (2006: 9). Perhaps, digital cinema, as in *Nemesis*, also heightens and intensifies the 'marginal' images in film that lie outside the habitual practices of interpretation and narrative. The cinephile is 'mobilised by discovery of what has been captured unexpectedly' (2006: 39). Again, we run into Bazin here, but it is a productive dilemma that allows us to take the final turn towards the cinephiliac possibilities of digital images and effects. It is difficult to argue that anything produced by CGI was done so 'unexpectedly', but not impossible.

Consider, for a moment, an anecdote from the making of the *Lord of the Rings* trilogy. If, as Keathley insists, 'our knowledge of how the photographic image is produced is crucial in our response to it' (2006: 57), then it may serve a useful purpose to consider the specifics of CGI animation. The animators on *Lord of the Rings* were attempting to generate one of the films' many epic battle sequences between warring armies. They programmed each soldier to think, act and fight for himself, so that the final effect of the epic images would be thousands of individual soldiers each fighting separately and uniquely. They programmed the soldiers to think independently, in the hopes of creating a more realistic battle sequence. Then, when the time came to send the men into battle for the filmed fight sequence, some of them amusingly started to avoid battle altogether, and even ran away. In other words, they were so autonomous that they refused to fight. This was captured, but unexpected. It was there, but unpredicted. How does this relate to Bazin? According to Keathley, Bazin believed that 'the cinema is a technology that writes even in the absence of an author' (Keathley 2006: 65). Computer images maintain the ability to create even without direction or planning. They can generate images objectively which weren't necessarily intended to be captured, like the cowardly soldiers from *Lord of the Rings*.

This is an extreme example, of course, and the artists retained the ability to remove these warriors from the finished film. Yet, this anecdote speaks to the ontology and power of computer-generated images in film – *the outcome of a program may differ from what was planned, allowing contingency to enter into the frame*. And 'it is details captured by the camera [or programmed in a computer] – not only *things* or *beings*, but also specific moments – that have fascinated viewers since photography's inception' (2006: 77; emphasis in original). Indeed, the more subtle and marginal such details are, the less likely artists are to notice their deviation – like the fragments of space ships' hulls floating up into space, or particles from a falling log in *Final Destination 2*. The designers of *Nemesis* may have wanted fragments to float up into space to simulate weightlessness, but they asked the computer to draw many of the fragments in for them. Neither could they control every single fragment's movement and direction, nor could they create the exact number of fragments. Working off the original models, the computer generated that automatically, and the results may have been even more effective than the creators had planned. To amend

Keathley's argument, I would argue that computer imagery is not antithetical, but necessary, for 'an embracing of film's inherent automatism [which] means opening oneself to those fortuitous, chance encounters that are regularly captured by the camera in spite of the operator's intentions, and that form the basis of cinephiliac moments' (2006: 65). Digital imagery can assume a place as a bearer of a new 'inherent automatism' in the cinematic image.

A NEW KIND OF CINE-LOVE

> For [Serge Daney], the cinema we once knew was based on the photographic registration of the world – a notion dear to his mentor at one remove, André Bazin. But with the digital image we can fake the world, paint the image. So what does this mean for our almost religious belief and faith in the cinema?
>
> – Jonathan Rosenbaum, *Movie Mutations*[6]

My larger intent in reviving the spectre of Bazin is to suggest how these issues of realism, raised in earnest, present themselves to us, whether we wish it or not. We are nonetheless still driven by the myth of total cinema, the distant unattainable utopia of mimetic realism, even as the cinema itself becomes increasingly digital. And of course the two no doubt go hand-in-hand. In the same article in which he attempts to revive cinephilia, Wollen also acknowledges the inevitability of digital media. He notes how, 'strictly speaking, we are moving away from cinema now [with media convergence and the emergence of digital effects, DVDs and the Internet], yet cinema itself is clearly mutating into a digital art, with its dependence on special effects and its potential for home delivery and interactivity. Digital technology is changing the whole nature of image-capture, allowing images to be changed, combined and appropriated' (2001: 126). A life-long cinephile, Wollen embraces the potential of digital effects in the future of the cinema, not falling into the more nihilistic and fatalistic trappings that beset others of his generation, even though he, too, used to experience cinephilia and the movies in a historically specific way. 'I used to think that film would become an extinct art – like stained glass or tapestry', he admits, 'but now I believe that film as a collective spectacle will continue, just as the theatre has continued, despite the coming of cinema … Technology has always been a part of the history of film' (2001: 126–7). For me, embracing the idea that the 'spectacle' will continue is necessary for the future of film, and this cannot be done without a sense of cinephilia. Cinephilia can operate as the 'ghost in the machine', that which compels new advances in technology and the love of these new advances. Wollen understands that cinephilia cannot stay trapped in a particular time because film technology does not and will not stay trapped in any time:

When Lumière and Méliès made their first films, the audience went for the spectacle – to see what the new medium was like, to experience the technology of
cinema itself. The cinema has constantly reconstructed itself through waves of
new technological innovation – sound, colour, wide-screen, 3-D, Dolby, Imax, digital
editing, new media. Experimental filmmakers, on the other hand, have exploited
its technical resources in their own subversive way, misusing (or travestying) them
even, not to submit them to the law of narrative, but to develop new forms of filmmaking, to create new beginnings for the art of film. (2001: 130–1)

Cinephilia is liberated from its temporal decay to embrace these 'new forms of
filmmaking' and 'new beginnings for the art of film.' And not just to embrace the
'experimental filmmakers', but to return to the roots (so to speak) of cinephilia,
where – according to Sontag – 'the distinctive thing about cinephile taste was
that it embraced both "art" films and popular films' (2001: 120). The history of
cinema is important; the history of cinema as *history evolving* is equally important, and probably more so. Even Sontag acknowledges that the 'cinema began
in wonder, the wonder that reality can be transcribed with such magical immediacy. All of cinema is an attempt to perpetuate and to reinvent that sense of
wonder' (2001: 118). Only by turning to the future can we re-attain that wonder
of 'magical immediacy'. To tie cinephilia to a particular moment in past history,
meanwhile, is to miss what film is and will be.

Thomas Elsaesser focuses on history as well, but only in how it leads to the
future of cinephilia, which has always been driven by a 'crisis of memory' (2005:
40), a fear of losing what once was or what was thought once to be. This, in turn,
led to 'the impossibility of experience in the present' (ibid.) instead of always
returning to the past. I have argued throughout this essay that cinephilia needs to
move out of this historical trap, and that such a project is no better realised than
(as Wollen implicitly acknowledges) by taking the issue of digital cinema head-on.
Elsaesser writes that older 'cinephiles were always ready to give in to the anxiety
of possible loss, to mourn the once sensuous-sensory plentitude of the celluloid
image, and to insist on the irrecoverably fleeting nature of a film's experience'
(2005: 27–8). A new cinephilia can do this as well. I cannot, for example, return
to that winter night in Stillwater. But what motivates me is not the desire to relive
that moment, but to articulate how a similar moment, with the next spectacle,
awaits me in the future – *a cinephilia of anticipation*. 'Since there exists, however,
no such thing as cinephilia, but rather forms and periods of cinephilia', Annette
Michelson writes, 'its complex history over its first century suggests, in fact, that
cinephilia may indeed have a future within the framework of its expanded construction' (1998:3). Hence, we turn back to the question of cinephilia as a theory,
which also may require ceasing to think in terms of histories and generations at
all, other than as being co-existent with the present and the future. According to

Elsaesser, 'cinephilia, in other words, has reincarnated itself, by dis-embodying itself ... into a new ontology of belief, suspension of disbelief, and memory' (2005: 41). Memory exists for Elsaesser as a contemporaneous concept. It is something of the past which simultaneously frames the present and future. I can only hope that this memory will continue to allow for the future of digital cinema, which is after all the cinephile's *only* future.

The possibilities, the potential, of digital effects contain within themselves the nostalgic tension of past and present, a nostalgia predicated on loss and revelation. According to Robnik, 'in *Titanic*'s [1997] narrative and audience address, we can see both Willemen's and Elsaesser's versions of cinephilia at work, two versions of remembering cinema from the vantage point of digitisation: There is the fear of losing it, losing cinema, losing history, losing memory of the revelation, which is, however, narratively translated into a discourse of revival inspired by the ability of digital cinema to remember this very fear' (2005: 61). Thus, the new cinephilia negotiates the past and the present, with effects such as CGI highlighting this tension. Overtly digital cinema can celebrate the past (including the past love for film), but do so in a way (technologically) that simultaneously cannot but help always already pointing to the future. In discussing the memory of an exclusively photographic image, Robnik adds that:

> It seems as if the cinematic image could survive and even contain digitisation. *Titanic*'s memorial image on the one hand folds digitisation into the splendour of 'great cinema' (the invisible special effect of sweeping 'camera travellings' above and around the ship); on the other hand, the film is able to remember a Bazinian ontology of the cinematic image. (2005: 62)

Robnik suggests that the images in *Titanic*, both explicitly visual and seemingly photographic, create a 'sensualism that remembers social and physical mobility in terms of the proto-tactile, moving mobility of the image' (ibid.). Here again we have an effect of realism, albeit computer-generated, whereby Bazin is still remembered (and memorialised), even while the medium itself challenges ontological assumptions about the cinema.

Michele Pierson writes in *Special Effects: Still in Search of Wonder* that 'what fan discourse on special effects reminds us is that whether they are recognised in these terms by the Hollywood film industry or indeed whether they are so recognised by contemporary film and cultural criticism, popular and mass cultural forms are sites for the articulation of modes of aesthetic criticism and engagement that speak of nothing so much as the longing for a kind of art' (2002: 168). In a way, we could read Pierson's observations as meaning that special effects spectacles are an ideal site for cinephiliac moments because most articulate the possibilities of a 'longing for a kind of art'. There is an emphasis on longing here in Pierson's work, but it is a longing for the future, not so much a longing for the past – 'the pursuit of aesthetic novelty, innovation, and invention that ideally characterises visual effects production also answers a cultural demand for the aesthetic experience of wonder' (ibid.). This wonder is compatible with a future-oriented cinephilia that can embrace and is produced by digital cinema. Cinephiles who delight in the revelatory moments generated by CGI long for subsequent experiences such as those they have enjoyed in the past. I personally hope to experience again something approximating the revelatory excesses I perceived in the weightless, random fragments in *Nemesis*. With the cinephiliac moments of CGI, we can begin to rethink film from the past to the future, with a renewed emphasis on wonder. The idea of the unique can be retained if the urgency of affect is foregrounded in the discussion. Different moments affect people differently – this is still an irreclaimable, fleeting moment which cannot necessarily be repeated, just as cinephiles cannot go back in time, except in memory. Perhaps, if digital spectacles do not hold up as much on subsequent viewings it is because they, more than anything, are destined to prompt that unrepeatable moment of joy of which cinephiles often speak. And what then matters is not returning to that moment, but awaiting the next. What I am advocating is a new cinephilia based not on what was but on what will be.

Wonder is not, of course, synonymous with cinephilia, but I think the emphasis on wonder in special effects discourses points to a similar desire to become captive to the cinematic image, in a manner not dissimilar to that which Sontag spoke of so lovingly. In special effects films, Annette Kuhn writes, 'Spectators are invited to gape in wonder and abandon themselves to the totality of the audiovisual experience' (1999: 5). Both in wonder and in cinephilia, there is an emphasis on the unique, unrepeatable experience – but what fans of science fiction films wish to experience is the next unique, unrepeatable experience, something most strikingly (though not exclusively) rendered through the possibilities of CGI. Pierson notes in *The Phantom Menace* (1999), 'the digital simulation of a special photographic effect, the flickering blue image generated by a holographic communicator, still looks special, its simulated degradation of an analogue image a rare curiosity' (2002: 152). It might be too much to say that Pierson experiences a cinephiliac moment here, but it is the simulation of a simulation within the film which creates for Pierson a new unique moment in the spectacle of *Star Wars*.

However, if there is a strong model in special effects research for the possibilities of cinephilia, it exists in the work of Scott Bukatman. In his book *Matters of Gravity: Special Effects and Supermen in the 20th Century* he opens with (what I see as) his own cinephiliac moment, describing the experience of watching Christopher Walken dance (and at times float through the air and up the walls) in the Fat Boy Slim music video, 'Weapon of Choice'. 'Alienation yields to shock', he writes, 'the bricolage of sampled tracks, acts of fantastic mobility, and perpetual surprise (with the merest touch of shock)' (2003: 2). Like a cinephile, Bukatman speaks in a deeply personal voice:

> It must have been my early love of planetariums that made me want to become an astronomer. So imagine my surprise, disgust, and resentment on discovering that astronomy consisted of something more than sitting in the dark and gazing upward into the abyss ... But here I am, attending to the discourse of science fiction cinema, still embracing that experience of sitting in the darkness and peering into infinity. (2003: 111)

Bukatman's work emphasises the sublime impact of special effects in a way that brings us seductively close to the affective powers of cinephilia. 'The sublime initiates a crisis in the subject', Bukatman writes in a separate article, 'by disrupting the customary cognised relationship between subject and external reality. It threatens human thought, habitual signifying systems, and finally, human prowess' (1999: 255). In other words, when confronted with the sublime cinematic spectacle, logic and intellect break down; what remains is the experience in place. Bukatman writes – not unlike Wollen, Mamet and Sontag – of the early wonders of the cinema. Though audiences were not duped by the images of the early spectacle, 'some pleasure, however, clearly derived from responding to these entertainments *as if they were real*' (1999: 249; emphasis in original). This reminds me of my first encounter with *Nemesis* – how the ships' collision 'felt' real, though it obviously was not. For Bukatman, the special effects film is a vast opportunity for the senses that redirects 'the spectator to the visual (and auditory and even kinesthetic) conditions of the cinema, and thus brings the principles of perception to the foreground of consciousness' (1999: 254). What Bukatman articulates (among other things) is the potential of special and visual effects films as an affective cinema: 'We are bombarded, stunned into submission, by special effects; technological space moves through our passive bodies. But we move with it and sometimes even move against its overdeterminism' (2003: 129). Thus, this new cinema engages our senses, perhaps even in excess of its own intended programming, but also compels us to respond to it. We are not passively in awe, but seek the joy of new discoveries and reject the ineffectiveness of blatantly fake, repeated and/or clichéd images. Cinephiliac moments as affect are moments of indescribable bliss, but they are also (productive) shocks to thought.

But Bukatman speaks in a language that resists thought: 'The landscape sublime is rooted in an activity of contemplation, in an attempt to grasp what, fundamentally, cannot be grasped' (1999: 257). He envisions 'an environment that we have made [which] has moved beyond our ability to control and cognize it' (1999: 266) – something highlighted by the emergence of the sublime. Bukatman feels the experience of the special effects cinema in a deeply, nonverbal, subjective way – and this in turn compels him to long for a utopia of new possibilities, which 'might be found outside the narrative in the embodied, kaleidoscopic perception presented through special effects' (2003: 12). Even when images of utopia are banal, the sheer power and possibility of these images suggests that 'the experience of a kinetic, delirious, immersive, and yet still magisterial vision retains its affect' (ibid.). Here we move fully into the unlimited potential of digital cinema – the possible landscapes that also contain and produce fragments within the as-yet-unimaginable promise so crucial to sustaining a cinephilia of anticipation.

Thus, not unlike Bukatman, I am imagining this utopia, a cinema of possibilities that 'is less a place, a fixed site, than a trajectory. Actually, it's a field of possible, and multiple, trajectories' (2003: 125). What drives Bukatman is, I suspect, a cinephiliac trajectory (among other adjectives). Thus a new cinephilia resists limits and embraces possibilities. 'With the kinesis of spectacular visual effects, often accompanied by a sense of utopian possibility', Bukatman writes, 'movement becomes a passage across borders that promise resistance to external control' (ibid.). This is simultaneously a resistance to intellect, and a compulsion to love what my mind tells me I shouldn't love. Moreover, this resistance suggests that more cinephiliac fragments, that which cannot be externally controlled, lay ahead. I long for, await, the next resistance, the next affect – unique perhaps only to me, but which also necessarily has the potential to affect others in some way. Audiences that embrace digital cinema follow a utopian trajectory of new possibilities. And the cinephile within me demands that I follow it, and demands that I write about it.

AUTHOR'S NOTE

This essay is very much a product of particular times and particular environments, and I would like briefly and belatedly to acknowledge my gratitude to them. This essay was originally written for Professor Barbara Klinger in a 'Media Theory and Aesthetics' seminar in the autumn of 2005 at Indiana University – Bloomington. I am deeply grateful to the long-time support of the CMCL department over the last three years.

A revised version was published in *Film Criticism* in 2007. My gratitude goes to Lloyd Michaels and Kristen Whissel for their support of the project there. In general, I am deeply appreciative of the ways in which *Film Criticism* over the last five years has been a generous and supportive venue for my work.

NOTES

1   Keathley (2006: 134–5).
2   According to Keathley: 'With the cinephiliac anecdote, the cinephile tells a story about
    – or a story that embodies – his or her relationship with the cinema, a story that has
    the effect of knowledge in the generalisable sense about its object, as well as in some
    personal sense' (2006: 151).
3   Though his book is about cinephilia in general, Keathley is referring in this particular
    instance to a moment with Sherlock Holmes in the short story, 'Silver Blaze' (1892).
4   I am using the term more or less as it was defined by Roland Barthes in *Pleasure of the
    Text* (1975). Barthes is referring to a moment of intense joy which defies language, but
    which inspires a unique response that cannot be repeated except in pleasure.
5   Certainly, what Mamet is ultimately regretting is the loss of strong narrative in film:
    'It occurred to me that Cinema is just going its own merry way, diverging from its
    momentary harness mate, the Drama, and slouching toward Bethlehem like the rest of
    us' (1996: 125).
6   In Rosenbaum and Martin (2003: vii).

REFERENCES

Barthes, Roland (1975) *Pleasure of the Text*, trans. Richard Miller. New York: Hill and Wang.

Bazin, André (1967 [1945]) 'The Ontology of the Photographic Image', in *What is Cinema?*
    Volume 1, trans. Hugh Gray. Berkeley: University of California Press, 9–16.

Bukatman, Scott (1999) 'The Artificial Infinite: On Special Effects and the Sublime', in
    Annette Kuhn (ed.) *Alien Zone 2: The Spaces of Science Fiction Cinema*. New York:
    Verso, 249–75.

____ (2003) *Matters of Gravity: Special Effects and Supermen in the 20th Century*. Durham,
    NC: Duke Univeristy Press.

Elsaesser, Thomas (2005) 'Cinephilia or the Uses of Disenchantment', in Marijke de Valck
    and Malte Hagener (eds) *Cinephilia: Movies, Love and Memory*. Amsterdam: Amster-
    dam University Press, 27–43.

Elsaesser, Thomas and Warren Buckland (2002) *Studying Contemporary American Cin-
    ema: A Guide to Movie Analysis*. New York: Oxford University Press.

Keathley, Christian (2006) *Cinephilia and History, or The Winds in the Trees*. Bloomington:
    Indiana University Press.

Kuhn, Annette (1999) 'Introduction', in *Alien Zone 2: The Spaces of Science Fiction Cin-
    ema*. New York: Verso, 1–8.

Mamet, David (1996) 'The Screenplay', *Make-Believe Town: Essays and Remembrances*.
    New York: Little, Brown, 117–25.

Michelson, Annette (1998) 'Gnosis and Iconoclasm: A Case Study of Cinephilia', *October*
    83, 3–18.

Morrison, James (2005) 'After the Revolution: On the Fate of Cinephilia', *Michigan Quarterly Review*, 44, 3, 393–413.

Norton, Bill (2003) 'Through a Glass Darkly', *Cinefex*, 93, 88–111.

Pierson, Michele (2002) *Special Effects: Still in Search of Wonder*. New York: Columbia University Press.

Robnik, Drehli (2005) 'Mass Memories of Movies: Cinephilia as Norm and Narrative in Blockbuster Culture', in Marijke de Valck and Malte Hagener (eds) *Cinephilia: Movies, Love and Memory*. Amsterdam: Amsterdam University Press, 55–64.

Rosenbaum, Jonathan and Adrian Martin (2003) 'Preface', in Jonathan Rosenbaum and Adrian Martin (eds) *Movie Mutations: The Changing Face of World Cinephilia*. London: British Film Institute, vi–x.

Rosenbaum, Jonathan, Adrian Martin, Kent Jones, Alexander Horwath, Nicole Brenez and Raymond Bellour (2003) 'Movie Mutations: Letters from (and to) Some Children of 1960', in Jonathan Rosenbaum and Adrian Martin (eds) *Movie Mutations: The Changing Face of World Cinephilia*. London: British Film Institute, 1–33.

Sontag, Susan (2001 [1996]) 'A Century of Cinema', in *Where the Stress Falls*. New York: Farrar, Straus and Giroux, 117–22.

Willemen, Paul (1994) 'Through the Glass Darkly: Cinephilia Reconsidered', *Looks and Frictions*. London: British Film Institute, 223–57.

Wollen, Peter (2001) 'An Alphabet of Cinema', *New Left Review*, 12, 115–34.

ONTOLOGIES

CHAPTER SIX
THE '*CAMERA* AS CAMERA':
HOW CGI CHANGES THE WORLD AS WE KNOW IT
Tobey Crockett

The first time I saw *The Lord of the Rings: The Fellowship of the Ring* (2001) was on a large multiplex screen, and about a week later I saw it again at the famous Cinerama Dome, now called the ArcLight Hollywood. I was fortunate to live for a time just down the street from the Dome, and have seen many movies screened there. I noticed right away that Jackson's effects were even more amazing and that they 'popped' in a slightly different manner on the curved screen. I was especially struck by a long sequence which caromed across an enormous expanse and then brought us flying down underground to the emergence of a dreadful army of golem-like warriors. Haunted by this single shot sequence for over four years, I will examine the changes in film making which occur when the mechanical camera is transformed into a virtual camera, and an entirely new set of sensibilities emerge to inform the filmmaking process. This transition from mechanical to virtual is a paradigm shift embodied in what I call the '*camera* as camera' argument.

Research into why the effects should look better in the Cinerama Dome than elsewhere has ultimately led to an exceptionally detailed article by George Kimble for *Cinema Technology* magazine. On the fiftieth anniversary of Cinerama, Kimble (2002) tells the back-story of Fred Waller and the invention of widescreen panoramic technology. Waller was the head of special effects at Paramount in 1924 and worked with the biggest directors of the day, such as D. W. Griffith, Cecil B. DeMille and others. He was a great innovator and inventor. Noticing some effects of 3-D vision in relation to screen size, he began a ten year study of perception. He ultimately came to the realisation that peripheral vision, produced on a curved screen, will create a 3-D effect without additional apparatus. This was the beginning of Cinerama, arguably one of the most exciting screen experiences yet offered to cinephiles.

Often castigated as being the least lovely of films, the special effects Hollywood blockbuster, made with the aid of Computer-Generated imagery (CGI), is also ostensibly viewed as the most commercially driven and the least auteur-like of any entertainment industry vehicle. Here, I hope to remedy some of these slights and even defend some aspects of the blockbuster film in critical and cinephilic terms. Such blockbusters, especially those with outrageous special effects, are in fact the potential site of an emerging subjectivity, one which we ought to recognise as a new posthuman author.

Perversely, discussions about CGI films often neglect the actual means of production which have changed their making. The 'camera as camera' argument sets out to remedy some of this lack, focusing specifically on the contributions of 3-D virtual spaces to CGI-driven productions. First and foremost, this 'camera as camera' argument establishes that, with the technological changes brought about by CGI, especially those derived from 3-D virtual worlds technology, we must now change what we mean by the word 'camera'. As will be explored in depth, these new cinema-inflected virtual worlds generate 'virtual camera' technology, such as that seen in the 'bullet time' of the *Matrix* trilogy (1999, 2003, 2003) and other special effects films.[1]

The mechanical camera is now effectively dead, and in its place the virtual camera rewrites both cinema and the world around us. Along with the practical changes, there are theoretical changes as well. I argue that we should be alert for the emergence of a new subjectivity which comes with the territory, for as 3-D virtual worlds facilitate ever more persuasive CGI effects, there are consequences that have far-reaching implications – not only for the cinema, but, more broadly, for the humanities and the sciences in general.

The special effects film, typically a Hollywood blockbuster, 'can't get no respect' from the auteur and cinephilia-oriented academy. Nonetheless, special effects films provide an excellent, stable and reasonably well-documented body of work through which one can study some of the foundational shifts which have occurred in the digitisation of the filmmaking process. While physical effects are still very prominently used in special effects films, their integration into the production as a whole – notably via compositing – is nonetheless a very digitised process. I have pinpointed seven tropes which characterise many 'camera as camera' productions. Usually several or even all of these may be present in a given film, and it is almost never the case that only one of these devices is applied in any given shot or sequence, as filmmakers have discovered that a bouquet of various illusion-making techniques will keep an audience more entertained and enthralled by the spectacle. Audience awareness of any one particular device (too much green-screening for instance) tends to mar the final result.

As John Knoll, visual effects director at Industrial Light and Magic and the creative force behind the effects for films such as the *Star Wars* trilogies (1977–2005), the *Star Trek* series (1979–2009) and the *Pirates of the Caribbean* trilogy (2003, 2006, 2007) says about director Gore Verbinski:

> Gore feels very strongly, and I agree with him, that it's important to have real elements in there. As much as you can do real, the more plausible and realistic the

final results will be. Gore's a strong proponent of trying to get practical elements on set, to get these as much on camera as you can and then use visual effects where you really need them. And also, not to rely too much on one technique. So in one shot, for example, you'll have a background extension that's a miniature, and in another shot we're doing something with computer graphics. As long as you're switching things around a little bit, the audience doesn't key into being able to see the artifice of one particular technique, and we end up with a better-looking result. In Anon 2007

The only way it is possible to wed all these various techniques together is via the digitisation of the filmmaking process, a means of production which in fact and in practice is now digitised all the way down to its very foundation. This has far-reaching consequences both in practical production terms and in more abstract philosophical and theoretical terms.

'I am a camera', wrote Christopher Isherwood (1963: 1), famously giving voice to the narrative connection between camera and subjectivity. What the 'camera as camera' approach discerns is that the virtual camera is not to be understood in the same terms as a mechanical device. Rather, the virtual camera is predicated upon intricacies of calculation which render any point in a given digitised space as if it were a camera. With every point in space newly capable of camera-like reportage in practical terms, each pixel is now possessed of agency and author-ship in theoretical terms as well. In short, each pixel is a subject, rendering the entire volume of pixels as a complex multiplicity of cameras, with far-reaching implications. I call this the 'camera as camera' because now the very space itself – what I am taking the liberty in calling by the Latin 'camera' for room or chamber – is now literally a camera. The camera is no longer an object (a passive, dead volume of space to be filled by others), but is now a subject (an active space constituted out of authoring agents).

As I will demonstrate, this is how CGI changes the world as we know it – by rewriting the subject-object split, and annihilating it. Rather than a Cartesian reality in which our human hegemony dominates all, we find that we occupy a 'virtual reality' in which every point – that is every miniscule, smallest unit pos-sible – is a subject, and we are rid of 'mere' objects all together. Pixels (short for 'picture element') are these same points; pixels are subjects in the 'camera as camera'. This foundational transition from object to subject occurs because there are technical differences between the capture of light and shadow intended to represent visual imagery in traditional media, and the generation of visual imag-ery in the new media. Every point, every pixel, is now an author. The camera as a mechanical device is dead, and is replaced by the plastic 'camera', a volume of multiple voices, seething and protean. Now the 'camera' is a camera, or, to return to Isherwood, 'We are a camera'. And while these dense voices of calculation currently serve as incarnations, literal avatars of our human storytelling, there is no particular reason why they will not wish to tell stories of their own in some very near future.

In order to recognise the workings of these multiple authors now obligingly masquerading as mere pixels, I will briefly examine the historical roots of the mechanical camera and then offer a brief overview of the aforementioned seven interrelated tropes which characterise the virtual camera and digital film productions in general. I will examine several films which offer insight into the actual application of those tropes, including the *Lord of the Rings* trilogy (2001, 2002, 2003), *The Polar Express* (2004) and the *Matrix* trilogy. The seven tropes are (i) overtly digital techniques such as 3-D pre-visualisation, motion capture, and the pervasive compositing of these elements into a seamless whole; (ii) theme park and ride-derived aesthetics; (iii) dynamic, physics-defying camerawork; (iv) the treatment of avatars as actors and vice versa; (v) the recognition of previously inanimate or multiple entities as subjectivities with new narrative powers; (vi) the intensely detailed development of new worlds and 'virtual realities'; and (vii) a sensibility which relies on the playful remix as a standard device.[2] Finally, the broader cultural implications of the '*camera* as camera' will round out my discussion of how CGI 'changes the world as we know it'.

HISTORICAL ROOTS OF THE '*CAMERA* AS CAMERA'

The first technical development of note for the '*camera* as camera' argument is the shutter speed technology originated by Eadweard Muybridge. As is by now well-known, one of the main impacts of Muybridge's animal motion photography experiments was the eventual development of moving images and the birth of the motion picture industry. This is slightly ironic because what interested Muybridge was the possibility of capturing what happened in the intervals *between* each moment, and not particularly in recreating motion, although he did show Governor Leland Stanford the reassembled motions of the first horse on a zoopraxiscope.[3]

The 'in between moment' which so enthralled Muybridge is now being used to great (special) effect with the 'bullet-time' illusion in movies such as *The Matrix* (1999). Triggering a series of still photos, but at the rate of 1,000 to 1,500 frames per second instead of Muybridge's own 12 or 24 frames per second, visual effects supervisor John Gaeta was able to reinvent the new look which the Wachowski brothers wanted for their posthuman film trilogy. As Gaeta explains in an *American Cinematographer* interview with Ron Magid, 'Larry and Andy [Wachowski] told me, "Our movie is about the complete manipulation of time and space in a simulated world. We need you to come up with a method of manipulating time so the camera can be moving while all of the high-speed stunt action is happening"' (in Magid 1999: 1).

Gaeta's innovation was to blend the high shutter speeds of modern cameras and the Hong Kong-style wire stunts of contemporary action films with the old-fashioned camera array of Muybridge. Referring to the link between his effects and the early experiments of Muybridge, Gaeta remarks, 'The thinking is literally that old, but it's only just recently that we could fathom how to plot out the positions of still cameras in such a way that we can capture a dynamic camera move from point A to point B and create moving shots of events that are simulated to be at a much higher frame rate' (in ibid.).

As Gaeta explains, he took the still shots which he captured with the Muybridge style array, but further curled them around the scene of the action so that a dynamic, motion-filled, 360-degree sequence was captured on film. This was subsequently animated to 'create virtual camera moves' and to fill in the spaces in between the still shots for a seamless sequence (in Magid 1999: 2). Gaeta referred to this innovation as 'Flo-Mo', while the Wachowskis called it 'bullet-time'. Added to this camera array technique was the extensive use of green-screening in order to combine actual film footage with the additional virtual footage, sometimes interpolating frames in order to lengthen or exaggerate elements for greater visual impact. It is worth emphasising here that Gaeta's innovation is completely dependent upon computer programming to co-ordinate and control the firing of the cameras, as well as to incorporate the footage into animated scenes via compositing. While the advantages of the Flo-Mo system are numerous, chief among them for the 'camera as camera' discussion at hand is the ability to move the camera in any conceivable pattern and movement, while potentially eliminating the need for cuts and enabling complex, one-shot tracking sequences with dynamic, and even balletic, camerawork.

This was amply demonstrated in the famous 'Burly Brawl' sequence in the second film, *The Matrix Reloaded* (2003), where the character Neo (Keanu Reeves) fights over one hundred Agent Smiths (Hugo Weaving) in an astounding one-shot fight sequence achieved as a combination of live action and computer-generated effects. At the beginning of the trilogy's production, though, it was enough that the virtual camera could perform so many exotic movements. As Gaeta describes it, 'Audiences aren't accustomed to seeing changing perspectives in hyper-slow-motion sequences, which sets these sequences apart from anything that had been done before. We would also shoot the scenes with a 1/500- or 1/1000-per-second shutter speeds, which completely eliminates all motion blur and creates this false stereoscopic feeling' (in ibid.).

Of particular importance for the 'camera as camera', Gaeta's innovation of a 'virtual camera' is central, for in so doing, he creates a virtual cinematography in which the entire space is digitised. This technological feat allows the filmmakers to generate imagery for the audience from any point of view they choose. Without the impediments normally associated with the physical realities of making a film, such as camera booms, giant lighting sails, extraneous crew members and so on, the directors and cinematographer have a new freedom to place and choreograph the so-called 'camera' as never before. Now the entire space is activated as a viewing space; it has in effect become a camera, a new kind of volume in which all visual imagery is generated by pixels, and in which every mathematically defined point (by definition, the very points which comprise the calculated volume of 3-D virtual space) is literally enabled as a *point of view*. This virtual camera is in contrast to a mechanical camera which captures the traces of light falling upon discrete objects located in physical space. As will become clear, this transition from mechanical to virtual camera, the '*camera* as camera', has tremendous impact on the final presentation of the film, and interesting psycho-analytic and philosophical consequences as well.

SEVEN CHARACTERISTICS OF THE '*CAMERA* AS CAMERA'

Writing on the impact that CGI and DVD featurettes have had on the film viewer's experience, Dan North, in his essay on *The Matrix*, observes that 'the spectator is equipped with an exponentially expanding set of extra-diegetic, revelatory inter-texts that enhance his/her ability to decode the spectacle' (2006: 52). For North, this observation underscores that the audience occupies two viewing positions simultaneously – enabling them to be borne away by the spectacle afforded by the choreographed fight sequence, yet to admire the artifice with which it is produced. North emphasises that this is not a defect but a necessity of such a cinematic viewing position. Certainly this new sort of technical pleasure, the admiration for a technical feat well done, seems to become ever more central to the cinephilia of CGI films.

Thus the featurettes and other 'behind the scenes' information which com-prise the mainstays of DVD extras stage a profound intervention into the recep-tion of today's films, demonstrating both the collaborative nature of filmmaking and the impact that the singular vision of a director has on the final outcome. Barbara Klinger (2006), among others, has remarked that DVDs have changed movie viewing, most obviously in the home environment, where viewers can now have a far more active role in the reception of the film than before. With many layers of the film's production newly revealed, some, myself included, may find the 'magic' of movies even more impressive than the more conventional reception traditionally granted a film in a single theatrical viewing. Among other sources, including the publication *Cinefex*,[4] my analysis draws extensively on the DVD commentaries by directors, writers and most especially production and visual effects design teams and supervisors. Their practical, hands-on experience with the creation of films in general and with virtual cinematography in particular is central to expanding the '*camera* as camera' argument.[5]

Before delving more deeply into the various tropes which reflect the new authoring environment of the 'camera as camera', I want to again emphasise the original, mechanical 'camera' as the locus at which the compositing of multiple technologies and endeavours combine into a collective subjectivity. Common, everyday language aside, it is by no means any longer clear that the term 'camera' is sufficient to delimit the purely photographic apparatus deployed for the purposes of capturing images whose reflections are captured on light-sensitive films some relatively short distance away. The sense in which I am interested in the operations taking place at the locus we can term for convenience as a 'camera' are ones which do not involve the science of light and optics, except to the degree that imagery can be a representation of those operations. While it is true that my description within this project is more of a technical and pragmatic one, theoretical arguments draw a similar conclusion.

For example, in *Projecting A Camera: Language-Games in Film Theory*, Edward Branigan contends that the definition of camera is undergoing a transformation and offers an in-depth analysis of the many ways this is so – but never addresses digital or virtual technologies. He offers that the camera is a 'viewing hypothesis' which 'can be used successfully to expose pertinent features of visual texts' (2006: 96). Branigan continues:

> Today the camera seems to be neither a machine nor an invisible witness recording facts of the world but, rather, an aspect of a collective subjectivity – a name for how we ourselves are talking and thinking about cinema at a particular time for a particular purpose. As a collective subjectivity, the camera's status fluctuates in the twilight area between material object and interpretive subject, between world and language. (Ibid.)

Branigan is deeply invested in the languaging of film theory and arrives at his argument in a very different manner than I do. However, with the exception of his final word, 'language', his statement reads remarkably well as a summation for the 'camera as camera'. Undoubtedly reflecting my own bias as a scholar of visual studies, I might substitute the word 'representation' for 'language' in reimagining Branigan's quote applied to the 'camera as camera' argument.

With the locus of the camera redefined as a meeting point of various technologies, let us now turn to the special effects film as the most productive example of the new kind of participatory, authoring and agency-laden camera which I am describing. Almost always a Hollywood blockbuster, a special effects-driven film often has multiple types of effects being presented in any given sequence or frame. There are so many technologies at play in the construction of even a single minute of George Lucas's *Revenge of the Sith* (2005) that the DVD featurette which explains the 'behind the scenes' labour required to produce that minute takes a jam-packed hour to list the contributions of the many teams whose work is condensed into a short moment in time. The featurette is hardly an exhaustive explanation of the process, but it does demonstrate how the point of assembly of visual materials which we call, for convenience's sake, the 'camera' is very far removed from those early boxes designed in the mid-nineteenth century to capture the reflections and refractions of various kinds of light (ibid.).

Just as in the era of cinema's origins it took some time for the vocabulary of camera movements to become established (indeed, taking some time for the camera to be moved at all rather than simply being stationary), so too now it is taking a while to recognise that, in the era of a virtual cinema, every point in space is up for grabs as a potential camera location (see Bazin 1967c).[6] Inevitably this will produce a new aesthetic and reveal to us an underlying philosophical position which we have not adequately considered. This is the essence of the '*camera* as camera' – a position which, among other qualities, implies a cinematic multiplicity wherein the power of authority is deconstructed, many points of view are plausibly honoured, and we can see things from a new kind of non-essentialising yet global perspective which we have not yet fully embraced. Despite objections to the contrary, there is still room for the notion of an 'auteur' in such CGI-dominated productions; indeed, one might argue that the expanded range of tools available to a director whose idiosyncratic style is virtually iconic (Steven Spielberg, Peter Jackson, George Lucas) is by no means eliminated in the dynamic storytelling of the '*camera* as camera'.[7] Is this André Bazin's 'total cinema'? That remains to be seen.

With a new understanding of the camera as already being more a term of convenience than a descriptive one for a particular apparatus, how does the CGI space of the *camera* act as a 'camera'? Films such as *The Lord Of The Rings: The Fellowship of the Ring* and the *Star Wars* series blend traditional and virtual photography with a variety of other image materials and techniques such as pre-visualisations, motion capture, scanning, matte paintings, digital animation and miniature photography. Contrast this with films which use an all-digital framework, such as Robert Zemeckis's virtual creation *The Polar Express*, which was produced without any film at all (see Kehr 2004). Digital film productions are not necessarily concerned with image *capture* so much as they are with image *generation*, contributing to a philosophical reassessment of authoring agency in film and beyond. After all, who is really making these images in an all-digital framework?

To answer this, let us look at what I call a 'rollercoaster set piece' in many of these special effects films. These 'rollercoaster' components can be reliably counted upon to entertain and thrill the commercial audience. Although such 'ride' sequences are often economically motivated (that is, they function as part of a cross-platform merchandising programme for studio-derived theme parks) they are also useful for thinking about the virtual camera. *The Polar Express* has a particularly effective one, seen as the train careens off the tracks and skids across a frozen lake on the way to the North Pole, but such sequences are evident in many other films such as the *Lord of the Rings* trilogy, the *Mummy* movies (1999, 2001, 2008) and Peter Jackson's *King Kong* (2005).

What is actually taking place in such a ride moment in a sequence produced by a virtual camera? It is worth repeating that there is no actual light falling upon an actual object – in its place is calculation. In CG effects, there is a factual absence of the camera piercing and penetrating through space as it moves. In its stead, we have a virtual camera for which the pixels comprising the dense digital space described by the x, y and z axes of a traditional Cartesian cube are actually performing as *if* the audience point of view were a camera. The pixels are regrouping and reformulating themselves for the benefit of the fourth wall as points of view in space for the placement of a virtual camera. The pixels themselves are static. They only change colour and appearance, not location per se, on command via calculation. This is similar in result to one of those stadium activities where people hold up poster-sized cards in order to make a giant picture of Mao, for example. Here, in the '*camera* as camera', when imagery changes on the screen, it is as if the baton of agency, the 'talking stick' if you will, is being passed among the pixels as they regroup and reformulate according to the needs of the viewer and director.[8] No movement is taking place, only camouflage – the changing of stripes, the chameleon-like transition – taking place at lightning speed.

This enables the dramatically dynamic camera moves increasingly favoured by directors such as Lucas, Jackson, Zemeckis and the Wachowskis. Certainly a kind of cinephilia is at play in appreciation of the increasingly long and complex tracking sequences and visual effects shots created for these films.[9] In the opening sequence of *Revenge of the Sith*, the 'camera' never breaks away from two small ships in a tracking shot that lasts well over two minutes. We follow along two small flyers containing Obi Wan Kenobi and Anakin Skywalker as they cover an incredible amount of space, over and under and between other ships. It is an unbroken shot such as no physical camera on a crane could ever provide, even assuming that the objects onscreen were real objects, which, of course, they are not. In fact, it is practically pointless to speak of the 'camera' as never breaking away, because what passes for the point in space designated as a 'camera' is in fact an agglomeration of visual materials, composited from at least half a dozen completely independent sources, much of it non-photographic in origin.

Rather than offer details of the remaining tropes here, I will examine two films which offer examples of all seven. As prescribed by the seventh trope, there is a real tendency to mix things up in order to keep the audience off guard, thus these examples almost never use one trope at a time, but rather frequently cluster these techniques in order to thrill the audience. As indicated by visual effects director John Knoll at the very beginning of this essay, the most effective, best-looking result is achieved by deploying a variety of techniques, plus hefty doses of the real, all at once.

THE LORD OF THE RINGS: THE FELLOWSHIP OF THE RING

The *Lord of the Rings* trilogy is a superb example of a variety of techniques, combining effects which are purely digital with composites of traditional photography along with digital manipulations of various sorts, being used simultaneously to provide a rich visual vocabulary. After an intense history lesson masquerading as a prologue, *The Fellowship of the Ring* opens with thirty minutes or so of a very pastoral and picturesque tour through the Shire. The art direction and re-presentation of the Shire is meticulously crafted down to the very last details, in keeping with the 'virtual reality' of the sixth trope.[10] There we meet all the main hobbit characters and see their moving interrelationships as Bilbo Baggins (Ian Holm) hosts a party and plans to retire in order to write his book, which will become the novel *The Hobbit*. Dark energies start to gather strength and percolate through the story as Gandalf (Ian McKellen) undertakes more research on Bilbo's (voiced by Alan Howard) mysterious ring. As we discover, the ring itself is exerting a strong influence on the course of the events we are about to watch for several hours.[11] The ring is in fact the One Ring of the Dark Lord Sauron (Sala Baker), which must be destroyed in the place of its origin, Mount Doom. Bilbo's nephew Frodo Baggins (Elijah Wood) volunteers to take the Ring to be destroyed. The fellowship, which is ultimately formed to help him accomplish this mission, provides the story of this long and complex trilogy.

Rather than detail the story further, I am going to assume a moderate familiarity with the film trilogy. The first real sense of the intensive effects do not come until the first encounter with Saruman (Christopher Lee) after he has revealed himself as a disciple of the 'dark side', signalled by the sight of his dark tower dominating the night-time landscape, a molten river of orange lava flowing over a cliff from which the structure rises like a maleficent being. It is this first fly-over with Jackson's signature dynamic camera which establishes the turn of events that will come to dominate the trilogy from its introduction here as a sharp punctum, terminating the Shire idyll, the place to which the heroes will yearn to return throughout their long journey to destroy the Ring.

This dynamic camera dominates the *Lord of the Rings* trilogy: a flying camera which is dramatically enabled by the compositing and pre-visualisation of the first trope, evidencing the transition from mechanical to virtual camera which we see throughout the entire production. Even when a mechanical camera is being deployed, which happens often for Jackson uses physical effects and miniature shots to great effect, it is still the process of digitisation which gets underscored by the dynamic, roving camera footage. This is then composited into seamless agglomerations of multiply-sourced visual materials now substituting for the locus of the pre-digital camera of yore. Returning to the Shire, we see Gandalf explain the problem of the Ring to Frodo, an extensive flashback that allows us to see more of the Ring's origin story. It is a great juxtaposition of the forces of evil in contrast to the protagonist, the seeds of conflict held in his own hand – the Ring, which the writers refer to as an 'agonist'.[12] This is the decisive moment in which the journey is set into motion. The dramatic staging of the golden circle and the flaming eye of Sauron occur throughout the film, and is intended to give the Ring the presence of an actor. While *The Lord of the Rings* is famous for the performance capture acting of Andy Serkis as Gollum, the writing of the Ring as a character also reflects a '*camera* as camera' value, attaching subjectivity to that which has previously only been considered as inanimate.

Shortly after leaving Frodo and the Shire, we next see Gandalf riding up to Saruman's Orthanc Tower in Isengard. The shot is entirely computer-generated, says Jackson – the tower, the trees, the rider.[13] Again, Jackson characteristically shoots by moving the camera in a dynamic manner and then edits so that it is cross-cut with small segments of action. We see the rider emerging from under the bridge, a quick cut takes us overhead, rising slowly into an overhead pan which watches the rider from bridge to tower while rotating, so that the camera now appears to abut the tower. When the rider dismounts, he is now nearly upside down and dismounting from between the wings of the tower. This last shot, the world turned upside down, then cuts to the very last shot in which this tower will look bucolic, blue sky and green trees framing Saruman and Gandalf in discussion. Normalcy is about to shatter and remain undone for the remainder of the trilogy. Saruman is shortly revealed as an evil henchman to the Dark Lord Sauron, and Gandalf is imprisoned on the top of Orthanc Tower.

The sequence involving Gandalf's imprisonment on Orthanc Tower stayed in my mind for four years and eventually led to my theorisation of 3-D virtual worlds as pure calculation and total agency. As it turns out, it is also one of Jackson's favourites, though he acknowledges that it flies in the face of accepted wisdom that the camera is not supposed to dwell overlong on a miniatures set and visual effects sequence. He went ahead anyway. He says the reason one is supposed to keep an effects shot short is that a long effects shot runs the risk of allowing the audience to see where the seams are, but he likes this shot because it 'just keeps going and going' and he finds it very persuasive.[14]

Sauron has commanded Saruman to build him 'an army worthy of Mordor'. As the scene begins, the underlings commence to tear down the trees from the surrounding keep, and Gandalf awakens to the sound of activities rending the night quiet. He is imprisoned on the top of Saruman's sanctuary, a tall spire. A god's-eye point of view hovering over Gandalf now reveals the scope of a new landscape taking shape beneath him. This is accomplished, Jackson tells us on the DVD commentary, by compositing a stage shot of the actor, imposed with a miniature and then adding a computer-generated shot wrapped around as the backdrop.[15]

Jackson reiterates that industry clashing with nature is one of J. R. R. Tolkien's main themes in the books, and we might say that the blending of physical and virtual effects in the film echoes the clash of civilisations as well. As we see onscreen, a once verdant treasure is being transformed into black oozing pits, torches and monochromatic mud. The orcs delight in tearing down the fine old trees which groan piteously as they are wrenched from the earth. The fluffy tree tops shiver down below Gandalf as he huddles against the cold and his own despair, and a pervasive feeling that the destruction of the trees is making him physically ill.[16] Then, a long travelling shot starts outside the gates of Saruman's new fortress complex at Isengard where he is raising the army. The camera travels over the gates, and swings across a large excavation now made in the ground where there was earlier only forest. Militaristic music starts to blare and we hear the sounds of hammering and labour, while dozens of Orcs pour out like ants from within the military complex. There is a vast scaffold and all manner of mining, smelting and forging operations going on, which produce smoke, fires and ash — all of which the camera takes in during a long-distance pan.

The camera continues to soar seamlessly up and as it does so, it intercepts the path of a large flying Luna moth which makes for Gandalf slumped at the top of the tower. We follow the moth, and the music changes to a sweet chorus of high, spiritual voices which clearly recapitulate the contrast of good versus evil playing out on the screen. In a purely pagan mode of animal communication, Gandalf whispers instructions to the Luna moth and sends it on its way. Jackson calls this a 'brave shot' and is pleased that they 'managed to pull it off'.[17] The camera lingers to witness this exchange, but as the moth flies off, the camera swandives down the entire length of the tower, approximately twenty or more storeys, in a meticulously detailed swoop down the side of the building and then, in a slow spiral, into the depths of the military operation below. This is a single seamless drop which ends at the anvil upon which the weapons of Mordor are being forged. The feeling is heightened by several near misses by the camera as it drops down, effortlessly averting close encounters with architectural ornaments shaped as horns, a bridge made of wooden slats and rope, a swinging crane and the raised hammers of the smithies pounding out sword blades on the anvil. This spot on the anvil, with its red-hot pounding of mythic proportions, is where the camera comes to rest before continuing a tour of the destructive progress and Saruman's evident pride as he witnesses the startling birth of new Orc soldiers from wombs of muck and mud. This is the rise of the fearsome Uruk-hai army which will be the enemy for the nine or more hours of the remaining trilogy.

It is a rollercoaster of a sequence, especially when the camera plunges off the side of the tower and drops into the molten foundry of the orcs. The scene is made up largely of miniatures and models, says Jackson, including one giant model which filled an entire car park.[18] *Cinefex* editor Jody Duncan reports it was a massive 35th-scale set, made out of concrete units, urethane and polyurethane foams, tinfoil and prop pieces of trees, dirt and industrial gear (2002: 97). Director of miniature photography Alex Funke explains, 'Peter wanted this huge camera move with the camera swooping up over the wall and then to the top of the tower. But it wasn't possible to do the camera move all the way to the top of the miniature tower because we couldn't go that high with our crane' (in Duncan 2002: 98). The moth and the orcs are computer-generated, while Gandalf is computer-generated for about half the shot. Then, as the moth gets closer, Gandalf the human actor is shot in close-up, and edited in from a live-action shot.[19] A live moth is used in close-up as well.[20]

When the camera appears to leap off the side of the tower into the plunging shot, this is accomplished by changing sets to a larger-scaled miniature and setting it on its side, so that it could be shot horizontally (see Duncan 2002: 97). On the commentary, we learn that the red-hot and molten metal was something which could not easily be faked up close, so they did the shots in the actual foundry where the armour was being made for the prop department and dressed the foundry workers as orcs.[21] The live-action set with the blacksmiths is then composited into the end of this long visual effects sequence. The rollercoaster component which is especially evident in this plunge off the tower will be picked up again as a central motif to the '*camera* as camera' discussion in *The Polar Express*.

Duncan reports that this 'Isengard fly-over' sequence was composited by Mark Tait Lewis, blending 'live, digital and miniature fortress and tower elements', as well as shots of the computer-generated moth, computer-generated orcs and 'atmospherics', which are filters and lighting changes done digitally (2002: 98). His expertise results in an effects shot which appears as a seamless, poetic and enchanting whole. This description marvellously captures the complexity of the '*camera* as camera', for it is an ideal example of how many elements are brought together into a new virtual whole which has been conceived of as an outgrowth of a virtual visioning process. The camera, as such, is purely a fiction; the space which surrounds it and is introduced into it, this multiplicity of spaces, is instead the author of all we are seeing on the screen. Magic indeed.

THE POLAR EXPRESS

Because of the rapid re-sequencing which produces the characteristic '*camera* as camera' rollercoaster moments, these ride-like tropes present a great opportunity to watch the calculations of CGI at their technical peak. The first of nearly a dozen rollercoaster sequences in *The Polar Express* is the 'ticket ride' scene (see Fordham 2005: 133). The sequence follows a golden train ticket which the animated protagonist Hero Boy (performed by Tom Hanks) loses to the wind. The train is heading to the North Pole on Christmas Eve and the opportunity provided by this lost ticket allows the filmmakers to set the scene by showing the winter activities of wild animals passed by the golden ticket on its two-minute adventure away from the train. Wolves running in a pack through the moonlit snow, a plunge down a waterfall, an upward yank into the grip of a bald eagle, the catapulting from the nest and subsequent brief life as a snowball plummets downhill and the final re-emergence of the ticket onto the train itself present an amazing backdrop to the dynamic movements of the fluttering ticket.

The audience's point of view, attached as it is to the ticket, literally flies through this magical animated world from the very top of the mountain to the depths of the valley, and from the passenger areas of the train to the undercarriage and even inside the heating system. It is a 360-degree tour of the virtual world of *The Polar Express*, passing through seven different 'subset environments' in a tight two-minute sequence which took 18 months to produce (see Fordham 2005: 133). It is only because of 3-D virtual animation that such sequences are even remotely cost effective, let alone physically possible, to produce.

Screenwriter William Broyles Jr, who wrote the adaptation of the popular children's story with Robert Zemeckis, comments on the freedoms and burdens of writing for a production of this virtual nature:

> To write a screenplay under these conditions takes some getting used to. Usually, as the time for filming approaches, you adjust your screenplay to what is possible. But with this, as the time approached, it became clear than anything was possible. At first, there was an incredible exhilaration, but then that was followed by the realisation that anything you imagine has to be in the service of the story. (In Kehr 2004)

There are many of these various rollercoaster moments in *The Polar Express*, but the ride effect when the train goes out of control at Glacier Gulch is another outstanding example. A point-of-view shot from the front of the train as it plunges down the tracks in a deep dive is a masterpiece of spatial illusion. Later, the entry into Santa's installation at the North Pole features another fly-over of the looping bridges and aqueducts which lead into town, the camera swooping over and under various pieces of civic architecture and passing directly above the train as it slides into a tunnel on its way to its final disembarkation point for the passengers. It is a wonderful loop-the-loop over and through the city, revealing once again that this technology is really well-suited to dynamic flying camera moves which are simply too difficult to achieve in the physical world.

And yet despite (or perhaps because of) its technical virtuosity, *The Polar Express* has been widely decried as being insufficiently warm and fuzzy. One reviewer went so far as to suggest that it should be subtitled, 'The Night Of The Living Dead', because the virtually animated characters are 'that frightening' (Clinton 2004). This is related to its 'performance capture' techniques, whereby the faces and bodies of the actors are marked with reflective light dots and digitally filmed, allowing their movements and facial expressions to be directly transferred to digital characters, much as a puppet master controls a marionette. Due to the primary technical limitation that no markers can be placed on the actors' eyes, the thought is that a 'dead-eyed' look makes for an eerie or uncanny performance which is off-putting. Not everyone feels that the look and feel is such a problem, but it has become a bit *de rigueur* to critique *The Polar Express* as a failure on this account. Subsequent productions, such as Peter Jackson's employments of motion capture and Zemeckis's *Beowulf* (2007) have actively worked to solve this problem.

I think to focus on this temporary drawback of the performance capture process is to miss the power of the virtual cinematography enabled by the new technology. As David Kehr of the *New York Times* describes it:

Now, the real fun begins. With his 3-D characters inside a 3-D environment, the filmmaker has a literally infinite choice of camera angles. He can place his virtual camera at any point in the 3-D space, much as players of video games, like the newly released 'Sims 2', can do, though the games have a restricted range of positions and much less detail. He can move the virtual camera in any direction, simulating pans and tracking shots, and even a jittery, hand-held effect. He can simulate the look of any known lens (as well as some unknown ones, as the extraordinary deep-focus effects in 'Polar' attest). He can alter the lighting at will, dropping in shadows and highlights that would take hours to reset on a traditional shoot. Instead of having actors sitting in their trailers, waiting for the crews to set up the next shot, they can stay on stage and in character and go straight from one scene to the next. And as Mr Zemeckis pointed out, he also eliminated the risk and bother of working with child actors, substituting the skill of one consummate professional who has the only acting credit in the film's advertisements. (2004)

Zemeckis's closing remark points to the potential devaluation of the actor into a mere avatar. But in response to this criticism also raised by Kehr, he suggests that:

I found in my big effects movies where I had to do a lot of major blue-screen work, like in *Contact* and in *Forrest Gump*, it's really hard to keep the energy from flattening out, because the first thing that happens is the actor now becomes a prop if you're not careful. It takes a lot of discipline for the director and the actor to rise above the tedium of doing this blue-screen work, but there's none of that here. Performance capture is different because it's all about the acting. Without the tyranny of hitting marks and leading the lights and worrying about the boom shadow and your makeup and your wig and the line on your wig and all that horrendous stuff that stifles an actor's performance. Or when they do the greatest take ever and they miss the focus. (In Kehr 2004)

Whether this technology really allows the actor to focus just on the acting relationship with the director remains to be seen. What becomes increasingly clear is that actors in big, Hollywood-style blockbusters will be working in special effects environments for the foreseeable future. These environments can either give them more or less to work with – or more or less obstacles to overcome – in giving their performances within a virtual context. Zemeckis believes that this digital future is here to stay, and even David Kehr starts his article by speculating that this kind of performance capture technology is bringing about the greatest transition in the cinema since the advent of sound in 1927 (2004).

Before closing this examination of *The Polar Express*, I want to explore the scene with the greatest emotional payoff: the meeting between Hero Boy and Santa, with both roles performed by Tom Hanks. This is the moment the entire film has been moving towards. At the critical moment when Santa finally comes to the square and the crowd goes wild, it is like Elvis is in the building. Hero Boy has a problem though. He does not have the true spirit of Christmas in his heart. Because of this, he cannot hear the sleigh bells; his view of Santa is blocked; and this moment of tribal ecstasy, in which every other person present is exploding in joy and happiness, is turning to sawdust and ashes for him. Then comes an unexpected event: a sleigh bell comes loose, flies through the air and falls at his feet. Still, he cannot hear it. It rolls, shiny and full of perfect reflections – a technically stunning demonstration of animation – to rest at his feet. He bends down to pick it up. We see him reach for it in a reverse shot – *from underneath the ice it is laying upon* – in a very nice '*camera* as camera' angle. This is technical beauty *par excellence* in this delicate story moment. We continue to see him and the bell from this scratchy, detail-perfect patch of ice up into his face and then we rise as he gets to grips with his leap of faith. He wishes and prays that he can believe in the spirit of Christmas. 'I believe', he intones fervently. He tries the bell one last time, and at last – the diegetic sound we have been waiting for – the bell chimes in a pure and crystalline tone. He looks at it in amazement and we see the growing reflection of Santa as he approaches from behind Hero Boy.

We know Santa is right behind him, but our protagonist does not – and all this is done in the reflections of this animated object, again, a very '*camera* as camera' tactic. We see the scene unfold as the reflection located on the virtual object – it is literally a mirror, except that once again we must remind ourselves that there is no light to be reflected and that this is simulated. The bell does *not* reflect – it authors. When Hero Boy sees Santa's reflection, he knows his big moment has come. Santa is as luminescent as an angel, an archangel even, as he is so large. His sonorous voice cuts to the chase – 'What was that you said?' A very touching exchange between the pair affirms that Hero Boy has finally found the true spirit of Christmas, symbolised by the sleigh bell he asks for and receives as a symbolic gift, and then the sleigh finally takes off. Of course, there are some wonderful flying sleigh shots, as one would expect in a movie which is taking full advantage of its '*camera* as camera' opportunities.

Zemeckis's long-time effects supervisor, Ken Ralston, is a five-time Academy Award winner and is the senior visual effects supervisor at Sony Pictures Image-works (see Fordham 2005: 114). Ralston and Zemeckis have been collaborating for nearly twenty years on such diverse projects as the *Back to the Future* franchise (1985–1990), *Who Framed Roger Rabbit?* (1988) and many more. *Cinefex* writer Joe Fordham chooses to give Ralston the final word in his article about the effects in *The Polar Express*:

> I always approach effects from the artistic standpoint first. Technology is the night-mare that follows. It was great having the control that we had over this world. Bob's vision was less contaminated by compromise than it has been in any other film. It really did become what he set out to create – a moving art piece. For a direc-tor with a very precise, very specific vision, it's possible to achieve that vision in this world. (In Fordham 2005: 170)

Regardless of one's opinion about the quality of the animation or the ultimate vision, it is still undeniable that Zemeckis has made an extraordinary product in a 3-D virtual setting – an entire world of his own creation – with dramatic camera moves, motion capture and all manner of innovations relevant to the '*camera* as camera'. As is by now surely crystal-clear, I do believe that this technology is in a kind of infancy and that we will be seeing many unexpected iterations devel-oping from these options. Zemeckis's film points to a different aesthetic use of dynamic camera moves and digital or synthetic actors than Peter Jackson's, but the technologies are remarkably similar. Both directors extract similar uses from the tropes made possible by the '*camera* as camera', but their final products are as distinctive from one another as can be. Their personal artistic voices find spe-cial expression in the mode of virtual cinematography which is afforded by the '*camera* as camera'. This demonstrates that the '*camera* as camera' sensibility is becoming a necessary component of any filmmaking toolbox, with implications for a changing notion of the subject found in virtualised conditions.

BACK TO THE BURLY BRAWL

Returning briefly to the Burly Brawl sequence in *The Matrix Reloaded*, I would like to summarise the importance of the actor as avatar and the converse. Martial arts films bring with them their own very relevant history and the *Matrix* films provide a perfect summation of the wired flight of kung fu masters flying through the air to achieve maximum impact. In the Burly Brawl, hundreds of Agent Smiths converge into the fight scene with Neo, bringing us full circle to the beginning of this discussion with the fight choreography of Woo Ping. Actors are made over as avatars in the form of digital doubles, virtual humans and stuntmen with exchangeable heads. Avatars are also made into actors, with varying dramatic capabilities. Just where, or even *whether*, the line can be drawn between real actors performing synthetic behaviours and synthetic actors performing real emotions is a major question raised by the '*camera* as camera'. In part, this development is indebted to the proto-digital environment of the martial arts wire work which grid the sound stage for impossible action, dynamic movements and miraculous fly-throughs. Thus, a strong argument can be made for the influence of Asian cinema aesthetics in the development of '*camera* as camera' productions – since the *Matrix* films were stylistically influenced by Hong Kong action cinema.

In the DVD featurette explaining the making of the *Matrix* trilogy, John Gaeta mentions, almost as a throwaway, that in creating the virtual camera which can film anything anywhere, the camera is now 'separated from the subject'.[22] While the traditional subject/object sits in alienation, wrapped up in a world that seems like an unrelated tableau, watched over by an equally alienated viewer with a god-like perspective as voyeur, in the '*camera* as camera', the subject/object *and* viewer are now virtually indistinguishable from the surrounding world and every other presence in it. Furthermore, each of these 'subjects' is likely to have a cast of various sub-personalities, as the multi-dimensional opportunities of cyberspace are renowned for bringing out multiplicity, both of viewpoints and users. Future filmic experiences will explore this in ways we can now hardly imagine, stuck as we are with our limited dialectics of subject/object, auteur/audience and action/narrative. If we look back at 1905 and chuckle knowingly to ourselves that they did not even move the camera let alone consider making a cut, what will future cinephiles be thinking about us once these equally simplistic constraints of ours are overcome?

CONCLUSIONS

In *The Myth of Total Cinema* (1946), Bazin describes the birth of cinema as being intimately entwined with the *idée fixe* that art can produce a complete illusion of life, and on this basis, he states that cinema has not yet been invented. To my ears, Bazin's mythic evocation of 'a recreation of the world in its own image'

(1967b: 21) goes beyond so-called virtual reality. The search for the 'complete illusion of life' sounds like a description of artificial intelligence (A. I.) or artificial life (A. L.), both of which are still in their infancies and yet discernible on the horizon. Software such as MASSIVE, which generates entire ecologies of information in order to populate the screen with sophisticated extras, points the way to something new in cinema. Perhaps surprisingly it is in the realm of special effects, with its 3-D virtual worlds, sophisticated compositing techniques and autonomous crowds of intelligent agents, that we are witnessing a radical shift in what we traditionally think of as the 'subject'. I would not have guessed that it would be under the aegis of Jackson, Lucas, Zemeckis and the Wachowski brothers that the world would take on an entirely new meaning, but that is what appears to be happening.

Like Bazin, I would suggest that we are still in the process of developing a desire to see a 'total cinema'. I propose that we are developing a new set of philosophical and aesthetic motivations which value the contributions, agency and authorship of every point in space, thereby discarding the longstanding romance with the lone figure set against a sweeping vista. Certainly, an expanded subjectivity for every point in space – what is in fact a posthuman subjectivity – challenges the traditional status quo, with implications familiar to scholars of postcolonialism, feminism and psychoanalysis.

Mark Poster writes in his 2000 essay for 'The Multiple and Mutable Subject' conference:

> As we move into digital authorship we can expect serious alterations in the author figure, in the readerly imagination, evinced by the mobile bits and liquid pages travelling at the speed of light. These natural laws of digital authorship are yet only in their beginning stage of development. We can expect that someday they will constitute the formative conditions for a new regime of authorship. (2001: 95)

In the 'camera as camera', the author is also an actor, an agent, an avatar, a posthuman. Poster echoes the writing of Michel Foucault (see 1984: 119), Roland Barthes and other critical theorists concerned with the changing roles of the author and reader, but brings the discussion into a digital and hypertextual context, wedding the theory and media issues into a single discussion. What I am proposing in the 'camera as camera' is a way of understanding the shift from object to subject, predicated on the actual constitution of 3-D virtual spaces as what could be called the dense voices of calculation, or new virtual subjectivities. The objectification which in the past derived from the quasi-scientific imaging of 'subjects' by mechanical means has now shifted to a recognition of new subjectivities emerging from actively authoring posthuman agents in an uneasy compromise with directors, writers and audiences.

I suggest we should neither essentialise nor ventriloquise for these newly recognised virtual entities who share perspectives with us, since, as non-virtual humans who do not inhabit cyberspace, we can not know what, if any, new parameters of so-called 'subjectivity' may be engaged by these brave new, post-human subjects. It seems a bit of a throwback to an old Enlightenment-era argument to say that these virtual entities, complete with agency and voice, are only authorised to express information useful to us, information which is all about us, revealing more about our human condition. And all the while we completely disavow their posthuman condition about which we know nothing. This is a very one-way conversation, a colonial presumption which should not go forward unexamined and unchallenged. In arguing for a putative subjectivity for these new virtual entities, it is then only a small leap to wonder at what point we will extend 'rights' to the posthuman. And inevitably, in that same process we must then retroactively consider the merits of improving the everyday transactions between non-technologically determined humans as well.

As philosophically and aesthetically there is no longer *any* point in space, occupied or otherwise, which may be considered as *in*capable of authoring or agency, the moving image, already manufactured with false boundaries for presentation to the fourth wall for many decades, has now lost all boundaries. In 'The Ontology of the Photographic Image' (1945), Bazin says that the most important invention for the plastic arts is the invention of photography because photography is like Nature, and can imitate not only life, but the artist as well. For Bazin, the photograph is not an exercise in human agency. Even at this early date, we have a critical sense that the camera itself possesses a form of agency.[23] When, in any given world, virtual or otherwise, the entire space and people in it are activated as potential cameras – seen as points in space with potential and valuable calculus attached to each one and are additionally granted their own voice and not essentialised or ventriloquised as the Other – then we have a very different universe than the one articulated by traditional Western perspectives thus far. We may take a new pleasure in relating to these new '*camera* as camera' subjectivities – we are indeed witnessing the birth of a new consciousness. This too should be a source of cinephilic pleasures.

NOTES

1   For a walkthrough of visual effects supervisor John Gaeta's work, please see the three short clips available at: http://whatisthematrix.warnerbros.com/cmp/sfx-bullet_videos2. html. Accessed 1 May 2003.

2   My unpublished doctoral thesis (2006) covers these seven tropes in greater depth.

3   Muybridge's photographs were the result of settling a bet with Governor Sanford over whether or not all four legs of a horse were ever off the ground at the same point during a run. For a fascinating read on the life and times of Eadweard Muybridge, Solnit (2003) is highly recommended.

4   *Cinefex* is currently published in Riverside, California, by Don Shay and edited by Jody Duncan.

5   Primary sources are especially important when dealing with the relatively new technologies of virtual cinematography; theorists have not yet had much time to weigh in on the critical implications of such foundational shifts.

6   While I think there is much to be said for deep focus as a revelatory cinema, some camera movement is nonetheless necessary for there to be an 'evolution of the language of cinema'. As Bazin makes clear, all the major discoveries for camera movement were in place by the end of the silent era. Other research indicates that both the first dolly shot and the first crane shot were used by Allan Dwan in 1915. Among other sources, see: http://www.answers.com/topic/allan-dwan. Accessed 11 April 2006.

7   Writer/director William Friedkin predicts that by 2012 there will no longer be directors as such due to the total takeover of the filmmaking process by digital means. He foretells the end of the cinema in favour of mere programming. I disagree completely. Friedkin appears as a guest on 'Cannes Special Report' (hosted by Peter Bart and Peter Guber), *Sunday Morning Shootout*. American Movie Channel, 3 June 2007.

8   The talking stick was used in Native North American tribes at council meetings. In my paper for the Refresh! Conference held in September 2005, entitled 'An Aesthetics of Play – Or How To Understand Interactive Fun', I suggest that learning to embrace an apparently more chaotic aesthetic is part of the challenges we face in embracing interactive media. I believe that in the near future, the '*camera* as camera' aesthetic will provide us with a new opportunity to re-evaluate our reception of many voices simultaneously, rather than considering the orderly aesthetic which has so long dominated Western European art history as the only mode of pleasing expression. Many media trends point in this direction.

9   As further evidence of a cinephilic influence, I must note that these directors are well-known for their nostalgic embrace of the Saturday morning matinees of their childhoods and while no one will ever confuse that with the great art of auteur-driven cinema, there is nonetheless a legitimate cinephilic undertone to their films in general.

10 DVD Commentary. *The Lord of the Rings: The Fellowship of the Ring*. New Line Productions Inc., 2001. Producer Barrie Osbourne ruefully noted that it took over two thousand people to make all the props and objects that established the character of Middle Earth and the Shire.

11 Indeed, were one to watch all three movies in the extended director's cut, the entire experience would last approximately eleven hours. This would not include the additional hours and hours of DVD extras, featurettes and background material, which contribute more than fifty additional hours of material.

12 DVD Commentary. *The Lord of the Rings: The Fellowship of the Ring*. New Line Productions Inc., 2001.

13 Ibid.

14 Ibid.

15 Ibid.

16 Perhaps the transition from mechanical to virtual camera may also leave some feeling similarly queasy; paradigm shifts are rarely comfortable.

17 DVD Commentary. *The Lord of the Rings: The Fellowship of the Ring*. New Line Productions Inc., 2001.

18 Ibid.

19 DVD Commentary. *The Lord of the Rings: The Fellowship of the Ring*. New Line Productions Inc., 2001.

20 Ibid. This was apparently a bit tricky as Luna moths live a very short while and only hatch a few days a year. This entire shoot was therefore structured around the life cycle of this rare and beautiful creature, a point about which several people make awestruck remarks during the various DVD commentary sections.

21 DVD Commentary. *The Lord of the Rings: The Fellowship of the Ring*. New Line Productions Inc., 2001. Talk about art imitating life!

22 DVD Commentary: Disc 2 'The Matrix Revisited: What Is Bullet Time?'. *The Ultimate Matrix Collection: The Matrix/Reloaded/Revolutions/Experience/Animatrix*. Warner Home Video, 2004.

23 I say early date here, because in terms of virtual technology, the year 1945 places this text at the dawn of cybernetics.

REFERENCES

Anon (2007) 'Production notes essay', *Cinema Review*. Online. Available at: http://www.cinemareview.com/production.asp?prodid=4132. Accessed 7 July 2007.

Bazin, André (1967a [1945]) 'The Ontology of the Photographic Image', in *What Is Cinema?* Volume 1, trans. Hugh Gray. Berkeley: University of California Press, 9–16.

(1967b [1946]) 'The Myth of Total Cinema', in *What Is Cinema?* Volume 1, trans. Hugh Gray. Berkeley: University of California Press, 17–22.

(1967c [1950–55]) 'The Evolution of the Language of Cinema', in *What Is Cinema?* Volume 1, trans. Hugh Gray. Berkeley: University of California Press, 23–40.

Branigan, Edward (2006) *Projecting A Camera: Language-Games in Film Theory*. New York: Routledge.

Clinton, Paul (2004) '*Polar Express*: A Creepy Ride', CNN entertainment news, 10 November. Available at: http://edition.cnn.com/2004/SHOWBIZ/Movies/11/10/review.polar.express/index.html. Accessed 20 January 2006.

Crockett, Tobey (2006) 'The Camera as Camera: Emerging Subjectivities in 3-D Virtual Worlds', unpublished PhD thesis, University of California, Irvine.

Duncan, Jody (2002) 'Ring Masters', *Cinefex*, 89, 64–131.

Fordham, Joe (2005) 'A Dream of Christmas', *Cinefex*, 100, 112–35, 169–70.

Foucault, Michel (1977) 'What Is an Author?', in Paul Rabinow (ed.) *The Foucault Reader*, trans. Josue Hariri. New York: Pantheon, 101–20.

Isherwood, Christopher (1963) 'A Berlin Diary (Autumn 1930)', *Berlin Stories*. New York: New Directions Publishing.

Kehr, David (2004) 'A Face That Launched A Thousand Chips', *New York Times*, 24 October, Section 2. Online. Available at: http://www.nytimes.com/2004/10/24/movies/24kehr.ht ml?ex=1099651934&ei=1&en=76189ca508c6660d. Accessed October 28, 2004.

Kimble, George (2002) '50 Years On ... "This is Cinerama"', *Cinema Technology*. Online. Available at: http://www.cineramaadventure.com/kimblepage2.htm. Accessed 10 April 2006.

Klinger, Barbara (2006) *Beyond the Multiplex: Cinema, New Technologies and the Home*. Berkeley: University of California Press.

Magid, Ron (1999) 'Interview with John Gaeta', *American Cinematographer*. Online. Available at: http://www.theasc.com/protect/apr99/trinity/pg1.htm. Accessed 1 May 2003.

North, Dan (2006) 'Virtual Actors, Spectacle and Special Effects: Kung Fu Meets "All That CGI Bullshit"', in Stacy Gillis (ed.) *The Matrix Trilogy: Cyberpunk Reloaded*. London: Wallflower Press, 48–61.

Poster, Mark (2001 [2000]) 'Print and Digital Authorship', in Vera Lemecha and Reva Stone (eds) *The Multiple and Mutable Subject*. St Norbert: St Norbert Arts Centre, 95.

Solnit, Rebecca (2003) *River of Shadows: Eadweard Muybridge and the Technological Wild West*. New York: Viking Books.

CHAPTER SEVEN
DÉJÀ VU FOR SOMETHING THAT HASN'T HAPPENED YET / TIME, REPETITION AND *JAMAIS VU* WITHIN A CINEPHILIA OF ANTICIPATION

Jason Sperb

> The pleasure of the text is that moment when my body pursues its own ideas – for my body does not have the same ideas I do … this text is outside pleasure, outside criticism, *unless it is reached through another text of bliss*: you cannot speak 'on' such a text, you can only speak 'in' it.
>
> – Roland Barthes, *The Pleasure of the Text*[1]

Cinephiliac love is a tricky thing – a passive/aggressive beast. It can disrupt the very same process (thought) it first triggered. When academics write about films, one can by no means assume that it is the work of a cinephile – or at least that it was a cinephiliac impulse that triggered the essay. I find myself confronting the question of what could be a model for writing about cinephilia within the rigours and defamiliarising revisions of academia. Then again – I am reluctant to frame it in those terms. There is still too much critical distance. I would prefer to think of it as how one writes cinephiliacally as an academic. Nevertheless, there is still the question of a model, or a theory. How does a scholar write as a cinephile? The short answer is that they do not. The longer answer is that they do. Thus, this essay does not offer much of a definitive solution, but instead points towards a more clearly articulated series of questions for such a model.

THE LOVE OF CINEPHILIA 'SCHOLARSHIP'

In *The Imaginary Signifier: Psychoanalysis and the Cinema*, Christian Metz writes about the presence of cinephilia and its tensions for those who wish to write critically about the cinema. In a section entitled 'Loving the Cinema', Metz articulates the removal of thought from the experience of watching cinema itself, such that thought becomes its own referent. Metz calls this writing 'an uninterpreted dream. This is what constitutes its symptomatic value; it has already said everything' (1982: 14). Writing about movies is too often caught up in established assumptions about ideologies brought to the cinema, Metz believes, rather than about the text itself. One thinks about *thinking* about various aspects of the cinema, which thus can be removed quickly from the particulars of cinematic spectatorship. On the other hand, not thinking reflexively about the cinema hinders the development of new ideas. This aspect is what makes loving the cinema problematic for him. Knowledge generates in some sense apart from this love, by considering the affective power of the text, but also by re-contextualising that power within a variety of intellectual and theoretical discourses. Only then does Metz famously proceed to assert that:

> To be a theoretician of the cinema, one should ideally no longer love the cinema and yet still love it: have loved it a lot and only have detached oneself from it by taking it up again from the other end, taking it as the target for the very same scopic drive which had made one love it. (1982: 15)

Repeating the love of the 'scopic' experience of the text, through a sort of doubling of critical thought, distances the theorist from the cinephile. Repetition is a recurring trend in discussions of cinephilia and psychoanalytic theory – but what is repeated and what is generated by that repetition is less clear. Peter Wollen has previously suggested that cinephilia is 'a desire to remain within a child's view of the world, always outside, always fascinated by a mysterious parental drama, always seeking to master one's anxiety by compulsive repetition' (2001: 119). In a kind of reversal of Metz, for Wollen it seems to be a *fear* of critical, reflective thought ('to remain within a child's view') which generates the need for a 'compulsive repetition' which will allow the cinephile to maintain some sense of innocence, free from thought. Although I do not mean to suggest that Metz and Wollen are taking up exactly the same issues, it is clear that for Metz and other psychoanalytic theorists it is the distancing effect of thought which could complicate – or be complicated by – repetition. Like Wollen's conception of the cinephile's childish desires, Metz argues that ideally one should not love the cinema to theorise it – because such love in isolation complicates the ability to think outside the cinema.

In contrast to the usual critical response to Metz on these points, let me start out by suggesting that here he is more right than wrong. Of course, an essay on/ within cinephilia that starts out by accepting Metz's theories on the matter will most likely not get very far. Perhaps this is because scholars and theorists seem to presume that Metz advocates that one should renounce their cinephilia to write about the cinema. This is only half true. What Metz suggests is a tension that I believe to be the dilemma of the film academic – one not writing about cinephilia, but one trying to write as a *cinephile*. There is always a tension between the two – writing about versus writing within. It may be easier for most cinephiles; they can just write. But how can a scholar (of the 'critical distance' persuasion) also write as a cinephile? Loving the cinema, for Metz, constitutes seeing the cinema as a special, mythic landscape immune from the traditional standards of scientific and intellectual rigour. So, one must stand outside their love. However, Metz is also careful to assert that such love still must be retained in some way. He is not suggesting that it is enough to write *about* cinephilia, as do almost all cinephiliac thinkers (like Paul Willemen[2]), to think of it as this mysterious terrain, within which they insert themselves almost ethnographically – only to retreat again with thoughts, observations and eventually theories ... *upon reflection*. This would be cinephilia 'scholarship' and its distance would be susceptible to various forms of nostalgia – intellectual, personal and historical.

Conversely, it is too easy to write simply as a cinephile without the self-reflexivity of pleasure required for cinephilia to regenerate and proliferate as something beyond itself. The scholar must 'no longer be invaded by [the cinephile]: not have lost sight of him, but be keeping an eye on him. Finally, be him and not be him, since in all these are the two conditions on which one can speak of him' (Metz 1982: 15). Metz describes writing critically about the cinema as the anxiety of the cinephile trying always to crawl back up a subjective slope of pleasure towards the objective of ideas, down which they would otherwise slide. Taken in all of its messy ambiguity, Metz's theories on cinephilia and writing retain a certain urgency, a certain legitimacy. But of course I wish to go further. How can a scholar write through the cinephile (in my case, he whom I keep an eye on) in such a way which will retain – at the level of language – a sense of the power of cinephilia, and which will keep 'the very same scopic drive which had made one love' the cinema in the first place?

Interrogating my own cinephiliac and discursive reactions to the franchise horror film, *Final Destination 3* (2006), this essay attempts to articulate a theory of cinephilia that – through repetition – rethinks the reactive power of nostalgia within the larger affective power of presence, all the while embracing the emotional and intellectual possibilities of the new.[3] Moreover, by focusing on a theory of affect, one might be capable of retaining through discourse something close to the cinephiliac experience. In a way, this is also an autobiographical study of one cinephile – autobiographical insofar as I wish to go without any sustained distance from the pleasures which gave birth to it. One cannot truly understand cinephilia by standing outside its flow, to write and rewrite the 'uninterpreted dream', or to think endlessly about one's own distanced thoughts. One needs to immerse their whole body into cinephilia, to feel its effects, while attempting to articulate it. It is not enough to think that one is a cinephile (closeted or not, self-admitting or otherwise). Any film scholar can retrospectively claim that. Regardless of the critic's motivation, to write about the cinema is not automatically the same as to love the cinema. This distinction must remain in place. Though the two are not easily severed, thought and discourse come before, during and after the experiences of pleasure. To study cinephilia requires interrogating one's own cinephiliac infection, accepting its presence and its dominance. And to accept that it afflicts thought irreparably. Then one can speak of cinephilia. We do not write from thought. We write from pleasure (even sometimes from the pleasure (bliss) of pain). Thought emerges from writing, from pleasure. But it is not simply a matter of repetition.

DIFFERENCES IN REPETITION

Repetition plays a key role in *The Four Fundamental Concepts of Psychoanalysis*. Here, Jacques Lacan returns to 'the function of repetition' (1978: 48) while discussing the *objet petit a* (the object of desire), desire itself, and the tensions between 'thought and the real' (1978: 49) as effects of the symbolic. Because the *objet petit a* is unattainable, because desire can never be overcome, repetition is always generated anew – the endlessly deferred, unsatisfied drive to fulfill desire. But repetition here is also an effect of the real. For Lacan, some aspect of the real periodically disrupts thought, but then takes us back to thought. 'The real', writes Lacan, 'is that which always comes back to the same place – to the place where the subject insofar as he thinks, where the *res cogitans*, does not meet' (ibid.). Put differently, the real brings the subject back to the moment where a split occurs between the real and what the subject *thinks* of as the real, without ever reaching the real. However, thought too is changed here, though it still does not (and can never) account for a trace of the real. It is not my intention here to do an exhaustively close reading of Lacan, but to illustrate the importance in psychoanalytic theory of repetition – which, to a degree, is also crucial (as Wollen suggests) to the cinephile. However, there is also a logic in which, according to figures such as Lacan, something generates in excess of that repetition, and that thus changes repetition. As Slavoj Žižek writes, 'Where do we find the *objet petit a*? The *objet a* is precisely that surplus, that elusive make-believe that drove the man [in Dashiell Hammett's *The Maltese Falcon* (1930)] to change his existence. In "reality", it is nothing at all, just an empty surface (his life after the break is the same as before), but because of it the break is nonetheless worth the trouble' (1991: 8). The disruption is as crucial as the repetition.

In addition, this 'surplus', this seed of thought, is that which is less considered when one writes on the repetition of cinephilia. This issue of thought and repetition directly relates to the question of memory. According to Lacan, habitual practices posit remembering as the focal point, the 'centre' (1978: 51) – in a sense, we are always already in a state of nostalgia. But this routine is disrupted by the real through experiences with the symbolic, which thus brings us back to the present. However, the subject resists this process by reacquiring a centre through the act of remembering. Actually, the real *is the present*, but we can only process it in thought as an approach to the present, and thus the subject quickly substitutes the experience of the real with memory. But Lacan believes that in this repetition knowledge accrues. At a basic level, he insists that the constant tension between a subject's thoughts and the experience of the real facilitates repetition, arguing that:

> It is necessary to ground this repetition first of all in the very same split that occurs in the subject in relation to the encounter … it is precisely in this that the real finds itself, in the subject, to a very great degree the accomplish of the drive – which we shall come to at last, because only by following this way will we be able to conceive from what it returns. (1978: 69)

In his formulation, the real brings us back to the same pre-conscious or prethought state. But it also triggers thought, triggers development through the drive. Through the repetition of desire, the subject can become something more; there is the potential to evolve. Moreover, I would add, the repetition of pleasure, motivated by this sense of the real, also contains the potential to generate a higher level of understanding, rather than just be the experience of enjoyment for its own sake. To this extent, I believe that Lacan's work here in some way points to a manner of conceptualising cinephilia which is neither pleasure (nor bliss), nor repetition alone – but rather a cinephilia where thought and knowledge accumulate. Moreover, this accumulation produces *anticipation*, another form of desire, because to look forward is also to become something new. 'Repetition', writes Lacan, 'demands the new' (1978: 61). And, as I will argue in the concluding section of this essay, this newness – which exceeds repetition – should change how scholars have traditionally thought of repetition as it relates to the cinephile. Indeed, with this emphasis on the new in mind, I wonder if we should begin to rethink whether or not to regard the cinephile in terms of repetition at all.

THE PLEASURES OF PAIN: *FINAL DESTINATION 3*

At this point, I turn to a specific example for what I am attempting to untangle, though it is my hope that this will open back out to larger theoretical questions. In February 2006, I was watching *Final Destination 3* over at the local multiplex in Bloomington, Indiana. This is my idea of fun after a typically hard weekend for a PhD film student of researching, writing and of otherwise having no fun whatsoever. Like the first two films (2000, 2003), *Final Destination 3* is about a group of people who escape a horrific crash because someone has a vivid, graphic vision of the disaster about to happen. We too in the audience see this vision along with the protagonist, and viscerally feel the motivation for the character to try and stop the tragedy from occurring. But the disaster still eventually happens, minus the people who unexpectedly get out of Death's way. And the actual disaster is less intensely visualised than the experience of the protagonist's premonition (the actual disaster – always foreseen – is a bit anti-climatic). Thus, the past (future past) is always already co-existent with the present in a narrative explicitly about the expectation of death. Some characters survive, but this momentary escape merely sets up each *Final Destination* premise – they survive only to have Death pursue them for foiling Death's plan.

There are two main reasons why I find myself attracted to this franchise, why it arouses a particular kind of intense joy within me. For one, it takes the admittedly absurd goal of most run-of-the-mill teen horror flicks ('What is the most grotesquely violent way we can think of for killing this poor kid?') and gives it a literal premise. This is to say 'Death' (as an actual, though always unseen, character) is *literally* coming to get these survivors, *no matter what*. The more they try to undermine or in some way disrupt Death's plan, then the more elaborately violent their own demise will be, because they are only making it that much more difficult for Death to get to them. Hence, it might be weird to know that I find the *Final Destination* films oddly *plausible*. That is, once I accept the premise that *Death itself has agency*, all the characters' eventual demises – no matter how elaborately conceived and overly contrived – make perfect sense. Extreme and absurd diegetic coincidences are almost always at play in horror films, and usually necessary for a truly spectacular and elaborate cinematic death. The *Final Destination* films work because that usual generic element of serendipity is completely eliminated by the films' identical narrative foundation.

So, in short, I immensely enjoy this franchise because I know someone's going to die. But the emphasis here is on the 'knowing', not on the fact that someone dies. Moreover, entering the theatre with a basic understanding of this formulaic premise, one knows it's going to be incredibly violent, with a long, slow, elaborate build-up. In this respect, I suppose I am typical of white Midwestern film geeks who grew up during the 1980s. And, on some level, it would seem to make *Final Destination* not that different from other franchises such as *Halloween* (1978–2007), *Friday the 13th* (1980–2009) or *A Nightmare on Elm Street* (1984–2003) – three series, I confess, of which I've never been a big fan. But, I should caution to add, what interests me about this particular horror franchise, and its preferred depictions of death, is not the extent of the gore, or even the violence at all. *It is rather the anticipation itself*, the way the film, narratively even, plays upon this anticipation very explicitly, prolonging the moment of the demise as long as possible – if anything, the actual violence brings an end to the build-up, and thus an end to the anticipation.

As the third film began, I started feeling a very intense anxiety in my stomach as I awaited that inevitable first, horrifyingly disastrous crash – this time, a rollercoaster crash. This bodily intensity was no doubt partly informed by my graphic memories of the first two films and their horribly violent crashes, but it was still something I was feeling more than remembering. What really drew me in was the anticipation of something *I had a sense of, but could not yet see*. Of course, the beauty of the '*Final Destination*' (that is, the beauty of the film's figuration of death) is that there really is no *final* destination. The 'final' death itself is prolonged literally in *Final Destination*. The last death, that of the main protagonist is always put off until after the film has ended. The sole survivor of the first *Final Destination* dies suddenly and unexpectedly three-quarters of the way through the second *Final Destination*. As we learn halfway through the second film, the people fighting off Death's design are also people who were supposed to have died as a result of events extending from the narrative of the first film – literally extending the possibilities of death into infinite diegetic directions. It isn't just that we as the audience know people will die because it is a horror film; *Final Destination*'s very narrative progression is that the characters themselves know that everyone is always *supposed* to die. Meanwhile, one of the presumed 'survivors' in *Final Destination 2*, after the film's climatic *dénouement*, dies unexpectedly in the last shot of the film, reminding characters and audience that the other two remaining survivors will shortly meet their end as well. And indeed they are nowhere to be seen in *Final Destination 3*, even though the disasters from the first two are referenced directly in the narrative.

The *Final Destination* trilogy is built upon endlessly deferred narratives of anticipation. If I were to say that I possess a deep attachment to this sometimes fairly creative but still mostly routine 'slasher' franchise, what does such devotion say about being a cinephile? In his brief but noted essay, 'Leaving the Movie Theatre' (1975), Roland Barthes compares exiting the cinema with the experience of awaking from hypnosis. Although Barthes is not speaking for the cinephile explicitly (though he too is one of the figures Metz specifically responds to in *The Imaginary Signifier*), he demands that one 'who speaks here … admit one thing: he loves leaving a movie theatre' (1989: 345). While critics and scholars have long acknowledged how Barthes articulates what one experiences after watching a film in a darkened theatre, less attention has been paid to his discussion of how one *approaches the film beforehand*. Barthes suggests that – looking to relax – we primarily come to the movies with a prepared condition already approaching something like hypnosis, lazily embracing the imminent dream state into which we will shortly enter. However, embedded within this rather passive conception of the spectator is also a parenthetical aside – the recognition of an alternate motivation for going to the movies, 'a more and more frequent one, it is true' (ibid.). To this end, Barthes concedes that some films are those that are actively 'chosen sought, desired, *the object of a genuine anticipatory anxiety*' (ibid.; emphasis added). While it is difficult to identify how much, or to what extent, these two opposing motivations activate the typical moviegoer (erroneously assuming of course that there is such a thing as a 'typical' moviegoer), this description of a text which is sought, desired, anticipated, does constitute, I would venture to add, the primary motivation of the cinephile.

But *why* it is sought, desired, anticipated, is itself a loaded issue, and I will only attempt to unpack one possibility among many. What generates that 'genuine anticipatory anxiety?' My memories of watching *Final Destination* and the first sequel were co-present with my experience, sitting in the theatre, of watching *Final Destination 3*. Waiting for the rollercoaster's inevitable destruction created an intense anxiety for me that night. Even the slow, patient, methodical clicks of the rollercoaster's trip up the ramp, before that first drop (mimicking too the affective experiences of an actual rollercoaster ride), heightened this anticipation. All too aware on some level of the spectacular disasters which opened the first two films, I knew a similar spectacle was coming; I knew it was going to be bloody and fantastically cruel; and I knew it was going to be realised in no small part by digital effects – yet I didn't know what exactly was going to happen, or how. And it was in some ways a bodily knowledge. I could not quite envision the deaths before they are shown, but I could feel anxiously the memories of disasters past. In all three *Final Destination* films, Death was (is) inevitable, but its forms remain unrealised to a point.

In this sense, I had visions of the *virtual* (in multiple meanings of the term) not unlike the film's lead protagonist does in the narrative, as all of the lead protagonists have in each of the films. This vision, and its very literal affect, was a source of anxiety for me. But that anxiety itself was also the cause of a tremendous amount of joy, because the anticipation of that crash was one of the most intense feelings I have experienced in the cinema in quite a while. It is very rare for a film to come alive, if only for a moment or two. Such an experience is very rare, but it does happen – *the film felt real*. The image was not real; the story was not real. We are still in the realm of the symbolic. But the affect of it, what was in excess of its representation, was the effect of the real. I could feel the anticipation in my stomach. But the pleasure, the *bliss*, was not derived from my consciously saying 'this is real'. *Consciously*, I was thinking something more akin to, 'this is just a franchise horror film to distract me on a cold Saturday night from my weekly stresses'. The pleasure derived instead from the thoughts of my body. And it was a joy based primarily on what could be – though also co-present with what is (the present narrative) and what was (the first and second *Final Destination*). I am not interested solely in what could be crudely called by others a bodily pleasure, but I am interested in how this effect of the real pushes me beyond the comfort of established thought, and in how this push is itself the source of a kind of cinephiliac pleasure. The narratives and affects of the *Final Destination* films provide an especially good way to think of the co-presence of past/present/future possibilities of intense joy in the cinematic experience – *a cinephilia of anticipation*.

THE CINEPHILIA OF ANTICIPATION

The cinephilia of anticipation is an endless stream moving forward, generated by the present cinematic image, but also looking ahead to what it is yet to be/come. It does not stop to reflect, even though it still carries in the present that which it picked up in the past – nostalgia, affect, imagination, all at once. One could say it is a cumulative effect of repetition. In my previous work on cinephilia (2007),[4] I attempted to suggest possibilities for a *future-oriented* cinephilia, as a means to move the logic of these sorts of writings away from the crippling effects that nostalgia seems to have had on this particular discursive tradition. But, of course, I was not suggesting that one can, or should, forget the past. So the question becomes how can we theorise cinephilia explicitly within an appropriately efficient temporal dimension? I was then more interested in scholarship on cinephilia, and how one could speak to it today. Only at the end do I raise the possibility of a 'cinephilia of anticipation', a concept which I expand upon here.

What is a *cinephilia of anticipation*? When the main character in *Final Destination 3* first sees the (soon-to-be-notorious) rollercoaster up close, she briefly pauses, as though intimidated and even terrified for a spell by the ride's potential, before then shaking her head. Her boyfriend (himself doomed) turns around, notices her momentary apprehension and then asks her what's wrong. She responds by stating that she was 'having that feeling like *déjà vu* … except for something that hasn't happened yet'. He tries to console her by suggesting she's only scared because 'they say the real fear with these rides comes from the feeling of having no control. Everyone imagines weird stuff when they get scared. But it never turns out to be what they imagined.' On one level, the statement proves to be ironic, because the horrific accident that does occur turns out to be almost exactly what she had imagined minus the people who end up getting off the ride because of her eventual panic attack. But, on another level, it turns out to be a fitting revelation for the film and for the franchise. The audience is driven by the possibilities of what they imagine happening to the characters in *Final Destination*, but the deaths never quite occur in the way we expect them to. In this sense, the 'feeling of having no control' is a part of the anticipation within and in excess of the film – as is anticipating an actual rollercoaster, where something will happen that we cannot quite completely envision. And only after the act, can we give a vision, a meaning and shape to it ('its symptomatic value'), through the repetition of thought.

But even more provocative in that dialogue exchange is her declaration of having experienced '*déjà vu* … for something that hasn't happened yet'. This is, I think, an effective way to articulate the temporal paradoxes and flows of a cinephilia of anticipation. And it points rather nicely to some of the filmic concepts articulated by the French philosopher, Gilles Deleuze, a writer (cinephile[5]) crucial to my theoretical work. The concept of *déjà vu* itself recalls Deleuze's discussion of recollection and the work of Henri Bergson. For Deleuze, *déjà vu* contains elements of the 'genuinely virtual' (1989: 54), meaning that the feeling of thinking one has been somewhere before touches possibilities of action and behaviour not yet actualised, or come into being. In other words, *déjà vu* does not refer to a past event that already occurred, but rather to a future event yet to happen. Thus, what does it mean to experience *déjà vu for something that hasn't happened yet*? It is, in a sense, a perfect illustration of Deleuze's formulation of *déjà vu* itself – *déjà vu* is more a possibility, less a memory. And, within this possibility, it pushes towards anticipation. We do not think to the past alone in *Final Destination 3*, when we hear this line. We as an audience look towards the crash yet to come. Deleuze's work on the cinema, according to Elizabeth Grosz, offers 'an orientation to the future, in which we are always out of our element' (2000: 216).

Looking toward the future, a cinephiliac conception of time here can be challenged further. More so than *déjà vu*, the opposite notion of '*jamais vu*' may be even more appropriate for the temporal presence of cinephilia. *Jamais vu* is the feeling of having experienced something for the first time, despite having actually experienced it before. Unlike *déjà vu*, the emphasis is on the unfamiliar, rather than the familiar. While *déjà vu* can operate as a centring orientation point of memory and is capable of being reassuring ('I've experienced this before'), *jamais vu* can trouble thought, taking us outside our comfort zones. *Jamais vu* can make us feel as though there is something now unaccounted for, even while we are on some level still in the realm of the habitual. In other words, *jamais vu* is the feeling of the new within repetition. The cinephile is immersed constantly in repetition – the reiteration of viewing, thinking and especially writing. However, it is the sense of something different, something unexpected, which provokes the most interest – the desire within Lacan's anticipation of the new. And it is that something which gives itself to thought, and then to discourse – that practice which should remain the pre-eminent goal of the cinephile.

Deleuze does not, to my knowledge, write about *jamais vu*, but he could and, perhaps, should have – although, of course, detractors nitpick Deleuze's theories at their own risk. In any case, *jamais vu* seems more in line with Deleuze's conception of difference *in* repetition, and with his fascination with the virtual as that affective something which (in time) waits ahead of the event of the cinematic time-image. 'Time', writes Deleuze, 'is revealed inside the event' (1989: 100). For Deleuze, the time-image is not something represented in the image, but rather generated by it. The time-image is the sense of temporal past/present/futures simultaneously in *the present image*. Time is not represented by the film; rather, the movement of the image generates it affectively as it moves from the past to the present. Better yet, it is the past in the present. This logic has, I would argue, a profound effect on the temporality of the cinephile. To a point, the past is unrepeatable – except as a present. Hence the past is unrepeatable. But the past always already informs the cinephile's present, even while the present can and should feel strangely unlike the past.

Building on these far-reaching but foundational notions of repetition, thought, writing, *déjà vu* and *jamais vu*, I would argue that cinematic experiences such as *Final Destination 3* open up this kind of Deleuzian time-image; they reveal *cinephilia as time-image*, and that this time-image too points towards the future. As only one example, we see the remembered encounters of *Final Destination* and *Final Destination 2* co-presently with expectations of *Final Destination 3*. It is the presence of the past that causes us to anticipate the future. We can say nothing fixed about time other than it never stops moving, that never can I quite pin it down. But we can say that this movement has a profound effect on the cinephile. In fact, the time-image *constitutes* the cinephile; it materialises, brings into being, the possibilities for the cinephile, whereby the repetition of past and present disrupts old thought and generates the potential for new thoughts.

As with Deleuze's conception of the cinematic image, there is no past before the presence of *Final Destination 3*. What might be in the past (the other *Final Destination* films) is still present in the third film. In other words, for the viewer, *Final Destination 3* does not refer back to *Final Destination 2*, but rather *Final Destination 3* opens out to *Final Destination 2* – in the moment of that symbolic experience, the second sequel presently generates in us a sense of its predecessor. This logic, moreover, begins to speak to the *flow* of the cinephilia of anticipation.

The past is always in the present, for Deleuze; however, *that* past and *that* present are both always already gone. By the time we understand it, it's gone. 'If the present is actually distinguishable from the future and the past', writes Deleuze, 'it is because it is the presence of something, which precisely stops being present when it is replaced by *something else*' (ibid.; emphasis in original). And so we too are experiencing something else by then (another film, another book, another thought), which itself we will never understand until it too is gone.

As I noted earlier, this isn't to suggest that the past is forgotten, only that it co-exists with the present, which will soon replace it (and itself will be replaced by future events). Yet all these layers work together to trigger thought. The recollection of past events, together with the effect of a present real, is what facilitates anticipation, hopefully for something a little different, or at least new. For the artist, writes Deleuze, 'there is no other truth than the creation of the New' (1989: 146). Like Lacan, Deleuze posits thought somewhere as an effect of the real, whereby memories are disrupted and mutated by the shock of present experiences. Indeed, it is only shock which *can* generate thought. Drawing from Antonin Artaud, Deleuze writes:

> If it is true that thought depends upon a shock which gives birth to it (the nerve, the brain matter), it can only think one thing, *the fact that we are not yet thinking*, the powerlessness to think the whole and to think oneself, thought which is always fossilised, dislocated, collapsed. (1989: 167; emphasis in original)[6]

It is the affective experience of the cinema which contains the possibility of thought. This may seem like quite a bit of theoretical lifting to dump on the shoulders of *Final Destination 3*, but there was something about the visceral experience – how it *felt* real (I was writing from the pleasure of pain) – which seemed to trigger for me larger questions about the nature of the cinema and of cinephilia. And, of course, as Lacan suggests, such immense questions can never be truly satisfied, which in turn regenerates the drive, the *anticipation*, for not only new experiences but also for new thought.

WATCHING *FINAL DESTINATION 3* AGAIN

Déjà vu for something that hasn't happened yet suggests the vague recollection for the cinephile of past experiences, but such is a recollection which serves the future ahead, and not the dead end of nostalgia. Now, a confession – I did not recall this wonderfully useful line from my first viewing while I began writing my initial thoughts about *Final Destination 3* in a blog entry posted later that week.[7] However, I would not discount the possibility that it did on some level play to my anticipation during that initial viewing, even if I did not consciously retain it.

Of course, I only remember this passage in the film in such detail, and can thus relate it out to Lacan and Deleuze, because I bought the DVD of the film when it was released about five months later in the summer of 2006. This is not an arbitrary autobiographical aside, because on some level the DVD version of *Final Destination 3* also ties into, and perpetuates, the cinephilia of anticipation.

This does, however, shift cinephilia further away from the cinema. What does such a move produce? Barbara Klinger has already suggested previously that cinephilia today is only at best loosely tied to going to the movies, and rather may be better thought of as a home-viewing activity. Indeed, in *Beyond the Multiplex: Cinema, New Technologies, and the Home*, Klinger specifically responds to the cinephiliac theories of Metz and Barthes. Traditionally, she writes, scholars 'regarded cinephilia as essentially and exclusively a big screen experience, absolutely dependent on the projection of celluloid within the public space of the motion picture' (2006: 54). Indeed, when talking of cinephilia and the nature of repetition (including, but not limited to, repeated viewings), it would be impossible to skirt around the issue of DVD, or at least VHS tapes – although the latter is on the verge of acquiring that certain rare aura which it was once thought to have robbed from the theatrical experience. For Klinger, the modern cinephile's behaviour is centred on his/her own collecting habits and on the 'hardware aesthetic' (2006: 68) – how the advent of home-viewing technologies (sound systems, big screen televisions) and DVD special features (audio commentaries, deleted scenes, and so forth) shift and shape the desires and tastes of the collector. The pleasure, in this formulation, quite often is in the act of collecting itself, in the *possibilities* of owning, as much if not more so than in the pleasures of the film itself.

To a certain degree, there's no doubt that I was so anxious to own *Final Destination 3* because I wanted to own that powerful affective experience which much of the film was for me. But that always already pushes me dangerously close to nostalgia. That is to say, there's a distinct chance that I wanted to own a moment in (past) time, and not an affect (of course it is impossible to *own* an affect). Then again, I also wanted to possess it because I had the vague sense even then that I wanted to write about the film, so I too was always already looking ahead to future projects, even while remembering the past experiences of the film itself. So was it an act of anticipation for the past? *Déjà vu for something that hasn't happened yet*? When I bought *Final Destination 3* that summer at a major US retail chain, there was a special offer which gave the consumer a choice of buying one of the other *Final Destination* films for only five dollars with the purchase of the third (as Klinger notes, the media industries themselves play a key role in crafting our collecting behaviour). And, indeed, that day I walked out with two *Final Destination*s rather than just the one I originally sought, though I'd like to think I bought the other because I genuinely enjoy that film too and not just because they 'made me'.[8] Anyway, it is important to note that, even in the promotion of *Final Destination 3*, there is a conscious awareness on the part of the studio that the presence of the previous ones is crucial in constructing an anticipation for the latest instalment in the series.

Repetition is important to the continued consumption of the film, but it is curious too how the DVD itself plays to the importance of anticipating the new. Arguably, the most notable special feature of the film's presentation is the 'Create Your Own Movie' aspect of the disc. As the back of the DVD's cover says, 'New, Interactive Viewing Feature Puts You in Control! Change the course of the film and design new character deaths and destinies.' In a sense then, the DVD packaging suggests that the viewer has not even yet seen the film, even if they did see it in the theatres. There are new versions ahead to be experienced by the DVD itself. Indeed, the disc does (relatively) live-up to the hype. While watching one version of *Final Destination 3*, the film will periodically stop, present a menu and give the viewer the option of choosing different ambiguous directions to go in, although one doesn't know right away how their choices actually affect the narrative progression. The actual changes are relatively minor; most characters simply die in different ways than they would have before. However, one character – who otherwise dies a particularly gruesome death in a fast food drive-thru – can be saved from his demise. And his renewed life serves as the source of several unexpected sequences later in the alternative narrative. Overall, though, not that much of the film can really be changed by the 'Choose Their Fate!' version. But the feature does take quite a few run-throughs to figure out all the different possibilities for how the various destinies of *Final Destination 3* could unfold. I cannot say for certain that I experienced them all. In any case, various aspects of the DVD and its presentation do prolong some sense of the anticipation for the film itself.

Ultimately, the greatest *sustained* pleasure in watching *Final Destination 3* would be through the repetition of a story whose surprises do indeed diminish with each viewing. This is not, however, to suggest that there is no pleasure in subsequent viewings, or that I caught everything there was to find in the film the first time through. It is just that there is (and was) only that one initial experience of anticipating the disaster that opens the film, and then the secondary anticipations of the DVD's special features. Something about the affect, and about the virtual once actualised, irreparably changes once one has seen a film. There was, of course, also my anticipation of trying to write about the film. In contrast to this, however, Klinger argues that repetition 'is a cornerstone of the consumer's experience of entertainment that has the potential to be as enjoyable as it is inescapable' (2006: 137). One cannot deny that on some level repetition – specifically, repeated viewings – are important to the enjoyment of the cinema. In another chapter, Klinger builds upon results from surveys administered to Indiana University students to explore how and why people of a particular generation (namely, children of the 1980s) watched certain movies repeatedly throughout their lives.[9] While some students claimed not to be interested in watching films a second time (because of such factors as the boredom involved in already knowing the plot), most apparently responded to the questions of repeated viewings enthusiastically. Examining the source of their pleasures and satisfactions, Klinger groups their responses under the following categories: familiarity, aesthetic appreciation, therapy, nostalgia and dialogue memorisation (which she refers to as 'karaoke cinema'). Repetition rewards all of these different factors for the viewers. Rather than criticise or even just view their responses sceptically, Klinger wants to embrace the potentially positive and reassuring feelings of comfort that repetition creates in the viewer. Certainly, there is a very real feeling created in repeated viewings.

Although Klinger clearly privileges the importance of repetition to the viewing experience as a source of 'comfort and mastery' (2006: 154) over a film's diegesis, she does allow for something that may be generated in excess of that repetition – something new and different. 'The ritual of return', she writes, 'may introduce more volatile dynamics into the mix, inciting reassessments of the viewer's self or worldview' (2006: 139). For example, repeated viewings can sometimes provoke spectators into rethinking their earlier assumptions – like viewing the 1980s and the era of Ronald Reagan and his politics nostalgically.[10] Klinger ultimately reads repetition ambivalently – it 'represents a means by which, over time, quotidian acts of film consumption in the home maintain the cultural status quo or, conversely, spark and sustain desires for change' (2006: 188). The former mode of repetition no doubt contains its own pleasures for most film buffs, but it also seems to deny the possibility of *new* thought in the theoretical sense – the kind of thought which emerges when and where habitual recollection is disrupted. If we hold on to (as I prefer to do) the latter for the purposes of the cinephile, where repetition can 'spark and sustain desires for change', one is left to wonder what, if anything, is really 'repeated'. To think that something is repeated is to think of it in terms of a past that one attempts in some way to return to. Hence, I am inclined to believe repetition alone is a cinephilia of nostalgia. Repetition as change, as the past creating the future, is the cinephilia of anticipation.

CINEPHILIA AS PLEASURE AND BLISS

If cinephilia is rooted in affect, if cinephilia is rooted in anticipation (the past creating present possibilities), then perhaps cinephilia is in some respects really rooted in the unrepeatable, just as the past is *unrepeatable*. The only thing to be repeated is the anticipation of that thing which has not been repeated yet. What *is* repeated is something else, something less in its affect (if not automatically less in its discursive possibilities) – something now afflicted by thought. And that particular thought, meanwhile, is removed from that unrepeatable experience which, as Deleuze would say, gave 'birth' to it. Of course, *Final Destination 3* does not hold up as well for me on repeated viewings. Pleasure is still there though, but the same level of affective intensity is not – the promise of the new diminishes. *Final Destination 3* has become more of an idea – *this* idea – than a cinematic experience for me. At the same time, this is not to ultimately criticise the aesthetic value (or lack thereof) in the film. Very few films have ever held up for me on repeated viewings, perhaps none, even ones I love infinitely more than any franchise horror film. Periodically, I may see new things, many new things, in subsequent viewings of a film that I missed the first time, but almost never in such an overwhelming totality which has mimicked the experience of that initial viewing. In any case, eventually the original power of the film wanes, and the only way I can come back to it again and again is by spending just enough time away from it (months, years even) so that it *seems* somewhat new again when I finally do watch it another time. In other words, I largely *have to forget a film* (or think I've forgotten a film) before I can want to see it again. And such amnesia is often short-lived once the film's narrative starts to progress again.

But still I wouldn't deny the pleasures of repetition on some level, though I believe it is not the primary motivation of the cinephile, and I do not believe it generates thought quite as much as the effect of the new does. Perhaps it is best to think of cinephiliac enjoyment in terms of its two (at least) subspecies – *pleasure* and *bliss*. The distinction is of course Barthesian, as most discussions of textual joy should be. Pleasure, according to Barthes, merely 'contents, fills, grants euphoria', whereas bliss 'imposes a state of loss, the text that discomforts (perhaps to the point of a certain boredom), unsettles the reader's historical, cultural, psychological assumptions, the consistency of his tastes, values, memories, brings to a crisis his relation with language' (1975: 14). Watching *Final Destination 3* that first time, the affect of the real, was a moment of bliss; watching again, writing and rewriting about it here, is pleasure. That moment when I first saw how it *could* link up with theories I have been attempting to untangle was bliss; trying to put it into an essay is pleasure. 'Pleasure can be expressed in words', writes Barthes, 'bliss cannot' (ibid.). Bliss triggered this cinephiliac essay, but the ideas, recollections, past/present/futures, have become something else. The affect of *Final Destination 3* triggered thought. Affect is not quite the same as bliss, but I believe it is the closest modern theory has come to a concept of bliss since Barthes. And affect may ultimately be more productive for the scholar trying to keep an eye on the cinephile within. This has been an essay on affect. But this cannot be bliss (for me). So the anticipation continues elsewhere, because 'bliss may come only with the *absolutely new*, for only the new disturbs (weakens) consciousness (easy? not at all: nine times out of ten, the new is only the stereotype of novelty)' (Barthes 1975: 40; emphasis in original). Consciousness, thought, become something else here. The cinephilia of anticipation generates desire, demands that we never stop. I wish to write something more, to extend the dream, but holding onto this any longer would be to slip back to nostalgia. Were the movement to stop, the cinephiliac stream would become dirty, stagnant. That present has been replaced. However, there is no danger of losing the moment/um. Moreover, there is no danger of losing time, for it is time which sometimes loses us.

NOTES

1   Barthes (1975: 17, 22; emphasis in original).

2   I call Willemen here a 'cinephiliac thinker' rather than a cinephile, because he does not consider himself to be a cinephile per se, but instead merely presents an argument which analyses it and seems ambivalent about its potential.

3   As the work of such writers as Christian Keathley and Paul Willemen (as well as other contributors to this volume) has suggested, 'cinephilia' today is increasingly being defined in terms of a rigorous theory, rather than as a historical moment.

4   A slightly extended version of this essay has been republished as chapter five in the present collection.

5   In an essay for the film journal, *Senses of Cinema*, Claire Perkins has previously suggested that Deleuze's philosophy on the cinema is inseparable from his cinephilia – both are revealed by the medium itself. In her essay, Perkins suggests that, for Deleuze, to approach the cinema is always to be motivated by love, writing that:

> in the [*Cinema*] books there is no theory 'behind' the system which, having come from cinema, has no way – or desire – to *explain* cinema. Deleuze proves how the purest theory of cinema is necessarily profoundly tautological, and it is this, at base, *cinephilic* attitude which must carry over to any approach to a text. (2000; emphasis in original)

Perkins discusses Deleuze's two well-known books on the cinema, *The Movement-Image* and *The Time-Image*. In particular, she is interested in articulating the tensions within the book between film theory and philosophy, but bridges the gap by arguing that Deleuze was motivated by an implicit cinephilia. His love of film opened out to the ideas he articulates in film. Perkins spends more time on unpacking Henri Bergson's influence on Deleuze, and on Deleuze's subsequent influences on others (such as Laura Marks and Elizabeth Grosz), than she does on the essay's issues of 'cinephilia and monstrosity'. Yet the essay is a valuable addition. No one else to date has investigated Deleuze's cinephilia – a formulation very useful in rethinking and overcoming the temporal limitations which still haunt the subject.

6   Deleuze then proceeds to argue that this question is the essence and function of cinema, even if not all films can achieve it.

7   See http://dr-mabuses-kaleido-scope.blogspot.com/2006/02/weird-feelings.html. Originally posted 14 February 2006. I'm still very sorry for snapping at Sarah in the comments.

8   For what it's worth, I ended up picking the second over the first.

9   Klinger ends the chapter by including a copy of the exact questions she asked the respondents, allowing the reader to reflect on Klinger's own methodology (2006: 189–90).

10 On this note, Klinger admittedly possesses a much less hostile attitude towards nostalgia than I do. She sees that it 'counterposes two or more eras, [and] represents the possibility of a critical reassessment of self and the world' (2006: 181). I, on the other hand, see nostalgia as denying a distinction between 'two or more eras', thus complicating such a reassessment.

REFERENCES

Barthes, Roland (1975) *The Pleasure of the Text*, trans. Richard Miller. New York: Hill and Wang.

____ (1989 [1975]) 'Leaving the Movie Theatre', in *The Rustle of Language*, trans. Russell Howard. Berkeley: University of California Press, 345–49.

Deleuze, Gilles (1989) *Cinema 2: The Time-Image*, trans. Hugh Tomlinson and Robert Galeta. Minneapolis: University of Minnesota Press.

Grosz, Elizabeth (2000) 'Deleuze's Bergson: Duration, the Virtual and a Politics of the Future', in Claire Colebrook and Ian Buchanan (eds) *Deleuze and Feminist Theory*. Edinburgh: Edinburgh University Press, 214–34.

Klinger, Barbara (2006) *Beyond the Multiplex: Cinema, New Technologies, and the Home*. Berkeley: University of California Press.

Lacan, Jacques (1978) *The Four Fundamental Concepts of Psychoanalysis: The Seminar of Jacques Lacan, Book XI*, ed. Jacques-Alain Miller, trans. Alan Sheridan. New York: W. W. Norton.

Metz, Christian (1982) *The Imaginary Signifier: Psychoanalysis and the Cinema*, trans. Celia Britton, Annwyl Williams, Ben Brewster and Alfred Guzzetti. Bloomington: Indiana University Press.

Perkins, Claire (2000) 'Cinephilia and Monstrosity: The Problem of Cinema in Deleuze's *Cinema* Books', *Senses of Cinema*, 8. Online. Available at: http://www.sensesofcinema.com/contents/books/00/8/deleuze.html. Accessed 10 April 2009.

Sperb, Jason (2007) 'Sensing an Intellectual *Nemesis*', *Film Criticism*, 32, 1, 49–71.

Wollen, Peter (2001) 'An Alphabet of Cinema', *New Left Review*, 12, 115–34.

Žižek, Slavoj (1991) *Looking Awry: An Introduction to Jacques Lacan through Popular Culture*. Cambridge, MA: The MIT Press.

CHAPTER EIGHT
SWIMMING
Zach Campbell

Tuesday, 24 January 2006

An interesting moment in Robert Breer's ostensibly atypical *Pat's Birthday* (1962), which follows Claes Oldenburg and friends as they celebrate Pat's birthday … we see an idyllic scene at a swimming hole, a waterfall, friends and children, a relaxed time. And I think I realised something about the rhetorical functions, in American film at least, of the 'swimming hole' and the 'swimming pool'. The hole can be a private place (as it is for Reese Witherspoon in *The Man in the Moon* (1991)) or a group one (*Pat's Birthday*), but it seems to serve many of the same functions regardless – it's peaceful, restful, primordial, upfront, it's where we 'get away' from life's harassments.

The pool, on the other hand, is just another source of life's harassments, its inanities (even when, as Herman Blume and Benjamin Braddock try to do in *Rushmore* (1998) and *The Graduate* (1967), respectively, one wants to use it to escape). The pool, when private, is a conspicuous sign of prestige – the great Jason Robards, as Al Capone, shows up on his Miami vacation in his swimming pool in *The St. Valentine's Day Massacre* (Roger Corman, 1969). When public, the pool is a veritable factory of hijinks, impersonality, manufactured emotion – above all, *performance*. Robards' Capone, in fact, has reporters over to his poolside as he gives a very 'performative' interview! (And, also, in contrast, in *Pat's Birthday* Breer has several shots of a public swimming pool – in long shot, impersonal, wearing none of the lyrical beauty of the swimming hole scene.) One can think of the great sequence in *The Cameraman* (1928) where Buster Keaton struggles to clothe himself properly and then, once in the pool, to keep his date – or one may also recall the plucky kids in *The Sandlot* (1993) (maybe only a movie people my age and younger know at all?!) among whom one, bearing a crush on a blonde lifeguard, schemes to get a CPR kiss by faking his own drowning, since the pool is apparently no place for honest admissions.

Reese Witherspoon's swimming hole is frank, earnest. The swimming hole is where one can be naked, where a glimpse (or more) of bare skin asserts some innocence and straightforwardness of its own. (Maybe it takes us back to The Garden.) If it's natural water, flowing water, if it's surrounded by trees, one 'goes back', or represents a 'going back', like Jodie Foster's semi-civilised Nell, or one's secrets are revealed, as with the young man and young woman in *Dragonslayer* (Matthew Robbins, 1981). Images from the opening of Sternberg's *Blonde Venus* (1932) flash through my head, too – but I can't bring back the narrative context!

The swimming *pool* sees nakedness only when it's 'naughty', that is, one does not emphasise anything *natural* about it – it's a performative opportunity, as the notoriously showy pool fucking in *Showgirls* (not to mention John McNaughton's *Wild Things* (1998)) demonstrates. Or if there's no performance per se, there's another kind of 'imaginary' at work here – like the famous Phoebe Cates fantasy sequence in *Fast Times at Ridgemont High* (1982).

And just to make myself clear: I'm not trying to celebrate the 'swimming hole' and damn the 'swimming pool' – I'm just trying to clarify the connotative spaces these two settings tend to make for themselves. (And the 'tend' is important – I make no claims to clear, cut-and-dried divisions here!) It's the same cultural, rooted ordering system which presumably assigns 'honesty' to the hole and 'performance' to the pool, if I'm even correct to propose these assignments. Perhaps I'll get comments from unconvinced readers with a laundry list of exceptions to disprove my 'rule'. Which would be OK, as at least it would mean I won't go on enamored of my own crackpot idea.

All of this ignores the figure of 'the ocean', which is something else altogether, but that's OK because it's clear that this is anything but a rigorous stream of thoughts...

(Posted by Zach Campbell)

CHAPTER NINE
CUSTOMISING PLEASURE: 'SUPER MARIO CLOUDS' AND THE JOHN FORD SKY
Robert Burgoyne

Christian Metz writes that cinephilia represents, in part, the impulse to preserve and protect the good object, to save it from obliteration – not the film itself, the celluloid, nor the institution, but rather the social memory embodied in the cinema-object. Two installations, 'The Five Year Drive-By' (1995) by Douglas Gordon and 'Super Mario Clouds' (2003) by Cory Arcangel, would seem to make this point explicitly. In both, the impulse to save and protect is linked to the artists' childhoods, and thematised in the texts that provide the artists with their source material – *The Searchers* (1956) by John Ford and the video game, *Super Mario Brothers* – both of which have plots that revolve around rescue. The two installations can be read as a way of maintaining these objects in what Metz calls an 'imaginary enclosure of pure love' (1986: 13).

'The Five Year Drive-By', a five-year-long projection of *The Searchers* on a drive-in-size movie screen installed, among other places, in the California desert, draws from the artist's memory of the powerful effect of the film when he first saw it as a boy. By slowing it down to the point that each frame is held for 45 minutes, it becomes a kind of Deleuzian time-image, a work that is centrally concerned with duration, the passing and arresting of time and self, the near-capture of a moment that is 'frozen in time'. It also suggests the disappearing social memory of the western, a genre that has almost entirely been erased from cultural memory. The installation in effect amplifies the theme and the plot of the film, which is centred on loss, memory and the 'saving' of the past.

Cory Arcangel's 'Super Mario Clouds' seems to draw from a different cultural encyclopaedia, but the sense of affect surrounding the work is similar. Isolating the moving cloudscape that serves as background to the early video game *Super Mario Brothers*, the artist eliminates the buildings, barriers and the figure of Mario himself to concentrate simply on the clouds drifting by in a serene blue sky. Projected on a large screen in a museum space, the installation suggests the earliest moments of video game culture, the primal scene of an emergent technology linked to the generational memory of the artist. Stripped of the linear forward momentum of the game, the screen becomes an image of transience, of fleeting impermanence, a loop centred on memory, duration and loss. Like *The Searchers*, the goal of the game *Super Mario Brothers* is the rescue of a woman, in this case the Princess Toadstool, who can be saved only after transiting a game space filled with hazards. By erasing the quest aspect of the game to concentrate on a fragment of *mise-en-scène*, the artist elicits an emotional connection to the past, to childhood and to early game culture.

In this essay, I explore the work of Gordon and Arcangel as a way of rethinking the issues circulating around the concept of cinephilia and pleasure. Many video and game artists make use of cinematic or electronic media in ways that are provocative and richly enigmatic. Although the gap between classical cinema and video games has been much emphasised in contemporary theory, a shared culture of art practice has emerged around these two dominant forms, a practice that uses the media as a type of 'ready-made'. One critic has called contemporary video artists such as Arcangel and Gordon the ideal children of the children of Duchamp. Reformulating well-known films, video games and television broadcasts, these artists provide a way of customising industrially produced pleasures, reconfiguring, in a personal and illuminating way, the objects of audiovisual culture.

Arcangel has worked in a variety of media, but his most evocative objects are the repurposed video games, which include a Japanese racing game, stripped of all but the endlessly scrolling road, moving hypnotically from the horizon towards the viewer in an unending loop, an installation he calls 'F-1 Racer', and a new computer program that he wrote for *Super Mario Brothers* called 'Mario Movie', in which Mario floats through obstacles, encounters antagonists drawn from Pac-Man, falls endlessly through video space, racing by game objects and game architecture, and winds up alone on a cloud, crying.

Gordon's work, similarly, centres on cinematic ready-mades, including, in addition to 'The Five Year Drive-By', the earlier '24 Hour Psycho' (1993), a slowing down of the Hitchcock film to a 24-hour running time, and 'Between Darkness and Light (After William Blake)' (1997) in which two films are projected onto the back and the front of a semi-transparent cinema screen so that the images bleed through and are lightly superimposed. The two films, *The Song of Bernadette* (1943) and *The Exorcist* (1973), are both films about possession. They are non-synchronised, and thus appear differently, with different combinations of images every time they are viewed. The images of Regan's demonic head superimposed on the images of a praying Bernadette, or of Bernadette's nineteenth-century peasant mother walking out of Regan's suburban mansion, are typical of the combinations created. As J. Hoberman writes, 'However much *The Song of Bernadette* and *The Exorcist* may crash each other's parties, they emerge as essentially the same movie – lit by candles, filled with crosses, endlessly talking about God and faith. Bernadette will never exorcise *The Exorcist*, but united as between darkness and light, they constitute a pageant' (2006).

Metz devotes a few, powerfully evocative paragraphs to cinephilia in *The Imaginary Signifier: Psychoanalysis and the Cinema*. Comparing the cinephilia of the film historian and the archivist, the cinephilia of the ardent champion of certain auteurs, and the cinephilia of the theorist, Metz makes the striking point that all cinephilia comes at a cost: the mystery and fascination of the cinema, in every case, is converted into something else. Depending on the particular form it takes, it can become a kind of fetishism, as in the obsessive drive of the collector or the extreme connoisseur; or it can become a kind of sadistic voyeurism, seen in the discourse of the 'expert' or the theorist who desires nothing more than to 'take the film apart'. As Metz writes, 'To study the cinema: what an odd formula! How can it be done without "breaking" its beneficial image ... by breaking the toy one loses it' (1986: 80).

In many ways, the art installations of Douglas Gordon and Cory Arcangel can be seen precisely as 'breaking the toy'. In Gordon's work, *The Searchers* is slowed down so that the illusion of human movement is reconstituted as a series of frozen images. The fundamental illusion of the cinema, the illusion of motion, gives way to an image that reads like sculpture. Arresting the narrative, the image becomes monumental. Gordon's work brings out the material quality of film, the fact that it is a petroleum product with light shining through it. Moreover, his work heightens our sense that the objects in film have been created in order to be photographed under intense light. As Joe Fyfe writes, 'In the old movies that Gordon likes to use ... the actors are powdered and then polished by light to read like an idealised version of what we look like, which is what traditional figurative sculpture does' (2007).

The nearly static images also call up the basis of film in still photography, reversing the transition from still to moving images that was still much emphasised in early film projections. Writing about the astonishment that attended the first film screenings, Tom Gunning (1995) argues that the audiences' sense of surprise and pleasure was enhanced by the dramatic, *trompe-l'oeil* presentation with which the films were introduced, a presentation that emphasised the moment of transformation from still to moving pictures. The first Lumière projections, for example, dramatised the instant when the static image burst into lifelike movement, as a still image was first projected onto a screen, held for a while, and then animated by the projector. Rather than a naïve belief in the realism of the moving image, the amazement that greeted the first moving image projections was more an appreciation of the feat of creating lifelike movement in a photographic medium. The 'birth' of cinema in 1895 was understood, Gunning argues, as a style of theatre comparable to prestidigitation, magic theatre and illusionism. And in his view, the key to the dramatic impression created by the first projected films was the showman-like heightening of the passage from static image to moving pictures.

Expanding on this historical insight, we can begin to think of the static image, the frozen tableau, as an integral part of the aesthetic of cinema, an element that was utilised in the first cinematic projections by the brothers Lumière and remains as the undertone or undercurrent of every experience of film. Usually a concealed part of the code of the moving image, the static image might be seen as an aesthetic potential, an always available aesthetic resource. In Gordon's work we have a reverse evolution, a recoding of the fundamental illusion of the cinema, returning us by an unforeseen path to the earliest days of cinematic projection, and reminding us of an element or experience that was emphasised in the earliest film projections – 'breaking the toy' in order to rethink the basic illusion of stillness and motion.

This idea has been explored by critics as diverse as László Moholy-Nagy and Laura Mulvey, but only in a fragmentary way. Mulvey writes of the advent of DVDs, and the ability to stop, rewind and freeze-frame at will, suggesting that 'this new, freely accessible stillness, extracted from the moving image, is a product of the paradoxical relation between celluloid and new technology. It is primarily the historic cinema of celluloid that can blossom into new significance and beauty when its original stillness … is revealed in this way. The cinema has always been a medium of revelation' (2007: 139).

A recurrent motif in certain styles of cinematic practice, the use of static images or frozen tableaux in film occurs in a wide variety of works. Striking uses of stillness can be found in the work of D. W. Griffith, in his restaging of Matthew Brady-style battlefield scenes; in the 1925 version of *Ben Hur*, with its extraordinary, near-frozen devotional images of the birth and death of Christ; in Cecil B. DeMille's *The Sign of the Cross* (1932), in the impossibly slow ascent from the dungeon to the arena floor; in the Soviet montage style, which is structured as a series of extreme dynamic contrasts between still images; in Sergei Eisenstein's *Ivan the Terrible* (1943), in the protracted operatic moments of Ivan's coronation and his reconciliation with the people; and in more contemporary works by Chris Marker, Andy Warhol and Jean-Luc Godard. In Gordon, the repurposing of existing film and media artifacts evokes an alternative aesthetic, present in embryo at the beginnings of the art form, an underground current of aesthetic design that moves to the surface from time to time within the mainstream traditions of film.

Gordon's installations, especially '24 Hour Psycho' and 'The Five Year Drive-By', communicate an understanding of the cinema that expands on the static, frozen tableaux that occur throughout the history of film, exaggerating the stillness, holding and stretching every moment in the films he treats, decelerating the films to the point that narrative disappears, restaging the fundamental opposition of movement and stasis. And it brings the latent content of the films to the fore. What is *Psycho* (1960), after all, if not a movie about embalming, the holding on to memory and the freezing of time? And what is *The Searchers*, if not a movie about the impossibility of moving on, the impossibility of leaving the past behind?

The return to the sources of the medium itself and to its fundamental mechanisms of fascination draws the cinephilia of artists such as Gordon into a kind of artistic dialogue with film history and film theory alike. Other artists, such as Matthew Buckingham, have also explored the underground resources of the cinema by looking to the earliest history of the medium. Buckingham has recently mounted an installation, entitled 'False Future' (2007), based on the work and the inventions of a filmmaker, Louis Le Prince, who may have preceded the Lumière brothers in presenting motion pictures by seven years. Le Prince developed a camera with 16 lenses that exposed 16 frames of film in a second, and later developed a single lens camera with a film strip running behind the lens that could also expose 16 frames per second. He made three eight-second films. The mystery of his life and of his inventions is deepened by the fact that he disappeared 'without a trace' in September 1890. In a short interview in *Sight and Sound*, Buckingham says that 'The single lens camera was found in his [Le Prince's] workshop and only one second from each of the films was preserved' (in Godfrey 2007: 9). One of these circa-1890 films was shot overlooking the Leeds Bridge in London. In 'False Future', Buckingham restages the one-second fragment, filming from the exact same location, making an extended take that runs for about ten minutes. The installation is his way of framing an unusual hypothesis: 'what people imagined motion pictures might look like before they existed' (in ibid.). He concludes that the driving impulse behind the invention of the cinema was the creation of a convincing illusion of motion, tricking the eye into perceiving motion where none actually existed. The impulse behind the creation of convincing stories was, in his view, a subsequent and secondary concern.

By holding fast to the fleeting, flickering images of classical films by Ford and Hitchcock, or by restaging and extending the one-second fragment of cinema's prehistoric past that has survived to the present day, these two artists valorise both the object and the social memory that surrounds it. They also suggest a poignant recognition that film has moved to the cultural position of the 'outmoded'. The cinephilia of Gordon and Buckingham subtly underlines the passing into oblivion of an art form whose cultural and social dominance seems to be disappearing. On the positive side, however, their art can be compared to Walter Benjamin's discussion of the 'outmoded' as a key feature of surrealist practice. Writing about André Breton, he observes that Breton can boast an extraordinary discovery: 'He was the first to perceive the revolutionary energies that appear in the "outmoded", in the first iron constructions, in the first factory buildings, the earliest photos, the objects that have begun to be extinct, grand pianos, the dresses of five years ago, fashionable restaurants when the vogue has begun to ebb from them … they bring the immense forces of "atmosphere" concealed in these things to the point of explosion' (1978: 181–2).

At first glance, the work of Cory Arcangel would appear to be driven by very different questions, and to refer to a very different cultural encyclopaedia. However, the game art of Arcangel, like the video and film art of Gordon, also involves the 'breaking of the toy', in this case, literally 'breaking' old video games. Arcangel's game art involves opening the game cartridge in old Nintendo or Atari games, removing the chip installed in them to delete some of the gaming code and then reformulating the work, soldering the pieces back together, in order to produce contemplative and very different moving image installations. The hypnotic movement of the endlessly scrolling road in 'F-1 Racer' and the oneiric horizontal drift of the two-dimensional clouds in 'Super Mario Clouds' offer a kind of precise analogue, expressed in the medium of game art, to Metz's comments: 'I have loved the cinema, I no longer love it. I still love it' (1986: 79).

As part of the installation of 'Super Mario Clouds' and 'Mario Movie', Arcangel provides detailed instructions on the technique of deleting code from the Nintendo chip, how to reprogram it, and how to resolder the new program back into the game console, demystifying the video game in order to re-illusion it. Arcangel also describes the complete digital formula for constructing both the original game as well as his own game art. The demystification of the computer code and the inclusion of programming instructions constitute a kind of semiotic analysis, the uncovering and description of the game's codes and subcodes. Rather than being directed to an increasingly esoteric understanding of the game form, however, the impulse behind Arcangel's gesture seems more in the spirit of open-source software, the democratisation of art. The computer games Arcangel treats appeared early in the history of the medium, and are thus relatively simple to program and to understand, which allows for a kind of primitive artistic appropriation and manipulation. Here, the hand of the artist returns in a medium that had been defined by digital code. Seemingly as far removed from the hand of the artist as they could possibly be, digital video games, in the work of Arcangel and other game artists, can now be linked with the return of craft-based art forms such as hand-made books, YouTube videos, sculptures made from repurposed materials, and audio remixes.

Arcangel's media hacks and rewrites are extraordinarily various. Beyond the recoding of video games, one of his recent installations stages a kind of assault by computer program on the artifacts of mainstream pop culture – more specifically, the cultural memory embedded in mainstream popular culture. For example, in the installation he calls 'Untitled (After Lucier)' (2006), he rebroadcasts in a continuous repeating loop the Beatles' televised performance on *The Ed Sullivan Show* in 1964, one of the most iconic moments in the history of the television medium. Over time, the video performance slowly decomposes; during the first week or so of its run, the historic video looks normal. As time wears on, however, the pixels shift shape, enlarging into blocks, distorting and making the four Beatles, their guitars and their signature haircuts almost unrecognisable. They become, as one writer says, 'increasingly indistinct and further from memory ... an artifact of digital compression and cultural disintegration' (Berwick 2006: 1). As Arcangel says, 'The longer it goes on, the better the piece looks, and the less embarrassing it is' (in Berwick 2006: 2).

The pace of spectacle and media culture, dominated by speed, novelty, and distraction, is replaced here by a contemplative work that unfolds over the course of weeks and months. In early modernism, as David Campany writes, the 'photo-eye and the kino-eye (film-eye) were the driving metaphors for a new and dynamic intimacy between "man" and optical machine' (2007: 10). The optical machines of contemporary video game culture, however, go well beyond this, incorporating an accelerated motor component, a heightened interactive merging of the tactile and the optical. For his part, Arcangel works in the opposite direction of the adrenalised thumb culture that has developed around video games: 'I like to take the interactivity out of things actually' (in Berwick 2006: 2). Working against the dominant current, he discovers a quality of slowness in video games and in the experience of the Beatles' television performance, a quality of slowness that reads as resistance to speed, a slowness that responds to the kineticism of media culture with hypnotic and repetitive loop sequences that impose a slow pace upon the viewer.

It is easy to appreciate the playful, innovative uses that Arcangel makes of mass media, the sense of reverie they induce and his seemingly sunny perspective on mass media culture as a playground for inspired invention. His is a perspective comparable to Roland Barthes' way of characterising his experience in the souk in Tangiers, where the myriad voices and languages of a bar in the North African square drifted around and through him: 'music, conversations, the noises of chairs, of glasses, an entire stereophony of which a marketplace in Tangiers ... is the exemplary site ... I myself was a public place, a souk; the words passed through me, small syntagms, ends of formulae, and no sentence formed' (1975: 67). But within the artist's exploration of the pleasure of the fragment, the bits of game code and the isolated segment, a certain elusive but powerful point about media culture can be discerned.

Victor Burgin describes contemporary visual culture as a 'cinematic heterotopia' (2007: 198), a network of overlapping but distinct cinematic interfaces and experiences. Drawing from Michel Foucault's description of heterotopias – a space where several sites that are incompatible in themselves are juxtaposed – Burgin focuses on the crosscurrents of the mediascape, and the way they converge in the typical, daily experience of the ordinary person. Television and the Internet, radios and cds, cellphones, mp3s and iPods, the cineplex, video games,

DVDs and websites – the extraordinary multiplication of audiovisual forms in contemporary culture has created a world in which we are now 'entertained from cradle to grave whether we like it or not' (MacCabe 2003: 301).

One of the consequences of this cinematic heterotopia, as Burgin describes it, is that films are now often viewed in fragments, rather than from start to finish. And they are viewed with varying degrees of attentiveness, ranging from indifferent observation to active engagement. The spectrum of media forms universally available in contemporary culture, that cross into the spectator's lives whether they seek out the film or not, makes the ordinary spectator into an unwitting mimic of one of the great avant-garde experiments of the early twentieth century, what the surrealists André Breton and Jacques Vaché called the 'derive', the practice of dashing from one cinema to another in order to achieve the disorientation that the surrealists believed could open onto a critique of everyday life. This once radical practice of disorientation has, in effect, become a mainstream activity, a powerful way to customise pleasure. In its passage to the everyday, the fragmentation and decomposition of film has, as Viktor Shklovsky says, 'completed its journey from poetry to prose' (in Burgin 2007: 198).

A number of recent theorists have expressed pessimism and alarm over the media's power over subjective life. The range and penetration of audiovisual culture has led some writers to argue that the cinematic now 'possesses' the spectator, that the 'society of the spectacle' has now installed itself in the unconscious psychic registers to the point that it is now 'in virtual command of our memories' (Burgin 2007: 204). Society, in this view, has become a homogeneous mass that comes to 'share an increasingly uniform common memory' (2007: 205). The philosopher Bernard Steigler uses the term, 'prosthetic memory', to describe the global audiovisual industry as producing a synchronised state of consciousness through the agency of 'temporal objects' – objects, like cinema or television, or a popular melody, that take shape only in relation to the consciousness that apprehends it, and that 'elapse' in synchrony with the spectator's consciousness. Cinema and television are paradigmatic expressions of the production of temporal objects, as masses of people tune in to the same television programmes at the same time, or flock to the cinema for the opening weekend of blockbuster films. Rather than community or collectivity, Burgin argues, the uniformity that results creates a 'homogeneous impersonal mass who come to share an increasingly uniform common memory' (2007: 206).

The control of subjectivity through orchestrated temporal experiences creates a kind of 'degraded' subjective environment, much as the biosphere is degraded by capital-intensive industries, and much like society is degraded by exploitation and vast inequality. This view accords with Félix Guattari's description of the contemporary world as defined by three 'ecologies', the environmental, the social and the mental, all of which are subject to what he calls 'integrated world capitalism'. The global audiovisual industry, for Steigler and Guattari, exemplifies the ecology of mind – which comes down to the control of memory and consciousness. As Burgin summarises: 'Renewing Deleuze's vision of a "society of control" Steigler's prospectus is bleak, it conjures a world in which the global audiovisual industries, now in virtual command of our memories, determine what is visible and invisible, what may be heard and said, and what must remain inaudible and unutterable ... [it] conjures a world in which the spectator is "possessed' by cinema"' (2007: 206–7). Metz, for his part, also hints at this in his opening remarks in *The Imaginary Signifier*. As he explains, 'The cinematic institution is not just the cinema industry ... it is also the mental machinery – another industry – which spectators "accustomed to the cinema" have internalised historically ... The second machine [is] the social regulation of the spectator's metapsychology' (1986: 7).

Against the gloomy prognosis of Steigler, Alison Landsberg (2004) takes a very different view of the power of mass-mediated 'prosthetic memory'. Employing the same terminology as Steigler, Landsberg argues that the 'prosthetic memories' created by the mass media allow spectators to identify with people they would not otherwise feel a connection to, creating possibilities of new forms of solidarity, a new public sphere based on memories that are not organically based, but that people experience with their own bodies, through the impact of the mass media. Landsberg's argument for mediated forms of memory emphasises the role of the mass media as a way of connecting people to the past, to past lives and past bodies, as a way of forging empathetic identifications where none existed before. The mass media, in her view, can serve as a powerful agent of connection and mutual pleasure.

Audiovisual control machine or the public sphere – the souk – of contemporary life? These two approaches to contemporary mass media seem irreconcilable. One approach emphasises the ways the cinema – and mass media generally – possesses the spectator, degrading the subjective environment, degradation comparable to the despoiling of the biosphere and the economic exploitation of populations. The other viewpoint emphasises the expanding range of experience and understanding made available through mass media, the forging of new solidarities through its carnal, somatic impact on the spectator. Like a hologram, contemporary media conveys radically different impressions depending on the angle from which it is viewed.

Artists such as Gordon and Arcangel may offer a way between these two starkly opposed perspectives. Both make use of texts that inform the common cultural memory of the contemporary period, works such as *Psycho* and *Super Mario Brothers*. Both create objects that reflect on aspects of cultural memory, and that focus on the interconnections of subjectivity and the media. The stripping away of narrative, the holding of an image, the reformulating of game art, the staged decomposition of an iconic performance; the reworking of media products into new, enigmatic forms can be considered a tactical move. By freezing the temporal flow of a film such as *Psycho*, or by drawing a work, such as *The Song of Bernadette*, into an asynchronous dialogue with its 'other', Gordon finds a means of customising the industrially-produced pleasures of classical cinema. By erasing the interactive features of a video game such as *Super Mario Brothers*, or by reprogramming films and videos so that their internal structural coherence is lost, Arcangel opens the spectator's 'mental machinery' to other possibilities as well.

As audiovisual forms continue to proliferate, with an increasing range and number of screens, or interfaces, defining the practices of everyday life, the work of artists at the edge of culturally dominant media becomes more important. The relevance of these works to contemporary screen culture is directly related to the pleasure they elicit. I began by discussing cinephilia as a protective, deeply personal preoccupation, one that sought to rescue and preserve the 'good objects' of the past from oblivion. However, the cinephilic gesture of drawing these works into an 'imaginary enclosure of pure love', as Metz describes it, seems to fall short of the discursive and imaginative resonance of the art I describe above. Gordon and Arcangel employ ready-made objects of media culture in ways that have little to do with the past, and everything to do with experiences of the present moment, a moment aptly characterised by Burgin as a 'cinematic heterotopia'.

Nevertheless, the pleasure and interest of these projects seems perverse and paradoxical. It involves a reversal of the kineticism, the speed and the almost tactile stimulation that Benjamin, among others, saw as cinema's vocation and the emblem of its modernity. Here, the fascination comes from slowness, from the stilled image, from absorption in a simplified set of looped images, from contemplation rather than distraction. And what also comes powerfully into view in these works, in another reversal, is a surprising sense of the return of the aura. What Benjamin predicted would wither away in the age of mechanical, and now electronic, reproduction returns with new force in the frozen images from *The Searchers* and *Psycho*, and in the disintegrating images of the Beatles. Ethan Edwards, Marion Crane, the Beatles, are rendered, finally, as the auratic figures they always were. Nor does the power of these forms derive solely from the original works, a kind of borrowed or 'acquired aura'.[1] Rather, it seems that the hybrid relation between film and electronic media opens up new areas of fascination, and new possibilities for seeing into the culture's images.

NOTE

1   This phrase comes from Douglas Crimp, quoted in Lunenfeld (2000: 63).

REFERENCES

Barthes, Roland (1975) *The Pleasure of the Text*, trans. Richard Miller. New York: Hill and Wang.

Benjamin, Walter (1978 [1928]) 'Surrealism', in Peter Demetz (ed.) *Reflections*. New York: Harcourt Brace Jovanovich, 177–92.

Berwick, Carly (2006) 'Open Source Art?' *DigitAll Magazine*. Online. Available at: http://www.samsung.com/Features/BrandMagazine/magazinedigitall/2006_winter/feat_02a.htm. Accessed 11 May 2007.

Burgin, Victor (2007 [2006]) 'Possessive, Pensive and Possessed', in David Campany (ed.) *The Cinematic*. Cambridge, MA: The MIT Press, 198–209.

Campany, David (2007) 'Introduction//When to be Fast? When to be Slow?', in *The Cinematic*. Cambridge, MA: The MIT Press, 10–17.

Fyfe, Joe (2007) 'JF Gordon'. Online. Available at: www.artcritical.com/fyfe/JFGordon. Accessed 11 May 2007.

Godfrey, Mark (2007) 'Time and Motion', *Sight and Sound*, 17, 5, 9.

Gunning, Tom (1995) 'An Aesthetic of Astonishment: Early Film and the (In)Credulous Spectator', in Linda Williams (ed.) *Viewing Positions: Ways of Seeing Film*. New Brunswick: Rutgers University Press, 114–33.

Hoberman, J. (2006) 'Twin Peaks: this season's smartest double bill is a match made in heaven and hell', *Village Voice Online*. Available at: http://www.villagevoice.com/film/0631,hoberman,74039,20.html. Accessed 11 May 2007.

Landsberg, Alison (2004) *Prosthetic Memory*. New York: Columbia University Press.

Lunenfeld, Peter (2000) *Snap to Grid*. Cambridge, MA: The MIT Press.

MacCabe, Colin (2003) *Godard: a Portrait of the Artist at 70*. London: Bloomsbury.

Metz, Christian (1986) *The Imaginary Signifier: Psychoanalysis and the Cinema*, trans. Celia Britton, Annwyl Williams, Ben Brewster and Alfred Guzzetti. Bloomington: Indiana University Press.

Mulvey, Laura (2007 [2003]) 'Stillness in the Moving Image', in David Campany (ed.) *The Cinematic*. Cambridge, MA: The MIT Press, 134–9.

BODIES

CHAPTER TEN
CINEPHILIA AS TOPOPHILIA IN *THE MATRIX* (1999)
Kevin Fisher

The Matrix (1999) has much to recommend it as an object for cinephilic analysis in the age of digital special effects. As Hollywood product, it has inspired two successful sequels, a considerable fanbase and culture on the Internet, and numerous highbrow commentaries from philosophers and cultural theorists as well as film scholars. Its reception recapitulates what Marijke de Valck and Malte Hagener identify as the 'double nature' of cinephilia in its 'French attire of the 1960s' (2005: 11). Namely, 'it dotes on the most popular genre film(maker)s of the most popular national film industry, but does so in a highly idiosyncratic, elitist, and counterintuitive fashion' (ibid.). This ardour of popular audiences and professional academics for *The Matrix*, like the fervour of 1960s cinephiles for their chosen love objects, has also been criticised by leading psychoanalytic film theorists as a form of capitulation to the ideological effects of the medium. Slavoj Žižek, in particular, seems to echo Christian Metz and Jean-Louis Baudry when he describes *The Matrix* as an ideological trap – a Rorschach test that seduces theorists of diverse callings to find within it a rendition of everything from Plato's cave to *Kulturindustrie*, while missing the more fundamental problematics whereby the film's revelation of the real world behind the virtual provides ideological support for the belief in a 'reality with no deadlock of impossibility structuring it' (1999: 11).

Examined from a different angle, the desire for the real behind the virtual that the film elicits, and Žižek's disappointment in its indulgence of such philosophical bad faith, are both characteristic of a 'disenchantment' which, according to Thomas Elsaesser, has always been an animating component of cinephilia. Disenchantment is at the core of the cinephile's peculiar receptivity to the image. It is thus, for Elsaesser, a 'productive disenchantment' that is the spark of the 'memory imagination', and serves as a principle of individuation which 'rescues the spectator's sense of self from being engulfed by the totalising repleteness, the self-sufficiency and always already complete there-ness that especially classic American cinema tries to convey' (2005: 40). However, unlike the cinephilia of the 1960s that clustered around the unintended moment in which the sublimity of the real shone through, there is little about a film like *The Matrix* and the cinephilia surrounding it that is unintended or surreptitious. Referring to the filmmakers' plans for ancillary markets and multi-platform spin-offs prior to the making of *The Matrix*, Elsaesser describes how 'the film comes with its own discourses, which, in turn, give rise to more discourses. The critic – cinephile, consumer guide, enforcer of cultural standards, or fan – is already part of the package' (2005: 37). This package would not be complete without the intentional simulation of the unintended fragments upon which the cinephile of old (media) cathected. The apparent ontological antithesis between the digital special effect and analogue cinematic fragment conceals a more important common feature that enables the former to function like the latter: the tenuous connection to narrative. I also hope to show how the narrative suspension of special effects lends them to reflexive allegories of the film experience, which challenge assumptions about spectatorship within prevailing discourses on cinephilia.

The sequence of Neo's (Keanu Reeves) first extraction from the matrix, which this study takes as its object, occurs during an ellipsis within the narrative. Morpheus (Lawrence Fishburne) has just confronted Neo with the dilemma of whether to take the blue pill (and remain in the world as he knows it) or take the red pill (and have the true nature of the matrix revealed). Neo sits in a chair, framed in close-up with electrodes attached to his neck, ear and forearm. The scene generates a sense of expectation. Morpheus's cohorts interact with various monitoring technologies around Neo, but it is unclear what causal relation they have to the transformation about to occur. Morpheus also informs Neo that the pill he took possesses no active ingredients or causal powers as such, but is instead a trace program designed to pinpoint his position inside the matrix.

Morpheus's emphasis upon Neo's unique position and individual perception, even within a simulation that has become the universal condition of humanity, begs comparison with the cinephile's situation within the cinema, reconstituting the meaning of the film experience from his/her particular vantage. The extra-narrative nature of the sequence is also prefaced by Morpheus's insistence that 'no one can be *told* what the matrix is, you must experience it for yourself'. Indeed, while Neo sits in the chair waiting for something to happen, his gaze – like that of the traditional cinephile – wanders the marginalia of his surroundings, lingering on architectural details of the once grand but now dilapidated chamber and settling upon a shattered mirror panel on a nearby wall in which his fragmented image is reflected. It is within the margins and the fragments that Neo finds himself reflected. The function of the mirror in this sequence is also diametrically opposed to prevailing accounts in contemporary psychoanalytic film theory. Rather than an instrument of illusion and self-deception, the mirror transmutes into an agent of dis-illusion and self-revelation.

As Neo stares into his reflection, the shatter-lines of the mirror magically weld back together and Neo's fragmented image resolves. Neo turns towards Morpheus and Trinity (Carrie Ann Moss) and verbalises an unfinished question: 'Did you…?' In separate reverse-shots, Trinity and Morpheus each look back blankly, seemingly unaware of what Neo has just witnessed. Although those around Neo are aware that he is undergoing a transformation, the experience is his and his alone. The film cuts back to a close-up of Neo's hand reaching towards the mirror. Instead of finding a solid object, his fingers penetrate through the reflective surface as if into a pool of mercury. His hand withdraws, but the surface of the mirror sticks to his fingers and stretches back in a conical shape. The cone is itself reflective and reflected, creating a continuum between Neo's visible body and its virtual image. Reflected behind Neo in the mirror, Morpheus speaks: 'Have you ever had a dream, Neo, that you were so sure was real?' Neo withdraws his fingers further until the elastic continuum breaks. Some of the reflective substance adheres to Neo's fingertips, while the remainder splashes back into the surface of the mirror, sending out circular waves like a drop in a pond. The surface undulates as Morpheus continues: 'What if you were unable to awake from that dream? How would you know the difference between the dream world and the real world?' The verbalised dilemma is itself reflected in Neo's encounter with his own mirror image, which, in responding not only to vision but also to touch, transcends the limits of the visibly virtual, throwing the reality of what is happening on his side of the mirror into question.

Neo holds his hand before his eyes in an extreme close-up as the reflective substance creeps downwards from his fingers. Incredulous, he utters another unfinished question: 'This can't…?' Morpheus's face appears visibly reflected on the back of Neo's hand and he responds: 'Be what? Be real?' A reverse-shot from Neo's perspective again figures his hand in extreme close-up. This time, Morpheus is directly visible standing in the background, while Neo's face is doubly reflected on the contours of his own palm. A series of shots alternates between Neo's body, as the quicksilver substance creeps up his arm and then onto his neck, and the interactions of Morpheus with the other crew members as they busily operate computers whose monitors display graphs and wire-frames of strange topologies. Neo shudders as the substance creeps up his neck: 'It's c-c-c-cold.' Neo's head tilts back in profile in an extreme close-up shot as the reflective substance rises over his chin and lips. He begins to scream. An abrupt cut follows as the camera plunges into Neo's mouth as if caught up in a wave, and flies down his throat against the force of his scream, the liquid metal streaming ahead just within the field of vision and into the darkness of Neo's body. As the visual field goes black, the sound of Neo's scream transmutes into a broken electronic tone, like the sound of a dial-up modem. The electronic sound then transmutes into the sound of bubbles as the black screen dissolves into a point-of-view shot of Neo looking down the length of his own body submerged in a luminous pink fluid with air bubbles rising in the foreground, and connected by his chest, abdomen, arms and legs to an array of black tubes.

The visibly reflective surface of the mirror commutes itself to the invisible reflective, reflexive and reversible contours of the interface that produces Neo's virtual body as mirror image and double of his 'real' body outside the matrix. Unlike the hero of Jean Cocteau's *Orphée* (1950), Neo does not simply move through the mirror, but rather the mirror moves onto, into and through his body. The mirror activates something beneath its visible surface, which is the very substrate of reflection, reflexivity and reversibility within and between virtual bodies and worlds. This substance also connects Neo and Morpheus as they appear mirrored on either side of Neo's hand, a reflection of the shot/reverse-shot structure that also secondarily identifies and doubles the spectator within Neo's subjective vision. Neo's body itself becomes the hinge and intermediary of reflection, through which he ultimately turns inside out and into a parallel world. Mimetic resemblance gives way to a mode of duplication, doubling and displacement that entangles the senses through the body and across the threshold between the virtual and 'real' world. Neo's extraction, like the cinephiliac moment, stresses the power of the medium to reveal reality. As Morpheus points out to Neo just before the extraction: 'Remember, all I'm promising you is the truth, nothing more.'

CHALLENGES TO PREVAILING MODELS OF CINEPHILIA

In what follows, I aim to show how the attempt to describe cinephiliac moments within digital special effects, and digital cinema in general, confronts the ontological and phenomenological assumptions of realist film theory that still underlie much of the discourse on cinephilia. I will also analyse how the mirror scene in *The Matrix* complicates Christian Keathley's attempt to remobilise André Bazin in relation to contemporary cinema. Despite Keathley's admonition that his 'study claims no position in phenomenological debates' (2006: 36), his privileging of Bazin presents overt obstacles for a cinephilia of digital effects, which follow from realist understandings of the ontology of the cinematic image and the phenomenology of the spectator's experience (see 2006: 37). Keathley de-emphasises these proscriptive aspects of Bazin's ontology, including the notion that the film experience situates the viewer in a transcendental position relative to the concrete realities onscreen. In this way, his attempts diminish the antipathy between transcendentalist and existentialist accounts of spectatorship. However, when cinephilia finds its moment within digitally-generated special effects, the obstacles of Bazinian realism become repronounced (something I will eventually address within the context of Vivian Sobchack's approach to the embodied film experience).

On the most general level, the digital moving image is not an impression of reality, but the transcription of light into immaterial binary code. No matter how 'realistic' in appearance, it will always lack the photographic indexicality that defines the ontology of film and the phenomenology of its experience for Bazin. Computer graphic special effects demonstrate the postfilmic nature of digital cinema by figuring the hyperplasticity of the image. Bazin argues: 'if cinema is committed to communicate only by way of what is real, it becomes all the more important to discern those elements in filming which confirm our sense of natural reality and those which destroy that feeling' (1967d: 110). But the destruction of Neo and the spectator's senses of 'natural' reality is precisely what the mirror sequence from *The Matrix* is about. The film undermines the cinematic distinction between dream and reality and, with it, the distinction between internal and external perception, revealing the pro-filmic world/image from which Neo departs as digitally-simulated unreality, and the digitally-generated world/image into which he emerges as unmediated reality.

For Bazin, 'essential cinema ... is to be found in straightforward photographic respect for the unity of space' (1967b: 46). Even the 'panoramic perception' that, for Keathley, sets the cinephile apart from the average film spectator through 'the inclination to fix on marginalia in the image or landscape' (2006: 44), still adheres to and respects the external surfaces of the world. In Neo's extraction from the matrix, the spectator's perception does not stop at the visible surfaces of the world and the body, but rather plunges across them. *The Matrix* utilises its special effects to divide space into two connected but distinct dimensions. Moreover, these worlds are transited only through the body of the character, wherein the 'micro-physiognomy' that Keathley associates with panoramic perception, and which posits the surface of the face as limit, cedes to a radically post-filmic simulation of inner experience leading paradoxically back to the 'real' world. The sequence is more characteristic of what Scott Bukatman describes as 'kaleidoscopic perception' native to the pleasures of contemporary special effects cinema and 'comprised of equal parts delirium, kinesis, and immersion' (1998: 76). More precisely, it is the topological transmutations of the threshold of immersion between the objective and the subjective, the visible and the invisible, the real and the virtual, to which the audiovisual pleasures of this sequence relate: what I am describing as a *topophilic moment*.

As I have already pointed out, the disunification of space(s) within the film is traversed by a shot that enters Neo's body to assume his literal point of view. Bazin explicitly rejects this type of shot, one 'that fits the point of view of a protagonist in a given situation' (1967c: 91). He holds *The Lady in the Lake* (1946) as exemplary of 'a puerile kind of identification of the spectator and the camera by means of a camera trick' (1967c: 92). Bazin's prohibitions against subjective cinema protects both the realism of the image and the transcendental status of the film's vision as 'the gaze of an invisible witness ... a spectator and nothing else' (ibid.). In its essence then, according to Bazin, cinema enacts 'a way of seeing free of all contingency [that] still preserves the conditions and the concrete quality of vision: its continuity in time and its vanishing point in space. It is like the eye of God, in the proper sense of the word, if God could be satisfied with a single eye' (1971: 81). The relation of visibly concrete reality and invisible witness taps into what he describes as 'the paradox of the cinema … rooted in the dialectic of concrete and abstract' (1967d: 110), committed to the representation of concrete realities, but only from the viewpoint of a transcendental subject having no corporeality or interiority apart from the external world it makes visible.

At first glance, Neo's extraction from the matrix seems to have much more in common with the psychoanalytic apparatus theory of Baudry and Metz which, during the late 1960s and early 1970s, launched a critical assault on cinephilia and realist film theory that would alter the terrain of film studies. Like the apparatus theorists, Neo must break from identification and encounter the apparatus in order to re-enter the matrix without loving it, achieving critical distance from its ideological effects so that he may work for the destruction of its pleasures. To whatever degree *The Matrix* may allegorise the spectatorial situation described by apparatus theory, apparatus theory provides no basis for the constitution of the film or my particular moment as love objects. Quite the contrary, apparatus theory would read any such love as symptomatic of the spectator's disavowal of his/her own simultaneous subjection by the apparatus, or else as productive of 'alienation effects' that would sever identification altogether.

Curiously, for all their apparent enmity, the rejection of this type of sequence by realist and apparatus theories reveals more in common between the two positions than might be expected. For instance, the two theories part ways less in terms of their basic description of the film experience than in their evaluations. Both realist and apparatus theory understand the photo-indexical realism of the image as a condition of identification. However, Bazin's assertion of the ontological revelatory power of the medium gets reframed by apparatus theory in metapsychological terms as a deceptive 'reality effect'. As Noël Carrol observes:

> Though most contemporary film theoreticians reject the realist ontology of the cinematic image, many psychosemiotic Marxists accept what can be called the realist phenomenology of the cinematic image … The realist theory is ontologically incorrect but nevertheless it does, for certain contemporary film theorists, afford an account of how spectators regard film images. That is, film images do not really duplicate reality; however they do give the impression that they duplicate reality. (1988: 113)

While Bazin celebrates the purportedly transcendental vision onscreen as a god's-eye, divine revelation of reality, Baudry and Metz condemn it as the fulfilment of a regressive infantile fantasy of scopic control. Transcendental impulse and ontological fulfilment become repressed unconscious desire and ideological effect. As a consequence, there also occurs a shift in focus within apparatus theory from 'reality effects' to 'subject effects'. In his essay 'The Apparatus: Metapsychological Approaches to the Impression of Reality in the Cinema', Baudry redescribes cinematic 'realism' as 'a simulation of a condition of the subject ... and not of reality' (1976: 107).

Apparatus theory's account of the spectator's experience of the correlation between visible 'reality' and transcendental subject also translates Bazin's description of 'the paradox of cinema as a dialectic of the concrete and abstract' into the psychoanalytic binaries of presence and absence. In this way, apparatus theory identifies Jacques Lacan's description of the infant's encounter with its mirror image as the prototypical form of the spectator's 'mis-taken' encounter with the cinematic apparatus (see 1977). Most importantly, however (and unlike the infant's mirror encounter), the cinematic mirror represents a world from which the spectator's body is the one entirely absent term, yet this is an absence (or opening) around which the entire visible world of the film is structured. This structured absence circumscribes the activity of a consciousness that stands behind and unifies every possible subject position within the film – without itself being subject to the existential limitations of being a visible object for others. As Metz remarks: 'the spectator *identifies with himself*, with himself as a pure act of perception (as wakefulness, alertness): as condition of possibility of the perceived and hence as a kind of transcendental subject, anterior to every *there is*' (1977: 48–9; emphasis in original). As the infant bypasses the 'where' of its own lived-body in order to identify with the unifying image in the mirror, the spectator dissociates from his/her own embodied situation in order to identify with the transcendental subjectivity produced by the film.

Thus, for both realist film theory and apparatus theory, the film experience requires that the spectator evacuate one's own body and not be identified too directly with any particular character's body onscreen. For Metz, as for Bazin, the conditions of primary identification prohibit the cinematic representation of characters' 'mental images', which produce 'alienation effects', frustrating the spectator's unconscious desire for 'objective reality' conformed to the imaginary requirements of the mirror (1977: 121). For Metz, 'the cinema is ... too "real" to translate effectively the imaginary view of its characters ... The image which aims at being subjective – at least in this sense – is always experienced by the spectator as objective in the same way as its neighbouring images and because of this it disturbs rather more than it enlightens' (1973: 46). Yet in the moment of Neo's extraction from the matrix, it is not the nature of the image that establishes its 'experience by the spectator as objective', but the way images are related to one another through the transition between virtual and real worlds.

SOBCHACK'S PHENOMENOLOGY AND FILM'S BODY

The non-pro-filmic aspects of this sequence that disqualify it as a (good or bad) love object in the eyes of Bazinian cinephilia and its psychoanalytic critics, take on a very different light in the context of Vivian Sobchack's phenomenology of film experience. According to Bazin: 'The history of the plastic arts is not only a matter of their aesthetic but in the first place a matter of their psychology, it is essentially the story of resemblance, or if you will, of realism' (1967a: 12). However, for Sobchack, what is realistic about cinema cannot be located, as for Bazin, in its photo-indexicality as visible object, but in the way it 'imitates' and enacts the irreducible phenomenological correlation of subject and object. She writes: 'while the "age-old striving" of the visual arts has always been a *mimetic* striving, it is bent less on imitating the nature of intentional objects than on imitating the function of human intentional subjects who engage those objects as significant' (1992: 249; emphasis in original).

Keathley draws upon Philip Rosen as 'a corrective to the various critiques of Bazinian realism' (2006: 59). He quotes Rosen to the effect that 'Bazin can almost always be read as analysing the status of the objective *for* the subject' (in ibid.; emphasis in original).[1] However, it is the status of this object/subject correlation that differentiates the phenomenology of Bazin from that of Sobchack. As noted, for Bazin, spectator identification occurs on condition of the photo-indexical realism of the image and with a transcendental subject: 'if God could be satisfied with a single eye'. For Sobchack, spectator identification does not depend on any particular quality of the image, and always implicates the spectator with and as an embodied situation. She argues that insofar as 'vision is an *act* that occurs from somewhere in particular; its requisites are both a *body* and a *world*' (1992: 25; emphasis in original), an observation that applies 'not only to the spectator *of* the film, but also to the film *as* spectator' (1992: 49; emphasis in original). It is thus that Sobchack describes the 'film's body', like the spectator's own lived-body, as primarily the active intentional correlation between a viewing subject (or 'viewing view') and visible world (or 'viewed view' (1992: 50)).

That this body has gone unnamed and unreflected upon within film studies is a function not of its absence, as the apparatus theory of Jean-Louis Baudry and Christian Metz alleges, but rather of its invisible, yet implicit and sustaining, presence – just as the human eye recedes from visibility in the very act of vision it enables. Both realist film theory and apparatus theory assumes that because the source of the film's vision is invisible it is thereby disembodied and transcendental. Sobchack responds by explicitly rejecting the reduction of the terms of visibility and invisibility to those of presence and absence. She argues that, 'the most forcefully felt 'presence' of such invisibility in vision is, at one pole, the unseen world, the *offscreen space*, from which embodied vision prospects its sights and, at the other pole, the very enworlded eye/I, the *offscreen subject*, who enacts sight' (1992: 292; emphasis in original). It is this 'other pole' of invisible presence across the 'fourth wall' of the visible filmic world that, for Sobchack, defines the distinct phenomenology and ontology of the film experience. She describes how the co-ordinated operation of camera and projector exchange the terms of visibility and invisibility so that the ordinarily transcendent and invisible subjective vision of another is made immanently visible onscreen for the spectator:

> Enabled by its mechanical and technological body, each film projects and makes uniquely visible not only the objective world but the very structure and process of subjective, embodied vision – hitherto only directly available to human beings as the invisible and private structure we each experience as 'my own'. (1992: 298)

In the cinema, one sees as another in a modality commensurable with that by which one sees for oneself. Intersubjective communication between film and spectator occurs through structures of *intra*subjective experience in what Sobchack describes as a 'double-occupancy of vision' (1992: 10).

For Sobchack, the essence of cinema lies in its ability to dynamically reverse the modalities of visibility and invisibility, not as distinct ontological orders of presence and absence, but as irreducibly correlated modalities of embodied existence. The reversibility of visibility and invisibility within the film's body becomes most demonstrably figured through the various mechanisms of secondary identification, whereby cinema uniquely makes visible both sides of the correlation between transcendence and immanence, between the lived-body as a subject and an object of vision. In so doing, it transforms the perennial philosophical problem of the relationship of transcendence and immanence into a formal and figural problem specific to the structure and materiality of cinema.

This overlooked dimension of secondary identification as a shifting and reversible relation between transcendence and immanence recalls Maurice Merleau-Ponty's description of the lived-body as 'flesh'. He observes 'a being of two leaves, from one side a thing among things and otherwise what sees them and touches them ... it unites these two properties within itself, and its double belongingness to the order of the "object" and to the order of the "subject" reveals to us quite unexpected relations between the two orders' (1968: 180). Merleau-Ponty explores the structure of these relations through phenomena such as 'double perception', of which perhaps his most famous example is the experience of touching one's hands together (see 1968: 133–4). The crux of this heuristic is that the line (or *chiasm*) between which hand is the subject (doing the touching) and which is the object (being touched) becomes reversible and ambiguous within the experience.

Merleau-Ponty designates the flesh of the world as 'the formative medium of subject and object' (1968: 147) in which both terms 'form a couple ... more real than either of them' (1968: 139). This couple is 'more real' because it is the source and expression of a 'fundamental fission' whose terms are reversible but never wholly reducible to one another (ibid.). In the chiasm can also be found a non-objective criterion for cinematic realism that locates it neither in the objective qualities of the image nor in its particular subject effects, but rather in the film's ability to animate flesh. We can even speak of a special 'flesh of the world' within the film, through which spectators become identified within the embodied consciousness of various characters onscreen. The uniqueness of the flesh of the world of the film has to do with the way it reconfigures the correlation of transcendence and immanence within the experience of film's body. Through processes of secondary identification film extrudes onto the plane of visible immanence both sides of a correlation that, in extra-cinematic experience, is always half submerged in the invisible transcendence of the other's lived-body. This is apparent in the typical shot/reverse-shot structure between two characters, which must create a spatial and temporal adjacency between two facets of experience (mine and yours) that otherwise sit simultaneously on either side of a dimensional divide. Thus, the typical shot/reverse-shot structure reveals not only another embodied outlook onto the external world of the film, but imputes an inner world to each and every character into which the chiasm of film's body flips or rotates – revealing yet another fold within the 'flesh' of its world.

THE MIRROR AS FLESH OF THE WORLD OF THE FILM

Neo's conversation with Morpheus just prior to his extraction is rendered through an extended shot/reverse-shot structure through which the spectator alternately sees and *sees as* each character by reversing the terms of visibility and invisibility. At the centre of this visual exchange, and at times mediating it, is the experience of the mirror, which (as I've already suggested) takes on a very different function in this sequence than that described in psychoanalytic theories of spectatorship. The topophilic fascination with the reflective surface as threshold hearkens back to attempts (from the late nineteenth century – contemporaneous with the advent of cinema) to visualise how the third dimension might relate to the fourth, and how two or more parallel three-dimensional worlds might be connected within a larger four-dimensional continuum. These thought experiments all proceed from the notion of 'elemental parallelism', which observes certain structural constants in the correlations between consecutively lower and higher dimensions (see Dalrymple Henderson 1983: 127). Of particular interest here is the elemental parallelism which states that any space of *n dimensions* rotates around an axis of *n-1 dimensions* within a volume of *n+1 dimensions*. Consider the following example from my article, 'Tracing the Tesseract: A Conceptual Pre-history of the Digital Morph':

> A line (of one dimension) always rotates around a point (of no dimension) on a plane (of two dimensions). A plane (of two dimensions) rotates around a line (of one dimension) in a space (of three dimensions). The next step would suggest that in an unknown hyperspace (of four dimensions), a volume (of three dimensions) would rotate around a plane (of two dimensions). It is simple enough to conceive of how a three-dimensional object rotates around a line within three-dimensional space; but the mind reels at how an object might *rotate* around a plane into the fourth dimension. (2000: 120–1; emphasis in original)

Popular theorists of the fourth dimension, such as Charles Hinton and Claude Bragdon, explored the figure and experience of the mirror as a virtual means for simulating a rotation through the fourth dimension otherwise not possible within the third. Bragdon writes:

> In the mirror image of a solid we have a representation of what would result from a four-dimensional revolution, the surface of the mirror being the plane about which movement takes place. If such a change in position were effected in the constituent parts of the body as a mirror image of it *represents*, the body would have undergone a revolution in the fourth dimension. (1916: 41; emphasis in original)

For example, there is no manoeuvre within three-dimensional space that will effectively switch the sides of one's face, or make the right hand into the left, in the manner of a mirror reflection. Indeed, as Linda Dalrymple Henderson points out: 'writers on the fourth dimension, following the lead of Möbius, would frequently use the three-dimensional symmetry of a pair of hands as an argument for a fourth dimension of space, through which one hand could be "turned" to coincide with the other' (1983: 18). The extrapolative power of the mirror for providing a representative glimpse of the fourth dimension has had a profound effect upon twentieth century visual artists such as Marcel Duchamp, who describes the function of the mirror within his work as that of a 'hinge-plane' (1973: 94). In Duchamp's parlance, the hinge-plane (comprised of only two dimensions) will always appear 'infra-thin' in relation to the three-dimensional spaces it divides and connects.

'Hinge' is also a term that Merleau-Ponty uses to underscore the reversibility of the chiasmatic junction of subject and object within the flesh. As hinge, the chiasm is located neither within the space of the objective world nor of psychic interiority, but is the two dimensional plane around which transcendence and immanence exchange positions as in the example of touching one's hands together. The figure of the mirror as inter-dimensional hinge-plane and Merleau-Ponty's example of double-perception within the flesh converge in my topophilic moment from *The Matrix* as Neo reaches out to touch the mirror image of his own hand. This compound metaphor prefaces the reversibility of transcendence and immanence not only within a body and world but, more radically, through a body and between worlds. The metaphor of mirror as hinge-plane between worlds is extended (quite literally) as Neo withdraws his hand and the surface of the mirror stretches back with his fingers, forming a conical shape that (reflected within the mirror) figures a closed continuum between two bodies: Neo's and that of his reflected image. The graphic shape of the two cones joined at the base suggests the geometrical figure a 'pseudosphere' imploding back across its plane of circumference (hinge-plane) in both directions towards vanishing points. The image of cone as vortex is also foreshadowed by Morpheus's observation: 'I imagine that right now you feel a bit like Alice, tumbling down the rabbit hole.' Another crew member's reference to the cone of the tornado in *The Wizard of Oz* (1939) is heard just prior to Neo's extraction: 'buckle your seatbelt Dorothy 'cause Kansas is going "bye-bye".'

For Merleau-Ponty, the chiasm as hinge-plane is not flat and static like Euclid's plane or the quotidian mirror. Rather it is a curved and transforming non-Euclidean topology tracing the contours of embodied intention. It is significant in this respect that the substance of the mirror migrates from the flat wall to the living contours of Neo's hand and body. Covered with the mirror substance that had previously reflected his hand, the image evokes another of Duchamp's metaphors of a four-dimensional rotation: that of a glove, which by turning inside out simulates the four-dimensional rotation of a three-dimensional object across its curving contours (see Dalrymple Henderson 1983: 153). When the substance creeps up Neo's neck and then streams ahead of the field of vision and down his throat, it is as if the film's body has inserted itself into Neo's body *qua* glove and turned it inside out – or in this case right side in – returning him from virtual to 'real' world. However, in the moment of passage between worlds, the glove turned inside out exchanges the reflecting surface of the mirror image for the image plane of the representation.

This reversible rotation across the 'hinge-plane' *qua* 'chiasmus' is most fully realised within Sobchack's description of the cinema:

> Through the respective mediation of camera and projector (mechanisms that intervene in acts of perception and expression, *both duplicating and reversing them*), the filmmaker and spectator are brought into indirect perceptual engagement with each other, and into direct engagement with a world that is their *mutual intentional object*. (1992: 173; emphasis added)

To grasp the radical nature of what Sobchack is describing would be to imagine that by touching the fingers of another's glove turned inside out one could directly experience what the other touched from the outside in: 'duplicating and reversing'. This notion of sensations turned inside out as four-dimensional rotation is also captured in Duchamp's poetic image of infra-thin. Changing sensory modalities from the tactile to the olfactory, he writes: 'When/the tobacco smoke/ also smells/of the mouth/which exhales it/the two odours are married/by infra-thin' (in Dalrymple Henderson 1983: 163).[2] The chiasmatic hinge-plane around which the three-dimensionality of the virtual and real worlds (and Neo's virtual and real bodies) rotates is also infra-thin in its two-dimensionality. Although figured through the mirror, this reversal refuses the reduction to pure vision characteristic of transcendental accounts of spectatorship. The reflective properties of the mirror are not merely specular, but are commuted first to touch and then in the dark depths of Neo's body – then, to sound and, later in the film, to memories of smell and taste.

Merleau-Ponty stresses the lateral intertwining and transcoding of the senses within the vertical exchange between transcendence and immanence. He argues that the 'equivocal status as touching and touched' is no perceptual anomaly, but rather 'a *structural* characteristic of the body itself' (1968: 143; emphasis in original) operative within and among all our sensory registers:

> [Just as] there is a circle of the touched and the touching ... there is a circle of the
> visible and the seeing, the seeing is not without visible existence; there is even an
> inscription of the touching in the visible, of the seeing in the tangible – and the con-
> verse; there is finally a propagation of these exchanges to all the bodies ... which I
> see and touch – and this by virtue of the fundamental fission or segregation of the
> sentient and the sensible. (Ibid.)

In her article 'What My Fingers Knew: The Cinesthetic Subject, or Vision in the Flesh' Sobchack locates the 'cross-modal transfer' (2004: 68) of the senses, or synaesthesia, as central to what Richard Dyer refers to as the elusive 'as if real' (in Sobchack 2004: 57)[3] quality of film experience – that which through sound and vision evokes other sensual registers within the spectator's lived-body. She describes how the embodied sensuality of cinema has evaded film theoretical discourses even as it recurs within personal and popular critical descriptions of the film experience. Apposite to the fate of cinephilia, Sobchack writes that 'the language used in the press to describe the sensuous and affective dimensions of the film experience has been written off as a popular version of that imprecise humanist criticism drummed out of film studies in the early 1970s' (2004: 58). Christian Keathley corroborates that 'much film theory of the past 25 years has been preoccupied with articulating and exposing the means by which dominant narrative cinema creates a world ... that we can step into and lose ourselves in. The cinephiliac anecdote, by contrast, seeks to illuminate the ways in which movies – especially moments from movies – displace themselves out of their original contexts and step into our lives' (2006: 152).

However, the criteria of Bazinian pro-filmicity lurking beneath Keathley's notion of the anecdote serves, perhaps unwittingly, to maintain an ontological and phenomenological divide between the 'cinephiliac moment' and the increasingly digitally-mediated and special effects-laden quotidian experience of cinema. As Drehli Robnik points out, 'if we equate cinephilia with liking certain movies, the term loses its meaning; but it also does so if we disconnect it entirely from the common habit of liking movies' (2005: 62). For Sobchack, the cinephiliac anecdote would constitute a hyperbolic example of the displacement that always occurs as the figures represented onscreen must literally 'make sense' within the broader sensorium of the spectator's uniquely situated lived-body. She describes the film experience as a cyclical feedback loop through which the spectator 'feels his or her literal body as only one side of *an irreducible and dynamic relational structure of reversibility and reciprocity* that has as its other side the figural objects of bodily provocation on the screen' (2004: 79; emphasis in original). According to Sobchack, this reversible relationship between the visual and the visible, the touching and the touched, is irreducibly a 'chiasmatic relation in which the subjective sense of embodied experience and the objective sense of representation are perceived as reversibly figure and ground and thus both commensurable and incommensurable' (2004: 74). The figures onscreen are commensurable with lived experience because we perceive them directly and concretely, in the sense that Bazin privileges. However, they are also incommensurable (displaced and displacing) insofar as the figures onscreen are never the equivalent of their lived experience, and the lived experience of cinema is never reducible to its figural representation onscreen.

The specific relevance of Sobchack's argument to the phenomenology and ontology of the film experience can be found in her claim that synaesthesia as chiasmatic exchange 'may, in fact, be especially heightened and privileged by the medium of cinema' (ibid.). She observes that although 'the sense I have of sensing at the movies is in some ways *reduced* ... because of my only partially fulfilled sensual grasp of the cinematic object of desire ... in other ways ... it is also *enhanced* in comparison with much direct sensual experience – this because my only partially fulfilled sensual grasp of the original cinematic object is completed not in the realisation of that object but through my own body, where my sensual grasp is reflexively doubled since, in this rebound from the screen, I have become not only the toucher but also the touched' (2004: 77; emphasis in original). It is thus that Sobchack renominates the film spectator as '*cinesthetic subject*' (2004: 67; emphasis in original). If this account of synaesthesia constitutes a structural characteristic of the film experience, the experience of cineph-ilia might be conceived in terms of its amplification, which is arguably enhanced rather than diminished through digital special effects.

For example, in his transition between the real and virtual world, Neo is exemplary of cinesthetic subjectivity, which is in turn commuted to the spec-tator through secondary identification. The exchange across sensory registers occurs most profoundly as the film's body travels down the throat of Neo's virtual body, into darkness and then out through the eyes of his 'real' body inside the fluid-filled pod. The passage is at once supremely carnal: entangling the senses, and yet not a literal movement through three-dimensional space – as if forging some unknown physiological conduit between the throat and eye. When dou-bled through character identification, the cinesthetic nature of mediation lends itself invariably to topophilia, fascination with the chiasmatic threshold that cin-ema uniquely hyperactivates. Although the precise moment of Neo's extraction across the hinge-plane is not made visible, it is expressed sonically through the transmutation of his voice from analogue scream to digital signal and then to the analogue sound of air bubbles inside the pod. This audio morph provides a sonic correlative to the liquid mirror in signifying the revelation of digital information as a hidden layer of mediation within and behind Neo's virtual body and world.

Information, like the creeping reflective substance, assumes the role of uni-versal simulator, revealing its uniform code behind all the sensual surfaces of the world, and underlying all media forms. As Morpheus tells Neo: 'The matrix is everywhere. It is all around us. Even now in this very room. You can see it when you look out your window or when you turn on your television.' Mor-pheus's observations are allegorical of how contemporary material culture, and of course cinema itself, is being translated into, and transubstantiated by infor-mation-based processes. That this transmutation cuts straight to the chiasm, both within the film and in the special effects that so uniquely simulate it, is a function of the 'infra-thin' nature of information. For as N. Katherine Hayles has argued, the transmutative capacities of information derive from its definition as a 'pattern with no dimensions, no materiality, and no necessary connection to meaning' (1998: 18). However, according to Hayles, information without a body is no less an abstraction than disembodied consciousness or vision: 'information, like humanity, cannot exist apart from the embodiment that brings it into being as a material entity in the world' (1998: 49). Rather, information must always be accessed through a material interface, however concealed as in the case of the matrix. Such concealment is not absence but rather the ability of cybernetic sys-tems to take on the role of a transcendent, sustaining presence supplemental to that of the body whose experience they mediate.

CONCLUSION

In exploring further how the cinesthetic subject and cinephiliac moment might productively relate in accounting for the love of digital special effects (such as seen with Neo's extraction from the matrix), it is worth addressing how Sobchack and Keathley both juxtapose each term to the function of metaphor, though for different but complimentary reasons. Keathley strives to differentiate the cinephiliac, poetic impulse to write about film: extending it metonymically into the domain of personal experience and association, from the critical impulse that seeks to interpret or 'ideologise' film by uncovering its proper metaphoric meaning – what it stands for. He writes: 'The critical move of ideologising is linked with metaphor because both approaches involve uncovering and articulating a text's meaning, its signified. Poeticising, on the other hand, means extending the effect of the text (or moment) via association, a move that involves sliding at the level of the signifier (of language or image)' (2006: 143).

If, as Keathley points out, 'metonymy leads to new metaphor' (ibid.), Sobchack identifies the phenomenological grounds and reservoir for this extension in the cinesthetic subject's chiasmatic exchange and conflation of the literal and the figural. She describes this sensual exchange within the film experience as a special case of 'catechresis' (sometimes called improper or false metaphor) through which a term is applied for something otherwise unnamed (she gives the corporeal examples of 'the head of a pin' and 'arm of a chair'), and in which the figural is thereby applied as the literal, rather than in place of another figuration as in metaphor proper (see 2004: 81–2). As she writes: 'Reciprocating the figurally literal representations of bodies and worldly things in the cinema, the spectator's lived-body in the film experience engages in a form of *sensual catechresis*. That is, it fills in the gap in its sensual grasp of the figural world onscreen by turning back on itself to reciprocally ... "flesh it out" into literal physicalised sense' (2004: 82; emphasis in original). Sobchack's analysis of sensual catechresis in the film experience also extends allegorically to the digital simulation of Neo's extraction from the matrix – as the mirror transforms from figured and figuring reflective surface to agent of literal reversibility across the chiasmatic hinge-plane of Neo's body. This is a movement that simultaneously draws the spectator across the hinge-plane of film's body, in order to 'flesh out' not only the gap between film and world, but also that between the virtual and non-virtual, between digital and analogue cinema. The moment of Neo's extraction from the matrix is reflexively demonstrative of how the neglected sense-making aspect of the experience of moving images, which Sobchack describes, may be amplified through digital special effects and other post-cinematic technologies.

NOTES

1   For the original source cited by Keathley, see Rosen (1988: 9).
2   For the original source cited by Dalrymple Henderson, see Duchamp (1973: 194).
3   For the original source cited by Sobchack, see Dyer (1994: 7).

REFERENCES

Baudry, Jean-Louis (1976) 'The Apparatus: Metapsychological Approaches to The Impression of Reality in the Cinema', *Camera Obscura*, 1, 107, 99–126.

Bazin, André (1967a [1945]) 'The Ontology of the Photographic Image', in *What is Cinema?* Volume 1, trans. Hugh Gray. Berkeley: University of California Press, 9–16.

_____ (1967b [1957]) 'The Virtues and Limitations of Montage', in *What is Cinema?* Volume 1, trans. Hugh Gray. Berkeley: University of California Press, 41–52.

_____ (1967c [1951]) 'Theatre and Cinema – Part One', in *What is Cinema?* Volume 1, trans. Hugh Gray. Berkeley: University of California Press, 76–94.

_____ (1967d [1951]) 'Theatre and Cinema – Part Two', in *What is Cinema?* Volume 1, trans. Hugh Gray. Berkeley: University of California Press, 108–24.

_____ (1971) *Jean Renoir*. Paris: Editions Champ Libre.

Bragdon, Claude (1916) *Four Dimensional Vistas*. New York: Alfred A. Knopf.

Bukatman, Scott (1998) 'The Ultimate Trip: Special Effects and Kaleidoscopic Perception', *Iris*, 25, 75–97.

Carrol, Noël (1988) *Mystifying Movies: Fads and Fallacies in Contemporary Film Theory*. New York: Columbia University Press.

Dalrymple Henderson, Linda (1983) *The Fourth Dimension and Non-Euclidean Geometry in Modern Art*. Princeton: Princeton University Press.

de Valck, Marijke and Malte Hagener (2005) 'Down with Cinephilia? Long Live Cinephilia? And other Videosyncratic Pleasures', in Marijke de Valck and Malte Hagener (eds) *Cinephilia: Movies, Love and Memory*. Amsterdam: Amsterdam University Press, 11–26.

Duchamp, Marcel (1973) *Salt Seller: The Writings of Marcel Duchamp (Marchand du Sel)*, ed. Michel Sanouillet and Elmer Peterson, trans. Michel Sanuouillet. New York: Oxford University Press.

Dyer, Richard (1994) 'Action!', *Sight and Sound*, 4, 10, 7.

Elsaesser, Thomas (2005) 'Cinephilia or the Uses of Disenchantment', in Marijke de Valck and Malte Hagener (eds) *Cinephilia: Movies, Love and Memory*. Amsterdam: Amsterdam University Press, 27–43.

Fisher, Kevin (2000) 'Tracing the Tesseract: A Conceptual Prehistory of the Digital Morph', in Vivian Sobchack (ed.) *Meta-Morphing: Visual Transformations and the Culture of Quick-Change*. Minneapolis: University of Minnesota Press, 103–30.

Hayles, N. Katherine (1998) *How We Became Post Human: Virtual Bodies in Cybernetics,*

Literature, and Informatics. Minneapolis, University of Minnesota Press.

Keathley, Christian (2006) *Cinephelia and History, or The Wind in the Trees.* Bloomington: Indiana University Press.

Lacan, Jacques (1977) 'The Mirror Stage as Formative of the Function of the I as Revealed in Psychoanalytic Experience', in *Écrits: A Selection.* New York: W. W. Norton, 1–7.

Merleau-Ponty, Maurice (1968) *The Visible and the Invisible,* ed. Claude Lefort, trans. Alphonso Lingis. Evanston: Northwestern University Press.

Metz, Christian (1973) 'Current Problems in Film Theory: Christian Metz on Jean Mitry's *L'Esthétique et Psychologie du Cinéma, Vol II'*, trans. Diana Matias, *Screen,* 14, 1–2, 40–87.

____ (1977) *The Imaginary Signifier: Psychoanalysis and the Cinema,* trans. Celia Britton, Annwyl Williams, Ben Brewster, and Alfred Guzzetti. Bloomington: Indiana University Press.

Robnik, Drehli (2005) 'Mass Memories of Movies: Cinephilia as Norm and Narrative in Blockbuster Culture', in Marijke de Valck and Malte Hagener (eds) *Cinephilia: Movies, Love and Memory.* Amsterdam: Amsterdam University Press, 55–64.

Rosen, Robert (1988) 'History of Image, Image of History: Subject and Ontology in Bazin', *Wide Angle,* 9, 4, 9, 7–34.

Sobchack, Vivian (1992) *The Address of the Eye.* Princeton: Princeton University Press.

____ (2004) 'What My Fingers Knew: The Cinesthetic Subject, or Vision in the Flesh', *Carnal Thoughts: Embodiment and Moving Image Culture.* Berkeley: University of California Press, 53–84.

Žižek, Slavoj (1999) 'The Matrix, or two sides of Perversion', *Philosophy Today,* 43, 11–17.

CHAPTER ELEVEN
CODE UNKNOWN: AN AUTO-DIALOGUE
Girish Shambu

A: So, as you know, I saw Michael Haneke's *Code Unknown* (2001) recently.

B: But you'd seen it once before, right?

A: Yes, I remember being a little dazed by it, especially its loose structure: 27 scenes, almost all shot in single takes without any cuts, ending brusquely by going to a black screen, sometimes in mid-sentence. I realised later that Haneke isn't interested in simply working on one level (the personal) but simultaneously on several (familial, social, ethnic, political, moral, philosophical), which the structure of the movie seems to accommodate.

B: Yes, but the multi-stranded narrative structure isn't necessarily better at this accommodation than a more stripped-down and familiar, thriller-genre-derived structure, as in *Caché* (*Hidden*, 2005).

A: True. And that speaks to Haneke's versatility. In *Code Unknown*, despite its structural singularity and sprawling, fragmented narrative, a remarkable coherence emerges. Haneke has spoken of his first three films (*The Seventh Continent* (1989), *Benny's Video* (1992) and *71 Fragments Of A Chronology Of Chance* (1994)) as being his 'emotional glaciation' trilogy, but it's clearly a theme that runs through his entire body of work. The idea is that human life in the industrialised Western world is narcotised and frozen. We live our lives separated from reality, without confronting the truths (personal, social, moral) that we should be alive and alert to. The media helps maintain us in this frozen state, giving us a bogus illusion of 'truth' by pretending to keep us 'well-informed' about the world's realities.

B: Yes. A good example of this glaciated state is the scene in which Anne (Juliette Binoche) is ironing her clothes to the accompaniment of 'noise' spilling quietly out of the TV. She hears loud voices, an altercation, a child's cries, turns off the TV, and listens – breaking momentarily out of this glaciated state – but when the neighbours fall silent, she spends a few quiet seconds in thought, then turns the TV back on and resumes ironing. The scene ends the way it began.

A: But in 'Haneke World', what does it take to finally break out of that emotionally sealed-off state into a state of awareness and engagement?

B: Well, in her case, the film shows several potential 'thawing' attempts. The first is the street confrontation at the beginning of the film that unsettles her a bit. Then we see a 'false' rupture of her equanimity in front of the camera when she is locked into the 'room of death'. But this occurs in a performance context, which is again sealed off from her real life. What it really takes is the arrival of the letter about an hour into the film. The event is a turning point of sorts for her; she begins to question her actions, and those of Georges (Thierry Neuvic). The supermarket scene follows. Then, the laughing fit during the dialogue dubbing scene, a sort of hysteria which indicates that she is no longer able to keep her real life and her performances apart. The thawing process is underway. Then, the scene in the subway that completes the melting. (Ice turns to water: she cries.) Anne emerges from the Metro, walks straight home, changes the code. Hopefully, a new (and more alert, aware and sensitised) life begins.

A: Interesting that the arrival of the video in *Caché* (the rupturing event, and the equivalent of the letter in *Code Unknown*) occurs at the get-go. Haneke is getting down to business sooner: introducing the alien element, spending the rest of the movie observing its effects. Once again, the couple in the film is named Georges and Anne…

B: What about the film-within-the-film, *The Collector*? She describes it to her friends at dinner as a thriller. Is it a by-the-numbers genre film or is it a stand-in for a Haneke film, a sort of *Funny Games* (1997)?

A: It's possible that Anne thinks it's a straightforward genre film – an impression supported by the casual, light manner in which she recommends it to her friends – but the words of the serial killer are tellingly spoken by the director behind the camera: 'Show me your true face', he says. This could easily be Haneke initiating the rupture of the character's composure to obtain, in effect, a 'genuinely human' response.

B: Of course, Haneke is also attempting to do to the audience exactly what he is doing to his characters. This is perhaps more viscerally apparent in his other films, like *Funny Games*, *Benny's Video* or *Caché*, which deliberately assault the audience and break through our coolness and complacency and the separation we feel between our lives and the comfort of what is 'just a movie'. He wants his films to disturb us, so that we carry them out of the theatre and into our lives like a wound we can't conveniently forget. But sometimes – and this is not really true of *Code Unknown* – I sense that Haneke derives a little sadistic relish from inflicting this punishment upon us, which bothers me a little. But I guess I admire his films enough to try to overlook this aspect. But: back to *Code Unknown*. What about the role of the media?

A: Yes. The media is a reliable Haneke *bête noire*. He worked in television for 15 years and reserves his choicest vitriol for it. All his films feature TV sets pouring soothing, sedating drivel into homes. And Georges, who works for the media as a war photographer, is frozen-up in his own unique way. 'I'm unfit for life in peace', he confesses, and when a moment of personal reflection about his war experience and his 'return to civilisation' crops up at dinner with friends (potentially breaking the frozen surface), it's quickly interrupted by Anne leaning in and asking for a dentist recommendation! There's the end of *that* conversation. In Paris, Georges jerry-rigs his camera to take secret pictures on the subway, a displaced act of aggression, a certain kind of rape, you could argue, an act of perversion, like those born of Erika's (Isabelle Huppert) sadomasochistic affliction in *The Piano Teacher* (2001).

B: Speaking of *The Piano Teacher*, civilisation (Schubert) and barbarism (S&M) go hand in hand in Erika's life. The 'room of death' in *Code Unknown* is, let's not forget, a wood-panelled, acoustically perfect *music room*. And *The Time Of The Wolf* (2003) erases civilisation in one quick stroke, leaving only barbarism.

A: Finally: communication.

B: Yes. Every household in the film is stricken with communication troubles. Georges and Anne's only (and doomed) attempt at communication takes place in the physical space of oppressively ordered and suffocating material objects – the supermarket. The film begins with deaf children signing, and ends with their reverting, along with their teacher, Amadou (Ona Lu Yenke), to a pre-verbal state of pure, ecstatic communion using the sound and rhythms of tribalistic drums.

A: Haneke banishes speech, returns to zero, and posits an optimistic building of the future by … children. A 'happy ending' if I ever saw one.

B: I agree. But can I bring up one thing that's always bothered me a wee bit about Haneke?

A: Uh-oh.

B: Don't get me wrong: I admire the guy, but that doesn't make him immune to scepticism, right? Here's the thing: Haneke is an old-fashioned European moralist. He makes didactic movies that he feels perform a useful social function. (*Code Unknown* is my favourite of his films partly because it appears to me his least overtly didactic.) This also means that often, after I've seen his films a couple of times to untangle their narrative complexities and apprehend the 'reasons for their existence', the films feel to me like they've … served their purpose, performed their function, exhausted themselves. Further visits yield – as the economists might put it – 'diminishing marginal returns'. The fact is, Haneke's characters seem like illustrative creations, intended by this stern, grey-bearded martinet to teach us lessons. This fact will always keep me at a slight remove from his (cold, cerebral, pedagogical) movies, especially because they also feel … anti-humanist.

A: But don't you see: Haneke makes us swallow the bitter pill because he is ultimately a humanist, even if his means (as in *Funny Games*) are anti-humanist. Above all, he wants us to see the errors of our ways…!

B: [sigh] Please: not another blogger rant, I beg of you…

A: [outraged] Sheesh. *Excuse* me…

B: [firmly] Thank you.

CHAPTER TWELVE

ANDY SERKIS AS ACTOR, BODY AND GORILLA: MOTION CAPTURE AND THE PRESENCE OF PERFORMANCE

Scott Balcerzak

> I don't see the difference between flesh and blood and motion capture. For me, acting's acting. What I've done with Gollum and Kong is no different to any other character that I've ever played. It's acting.
>
> – Andy Serkis[1]

Considering the complicated technology involved in the process known as motion capture or 'mo-cap', I find it difficult to take Andy Serkis's words at face value. The actor has emerged as a strange breed of star (or, more accurately, character actor) ever since his critically acclaimed performance as Gollum in Peter Jackson's popular adaptations of J. R. R Tolkien's *The Lord of the Rings: The Two Towers* (2002) and *The Return of the King* (2003). With these films, he was widely heralded by critics as the coming of a new kind of cinematic performer – a designation not so much determined by his acting prowess, but by the technology involved in creating the image of the character that we see onscreen. With the release of *The Two Towers*, New Line Cinema launched an Academy Award campaign to have Serkis nominated in the supporting actor category. Jackson also supported the idea, stating in an interview that he believed the dramatics to be 'as relevant an acting performance as *The Elephant Man* [1980] with John Hurt [who was nominated as best actor in 1981]' (in Stout 2003: 12). The director's comparison of the two actors was based on Hurt's heavy prosthetic make-up in David Lynch's film, made of inches of thick rubber, and how he had 'to use his acting skills to push this prosthetic around and fuel the character' (in ibid.). To Jackson, Serkis is simply using a similar technique, but this time as 'the driver manipulating this pixilated skin that we see in the film' (in ibid.). Ultimately, the Academy Award campaign was unsuccessful, but Jackson had found his motion capture star. When he began his ambitious remake of *King Kong* (2005), he approached Serkis to play the title character.

Despite all this excitement over the actor and the technology, I have to question if mo-cap really is the same as, to use Serkis's words, 'flesh and blood' performance. The filmmakers and other supporters of the process have certainly tried to sell it as simply a new form of acting – a kind of inevitable evolution for the art of performance in cinema. Such a characterisation of mo-cap as preserving the supposed autonomy of the actor was typical in the press for *King Kong*, where Serkis often found himself promoting the process as a legitimate form of acting. After suggesting some reservations about returning to mo-cap, Serkis stated in a 2005 interview that he agreed to the role through the promise of creative freedom: 'I became very excited about making him a creature that was driven by an *actor's choices*, although finally manifested in CG' (in Wake 2005: 204; emphasis added). Jackson's own characterisation of Serkis's Gollum as Oscar-worthy also follows this trend, with the suggestion that the actor is driving a 'pixilated skin', as if a type of digital prosthetic has been added to the body in post-production. A few critics also expressed their need to humanise the technology by suggesting it was simply adding a kind of digital enhancement to the actor. Gary Johnson (2005) writes in praise of Serkis that he 'gives a marvellous interpretation of Kong with his presence and actions enhanced by computer graphics'. Philip Wuntch (2005) also suggests a physically material presence onscreen, stating that Serkis's 'eyes register the ape's bewilderment at his unexpected love for Ann and his painful confusion among the stone and brick canyons of New York City'.

But on a close examination of the actual process, I find that the technical realities of mo-cap actually complicate these characterisations. The technology, which has been around since the 1980s, consists of situating numerous markers on a performer's body, placed on the joints and other key areas. Multiple lights reflect off these markers and, then, these reflections are captured and fed into a computer as the performer moves around the capture stage. All of this information is applied to a virtual 3-D body, which is then instantly mapped onto a kind of digital puppet. With Jackson's employment of the technology, there were also separate sessions with multiple cameras focused tightly on Serkis's marker-covered face to capture realistic expressions. Jackson then employed a process known as key-frame animation to stylise facial expressions, along with mo-cap editing and general CGI animation to perfect larger movements.[2] The result was a technological marvel with a stylised (yet oddly plausible) creature seamlessly interacting with the actors onscreen. Thus, mo-cap takes one essential externalised aspect of performance (realistic movement), separates it from the body, and uses it to guide the special effect. This process shows Jackson's comparison to *The Elephant Man* as lacking, since the viewer recognises that John Hurt or somebody does exist underneath the inches of prosthetics. Heavy make-up alters the appearance of the body, while mo-cap removes the physical reality of the body and replaces it with something or someone digital. The entire philosophy behind the technology is not about a digitisation of the human, but the humanisation of the digital through the addition of supposedly real movement. It is a process developed to make the special effect perform realistically as opposed to, as suggested by many, digitally enhance the actor.

For this reason, as opposed to examining the equally innovative *Lord of the Rings* trilogy, I want to solely consider Serkis's contribution to *King Kong* – which Jackson directs as a cinephilic conversation with the 1933 version, a film many see as containing the defining artificial performance of Hollywood's Golden Age. The director's initial plan to remake *King Kong* was greenlit in 1996 by Universal Studios and actually contained a vision of the title ape steeped more in the pure artifice of the original, using a combination of stop-motion animation, animatronics and digital effects. Jackson commented at the time, 'In a way, the artifice is still what's exciting about stop motion … You're bringing inanimate objects to life and you can invest them with a personality' (in Wake 2005: 2). Both small models and full-sized animatronic versions of Kong, along with the other inhabitants of Skull Island, were created before the studio shelved the plan six months into pre-production. With his post *Lord of the Rings*-clout, Jackson returned to Universal with his dream to remake *King Kong*, but this time with a definite turn towards realism as a goal, something he claims to have adopted from his work on the *Lord of the Rings* trilogy. He stated, 'we ultimately rewrote *Kong* by making it a little more real at its heart … making the characters more real, making the dynamics between the characters more centred and more focused' (in Wake 2005: 9). This change can be found most significantly in his new approach to realising the giant ape onscreen, adopting mo-cap to refine the special effects performance into something more realistic in its movements.

With Serkis's contribution to this film, we have a significant opportunity to reopen the question of what the actor means onscreen – as supposedly a 'flesh and blood' entity and as presence in a more intangible sense. In what follows, I will explore the technology of motion capture as it complicates our perceptions of acting as a process and, more importantly, as an onscreen construct. When examining the most workable theories of cinematic performance, there is a defining importance surrounding the actor's body – a theoretical tendency that becomes intensely problematic when considering mo-cap, which removes the physical reality of the body and replaces it with something or someone digital. By analysing Serkis's Kong, with a focus on the production diary's record of the mo-cap process, I will show how this absence of body does not allow for the crucial physical process of performance to dissipate. Instead, these basic movements become a technologically-enhanced tool for Jackson and his team of technicians to manipulate, thereby heavily emphasising the gestured fragments of performance that have long-defined the onscreen illusion of cinematic acting. As a result, Serkis's Kong forces us to reconsider performance itself as a cinematic component in the digital age.

Since newer technology has redetermined the boundaries of the onscreen body, our own definitions of the actor's presence ultimately must move beyond their original defining boundaries as well. What we see with the mo-cap-enhanced digital creature is how the technological process repositions the body of the actor within new spatial definitions – a position for Serkis that straddles the ever-evolving temporal and spatial 'presences', as explored in Vivian Sobchack's work on technologies of representation (see 2005). Through the motion captured by mo-cap, Serkis's performance as Kong transcends him simply being a digitally-enhanced actor. Instead, his 'presence' in the film allows us to examine something much more exciting in its formulation. We can now consider what the actor means onscreen when filmmakers remove 'flesh and blood' and allow 'presence' to exist as pure kinesis. As the onscreen body becomes more and more challenged by the technology of the digital age, our response to the performer onscreen can transcend the bodily and move completely into the realm of the spectral. To comprehend this monumental change, we must examine Serkis as he exists within three conceptional manifestations – as actor, body and onscreen gorilla.

ANDY SERKIS AS ACTOR

Andy Serkis's discussion of an 'actor's choices' driving his performance as Kong is nothing new in the popular discourse of acting. The performer's free will, to varying degrees, has been a mainstay in discussions of performance for over a century now, beginning with Constantin Stanislavski's experiments at the Moscow Art Theatre at the turn of the previous century. Stanislavski's System was developed to defeat artifice by accessing an 'inner truth' on a stage then dominated by pictorial displays and declamatory acting. The experiments highlighted the concept of an actor's *control* over his self-expressiveness, with Stanislavski writing that the 'artist of the stage must be the master of his own inspiration and must know how to call it forth when it is announced on the posters of the theatre' (in Blum 1984: 3).[3] Based upon the director's years of experimentation, the most famous technique for fostering this control is through using psychological reality as a groundwork – or employing emotional memories to expand one's 'inner technique'. But it is important to note that Stanislavski, from early on, meant the actor to be proficient in both inner and external techniques, writing in the late 1920s in 'The Art of the Actor and the Art of the Director', that the inner technique should correspond with 'the development of an external technique – the perfecting of a physical apparatus' (1958: 178). This aspect of his theories became so important to Stanislavski that, after many years of experimentation, he actually reversed his emphasis on the inner technique and concluded physical actions provided a greater access to truth on the stage.

This transition from the interior to the external was not to necessarily forgo honest psychological emotionalism in performance, but rather to facilitate a type of physical sense memory. In *Creating a Role* (1926), Stanislavski concluded that the actor 'need only sense the smallest modicum of organic physical truth in his action or general state and instantly his emotions will respond to his inner faith in the genuineness of what his body is doing' (1961: 150). The body itself, reflected through movement's complex rhythms, dictates an avenue to emotional truth – thus, you 'cannot master the method of physical actions if you do not master rhythm. Each physical action is inseparably linked with the rhythm which characterises it' (in Benedetti 2000: 92). The intricacies of mastering a physical rhythm ultimately became what splintered the American Method away from Stanislavski's System. When Stella Adler, who was working with Stanislavski in Paris, outlined the new Method of Physical Action to Lee Strasberg in 1934, he rejected it and embraced the recollection of the purely psychological memory. Ultimately, Strasberg saw the methodology of the external technique as constricting, stating that 'we would never get on with the business of acting' if Stanislavski's focus on physicality was heavily incorporated into the Method (in Blum 1984: 4).

Frequently mentioned in the publicity for *King Kong*, Serkis's explanation of his craft proves telling in the way it reflects Stanislavski's later Method of Physical Action. According to Serkis in a 2005 interview, the initial challenge of Kong was attempting to 'convey that range of emotion with a so-called mute' (in Fischer 2005). His approach to the role involved observing actual apes' movements for months on end, first at London Zoo and then in Rwanda with the Dian Fossey Gorilla Fund International. Through this research, he found the key to performing as the ape realistically through another sort of vocalisation and breathing, since actual gorillas 'sing, they chuckle, they have very specific ways of communicating within a group. And they just breathe, actually' (in ibid.). The idea of controlled breathing became crucial to his characterisation since 'on the motion capture stage they recorded sound as well. So the sound is linked to physicality. The chest expands and contracts. You'd have that breath happening for real and being recorded' (in ibid.). The technological manipulation of these recordings was also used as part of his process; as he explains, the sound 'was enhanced of course. It was beefed up and amazing things are done with the original sound that I made ... But it emanates from a living, breathing creature, i.e., a human being creating those sounds in sync with a physical performance' (in ibid.). As suggested by Serkis, this focus on breathing is a clear method of rhythm control (an essential component of Stanislavski's external technique) which basically dictated his ability to embody the character of Kong.

Only after explaining this physical manifestation of the character does Serkis finally address a deeper internal motivation behind Kong, which, given the fact that he is portraying an ape, is based in animal behaviourism. In the interview, he moves on to the internal only when discussing his interaction with Naomi Watts, who plays Ann Darrow. He reveals about the Kong/Ann relationship, 'although it's in gorillas' innate desire to connect with other beings, he's just not used to it. The only contact he has is with creatures that are trying to attack him or threaten' (in ibid.). Serkis then describes the ape, fittingly enough, as 'an old psychotic hobo' (in ibid.), a fascinatingly humanised explanation of the character's psychological make-up, but one still innately tied to outwardness as opposed to the ape's internal motivations. Notably, in *King Kong*, Serkis portrays two roles – the digital Kong and the live-action Lumpy, the ship's cook who dies midway through the film. Staying true to the promotion of mo-cap as 'legitimate', Serkis suggested in interviews that there was no difference in his approach to the two roles: 'He [Lumpy] has a physicality and a way of behaving which is built up around his experiences of life and what he is, and Kong the same' (in Ammes 2005). What proves most fascinating about this supposed similarity in approach is that Serkis still focuses upon physicality even when describing his live-action role. Interestingly, in other interviews, Serkis does discuss how his previous pre-mo-cap acting onstage and onscreen often took on a methodical (that is, internal) Method approach. It might be safe to assume that motion capture generally requires more externalisation from the actor – something, possibly, important as well in crafting the cartoonish Lumpy – an essentially 'Old Salt' seagoing caricature.[4]

On the detailed post-production diaries for *King Kong* (originally web broadcasts, now DVD extras), we see how the physicality of Serkis's performance as Kong plays out on the mo-cap stage as the actor dons the long extended arms of a gorilla and arches his body to mimic the animal. He beats his chest and, much like suggested in the interview, breathes loudly as he dominates the space through sheer physicality. More importantly, the video outlines how Serkis gave complete control over to Jackson and his team of technicians and animators to polish and, often, completely change this performance. Mo-cap technicians, many times, determine the larger movements of the ape – employing the motions captured from Serkis's body, but still taking great creative liberties during physically complicated sequences such as fight scenes. Beyond the mo-cap editing, key-frame animation is also used to perfect Kong's more nuanced performance. Most close-ups of the giant ape begin with Serkis's face covered in numerous markers and shot with multiple cameras. As the video diary shows, the actor sits uncomfortably, with large false gorilla teeth in his mouth and dozens of markers on his face. Serkis looks into the video camera, realising how ridiculous the process appears at this early stage and cracks, 'It's times like this when you really do wonder what you are doing with your life.' Mark Sager, a digital effects supervisor, then explains how these dots are used to create a mapping for Kong's face, which is a more intricate version of the process used to create the gorilla's larger bodily movements. Basically, the reflections are captured off the reflectors and fed into a computer – then eventually grafted onto a digital ape's face.

As the video explains, this process needs excessive tweaking to seem realistic. The facial movements captured by mo-cap are not enough to totally animate realistic expressions, thus the processes of motion editing and key-frame animation are employed. Motion editing is a fundamental step in manipulating the performance through manoeuvering the digital puppet of the ape. As Dejan Momcilovic, mo-cap supervisor, explains, this process is essentially based in perfecting more realistic movements and expressions, often on the face, since the technicians 'typically need to polish the performance of Andy. Or change it. Modify it.' The video then shows Kong's face displayed on a computer screen with a mapping of facial muscles over the image. Another technician reveals how, even though Serkis's expressions dictate many of the eye and brow movements, they can still control much of the face by clicking on the keyboard. With the video focused closely on the computer screen, they illustrate how they can make Kong 'happy' or 'angry'.

Beyond the mo-cap editing, key-frame animation is also used to perfect Kong's performance. Once again, much of the production video focuses on the facial movements of the ape to illustrate the tool's purpose. 'The mo-cap is great because it is the performance that Pete [Jackson] wants', explains Stephen Buckley, animator, 'but the motion capture that they did cannot really get, you know, brow and nuance. So with what the motion capture can't do, we can do by hand.' Overall, this stage of the process resembles a more traditional animation, something akin to the 1933 stop motion version of *King Kong* where the filmmakers used their own movements as inspiration. The video shows footage of animators snarling into mirrors to craft expressions and frantically moving like apes to understand larger movements. The animators then use intricate manoeuvering of the digital ape image to reflect such performances. Thus, the final version of Kong becomes influenced by multiple sources along with the centralised 'performance' of Serkis – including mo-cap editors, animators and, of course, Peter Jackson who oversees the entire process. Momcilovic explains what could be seen as the philosophy behind this – essentially, performance by committee: 'If the thing looks good, it doesn't matter if its motion capture or animation. So as long as the mo-cap is used where it really fits, it's a great tool.'

Fascinatingly, despite the Stanislavskian approach to physicality within Serkis's 'in-the-moment' performance, the overall philosophy behind creating the digital ape actually embraces a more Strasbergian view of cinematic acting. As Sharon Marie Carnicke suggests, Strasberg better fits the process of filmmaking, since in the Method, the actor may be central, but the director is the clear auteur:

> Strasberg, in contrast, shifts responsibility for the interpretive shaping of performance to the director, a shift clearly sympathetic to film. In the Method, the actor may be central, for the actor is the object of the audience's attention, but the director is 'auteur', sculpting the role's dynamics from the actor's credible, 'real', emotional life as if from living clay. (1999: 78)

In this often overlooked aspect of Method training at the Actors Studio, Strasberg insisted on the authority of the director, even stating that he considers the 'problem of acting solved' when the actor 'is capable of giving to the director anything that he wants' (in ibid.). Stanislavski believes the actor to be an autonomous artist who freely collaborates with the director in analysing and creating the character onstage. But this relationship fundamentally becomes problematic when considering film. As Strasberg observed in 1957, 'It is possible to put strips of film together and create a performance that never was actually given' (in Carnicke 1999: 76). In many ways, mo-cap *aggressively* positions Serkis into what can already be seen as the easily-manipulated position of the cinematic actor, exemplifying the performer's loss of control.

In *Acting in the Cinema*, James Naremore suggests that despite the influence of Stanislavski and Strasberg on process, the seemingly antiquated idea of François Delsarte and Charles Aubert's nineteenth century style of acting – where standardised and categorised gestures and expressions forgo psychological realism – still appears generally in the fragmented nature of filmmaking, with its 'brief shots which are photographed out of sequence' (1988: 64). Naremore contends that 'actors continue to practise the rhetoric of conventionalised expression; most of them simply explain their craft in a different way, exchanging old gestures for new' (ibid.). The process of filmmaking itself creates fragmentation, thus never allowing for a complete approximation of neither Stanislavski nor Strasberg. In a potent sense, mo-cap only aggressively heightens this disempowering of the actor. It allows for the performance, with all its Stanislavskian physicality, to exist 'in the moment', but gives greater control to the filmmaker to manipulate the fragments of this performance. When applying this idea to Serkis, it is the essence of these fragments, now purely kinetic in nature, that proves most significant in changing our perception of the actor as an onscreen construct. To understand this now aggressive diminishing of the autonomous actor, we must examine the *process* of mo-cap itself in direct relationship to the body of Andy Serkis.

ANDY SERKIS AS BODY

Watching Serkis perform on the production diaries video before the motion capture has been properly recorded and stylised shows a fascinating, if somewhat comical, simplification of the human form. Within a large converted warehouse of a studio, the video follows Serkis as he arrives at work only to be zipped into his black and blue lycra suit and covered with markers by the crew. In an accompanying interview, John Curtis, mo-cap technician, explains the technological specifics of the process, all of which illustrate the literal removal of the physical body. As the video cuts to explanatory shots of the equipment, Curtis tells how the process employs 52 cameras, each with a bright ring-light meant to reflect off the reflectors. Each monitor attached to the cameras records the single bright reflections which, in Serkis's words, lights him up 'like a Christmas tree'. When the video finally shows how this data looks when initially fed into the computers, the effect is startling in its simplicity of design. On a blue grid, we see Serkis's pure movements completely stripped of physicality in the form of small dark dots. The image resembles a star constellation, with the stars yet to be traced into a recognisable shape. Curtis explains that because of the large number of cameras completely encircling Serkis, 'you can actually track the dot in 3-D'. Therefore, when watching the basic pattern of captured lights, you see the points move, but the image largely resembles a twirling of dark dots. It takes a stretch of the imagination to provide the connections – something similar to a child's 'connect the dots' puzzle though more confused, since the 3-D effect of multiple cameras often shows dots in the fore- and background. Notably, only upon the intervention of human technicians does the process add even the most simplistic of bodily forms, which, at this very early stage, are pure digital artifice. As Curtis explains, 'once we've captured this *marker cloud*, which represents where Andy is, we map it onto a human body' (emphasis added). As we see on the production video, the 'human body' is actually a crude digital character designed by a computer programmer and little resembling Serkis, whose primary purpose in the process is to provide, as Curtis so fittingly characterises it, a marker cloud of movement – a record of the physicality of externalised performance. The digital human body is then fitted onto an equally crude digital gorilla body, all of which happens instantaneously and can be viewed as immediate playback on the monitors. So what we have with the mo-cap process is a literal removal of the corporeal body. Serkis's body is present to create a marker cloud of movements, but not to record a physical presence in any traditional sense.

This process – where, almost paradoxically, movement is valued over body – has resulted in a confusion over how to actually define the presence of Serkis onscreen. In response to *Lord of the Rings*'s Gollum, Stacey Abbott writes that the 'significance of these layers of techniques used to create Gollum is the degree to which the actor/character truly reflects a cyborg existence' (2006: 108). This equivalency of the mo-cap process with the cyborg was inevitable, since the term has become a mainstay in film studies as the cinematic cyborg, in such films as *Blade Runner* (1982) and *The Terminator* (1984), entered the popular imagination. Scott Bukatman outlines how the image of the humanistic machine in science fiction constructs 'a new subject-position to interface with the global realms of data circulation', which he famously calls 'terminal identity' (1993: 8). In this sense, Abbott's association between Peter Jackson's use of mo-cap and the cyborg is understandable, since the process employs both the human body and the digital to create its effect. But this association becomes compromised when considering mo-cap beyond these necessary components to honestly acknowl-edge the erasure of the human form itself. Motion capture might employ man and technology, but the effect is far from creating a 'new subject-position' in the same sense of Bukatman's influential readings of science fiction literature and cinema.[5] Problematically, in the *Lord of the Rings* films and *King Kong*, Serkis exists as an actor without a corporeal body, instead stripping the subject down to recorded movements (a marker cloud). Thus, a merger in the sense of a true cyborg existence fails to occur. In a way, even Abbott briefly considers this complication, but never develops the idea past the limitations of the cyborg model – writing that 'the character is not only a fusion of flesh and machine (Serkis and the computer-animated Gollum), but the expression of a range of representational technologies' (2006: 10). I would go further to suggest that mo-cap does not illustrate any fusion of man and machine, but must be considered *solely* within the realm of representational technologies since the physical body is totally erased. Instead, the process excitingly moves the actor beyond the bodily and, thus, even beyond the physically-mechanised into the realm of purely digitalised presence.

In 'The Scene of the Screen' (1994), Vivian Sobchack explores how the ever-evolving technologies of cinematic and electronic representation have been '*subjectively incorporated*, enabling a new perceptual mode of existential and embodied "presence"' (2005: 129; emphasis in original). As discussed in this piece, unlike cinematic representation, where spatiality and materiality foster a more inherent sense of dimension, electronic representation 'by its very struc-ture phenomenologically denies the human body its fleshy presence and the world its dimensions' (2005: 139). Sobchack's differentiation of the cinematic and electronic body is based in how the body is seen projected on a movie screen or, alternately, pixilated on a computer or television screen. As Sobchack relates, 'However significant and positive its values in some regards, the electronic trivia-lises the human body' (ibid.). As seen with the process outlined in the production diaries of *King Kong*, this trivialisation of physicality unfolds in a shockingly simple display. Serkis externalises his performance to realistically move like the apes he studied. Then, with reflectors placed upon his body, the cameras capture the lights and feed the movements into the computer. Now, the computer program reads the performance not as the physical body but as the marker cloud without bodily presence. On the blue grid displayed on the monitors and even when mapped onto preliminary digital bodies, the image is distinctly non-cinematic. Sobchack writes on electronic presence:

> What I am suggesting, ungrounded and uninvested as it is, electronic presence has neither a point of view nor a visual situation, such as we experience, respec-tively, with the photograph and the cinema. Rather, electronic presence randomly

disperses its being *across* a network, its kinetic gestures describing and lighting on the surface of the screen rather than inscribing it with bodily dimensions … Images on television screens and computer terminals seem neither projected nor deep. (2005: 138; emphasis in original)

With the process of motion capture, we see the actor wilfully surrendering his body to become a *purely* electronic subject in startlingly real ways. Rather literally, he is stripped down into a pattern of 'kinetic gestures' – a marker cloud to be employed by the director at his or her will. The presence of Andy Serkis loses the true bodily dimensions that are usually recorded in a traditional film performance, leaving only a streamlined electronic presence divorced from the body. All that is left is the kinetic residue of performance.

ANDY SERKIS AS GORILLA

While Serkis's transformation into electronic presence certainly describes the mocap process, what of the *product* – the image of the actor onscreen? The signs of acting, what we as viewers register as performance, remain in Serkis's Kong, but in a fascinatingly paradoxical manner. Richard Dyer summarises that the signs of performance are 'facial expressions; voice; gesture (principally of hands and arms, but also of any limb, e.g., neck, leg); body posture (how someone is standing or sitting); body movement (movement of the whole body, including how someone stands up or sits down, how they walk, run, etc.)' (1998: 134).[6] As this list suggests, our response to an actor ultimately revolves around the physical body of the performer, his or her movements and our culturally-dictated reactions to these movements and sounds as signs. This focus upon the physical is a common theoretical approach to the actor. When John O. Thompson attempts a semiotic comparison of classic movie stars in his 'Communication Test' (1978), his criteria are largely dependent on 'distinctive features' of the physical body, from slight facial expressions to broader physical differentiations that serve 'as a potential distinguisher both within the film itself and in the indefinitely extending space established by viewers' familiarity with cinema in general' (1991: 186). In a sense, this body-conscious approach to cinematic performance feels logical – since the body has long been theoretically linked to historical, political and philosophical systems in thinkers as diverse as Jean-François Lyotard, Gilles Deleuze, Luce Irigaray, Jacques Derrida, Jacques Lacan, Michel Foucault and, of course, countless others. As Elizabeth Grosz summarises, 'The interlocking of bodies and signifying systems is the pre-condition both of an ordered, relatively stable identity for the subject and of the smooth, regulated production of discourse and stable meanings. It also provides the possibility of a disruption and breakdown of the subject and discourse's symbolic registration' (2001: 141). If we are to apply this broad, yet warranted, summarisation to film studies' approach to the cinematic actor, we see why the body exists as the central component in the discipline's attempt at systemising performance onscreen. It allows for the stability of meaning, something attempted in Thompson's tests and, to a lesser extent, even in Dyer's summary of the signs of acting. The body also allows for examinations of potent exceptions to the rules, with actors' bodies that transcend popular social systems of representation.

More importantly, these bodily signs of performance provide one of the clearest ways we as viewers conceptualise the cinematic image as recording temporality itself. In 'The Ontology of the Photographic Image' (1945), André Bazin marks 'preserved' temporality (duration) as the key difference between the photo and cinema, contending that 'film delivers baroque art from its convulsive catalepsy. Now, for the first time, the image of things is likewise the image of their duration, change mummified as it were' (1967: 14–15). In this sense, we can see the supposedly 'real-time' recordings of performing bodies as easily identifiable markers of what the viewer recognises, on some level, as what film 'preserves'. Perhaps this is why actors' performance has often been used in discussions of the cinephiliac moment. In Paul Willemen's discussions with Noel King on cinephilia, many of the points on cinephiliac responses focus upon the performance choices of popular actors, particularly Method actor Marlon Brando in *On the Waterfront* (1954). The piece discusses at some length the famous moment when Brando improvised picking up Eva Marie Saint's dropped gloves in the middle of an intimate scene. To Willemen, this moment's power exists squarely in the actor as a real figure beyond the character created onscreen, contending that 'the main point is that at that moment he does something which allows you to glimpse Brando incarnating a character. There is a moment of doubling, of ghosting, as they would say in photography' (1994: 239).

This concept of a *ghosting* of the actor might help to explain how the presence of Serkis still works on some level in *King Kong* – even though his bodily image is not preserved onscreen. We must first contend that the potency of the actor as designated by Willemen is based upon an illusion of autonomy – since a director can easily cut such individualistic moments like Brando's improvisation and use whatever fragments he or she wishes. Therefore, the onscreen image of the digital character in *King Kong* does not necessitate a complete rejection of the human actor as presence, since the process allows for the most externalised aspects of performance still to surface. In relation to Bazin, what we logically have to ask with mo-capped performance is what aspect of the real is now being *preserved* when we watch the digital Kong onscreen? Ontologically, the effect onscreen can provide a heightened spectral quality for the viewer – an aspect in digitally-enhanced scenes that has been noted by Jenna Ng as 'ghosting the image'.[7] In direct relationship to the actor's contribution, while the image of the corporeal body is removed, the temporality inherent to all recorded performance still materialises at least to some extent. As outlined on the production diaries video, Serkis does dictate many aspects of Kong's performance, thus still maintaining partial autonomy as a performer and, in small moments, preserving temporalities through the promise of recorded movements (each with their own durations). Thus, even as compromised and manipulated as they are by technicians, the records of the actor's movements (and moments) suggest the aura of a performing body – allowing for a streamlined *kinetic* 'ghosting' of the performer. Mo-cap aggressively positions the actor as a type of spectral kinesis – a movement-based, yet always artistically compromised, possession within a digital image.

Hence, while the technological process might exemplify, in Sobchack's definition, the *electronic subject*, the product (the image of the character that we eventually see onscreen) often feels more traditionally *cinematic*. Partly the reason for this distinction is that Jackson's *King Kong* is in such a direct cinephilic conversation with the original – which, through the animation of small figures, kept striving for a distinctly cinematic vision. Stop motion (perfected by Willis O'Brien), by its very definition, is a process only made possible through the frame-by-frame illusion of movement facilitated through cinema as a mechanical process. It consists of filming models one frame at a time, repositioning them slightly between each exposure. The footage is played back to give the illusion of the gorilla's movements. In the documentary *RKO Production 601: The Making of Kong, Eighth Wonder of the World* (2005), Jackson, along with various other filmmakers, reflects on the significance of the original character of Kong as an emotionally effective special effect performance. Jackson contends, 'You cry when Kong falls off the Empire State Building because he is such a well-realised visual effect. And that is the first time in filmmaking that had really occurred.' Of course, the original Kong's 'performance' was more or less a form of visual trickery rather than acting in a traditional sense. No matter how emotional the original Kong seems onsceen, the fact remains that it is animation without a bodily presence and remains clearly artificial to the viewer. Each movement and facial expression was largely determined by animator O'Brien and producer/director Merian C. Cooper. As Ray Morton writes, 'People who worked on the film claimed to have recognised aspects of both Cooper and O'Brien in the giant ape' (2005: 38).

Despite these personalised touches, the manipulation of the small model cannot be viewed as a performance even in the sense of puppeteering, where the artificial figure can exist as an extension of the puppeteer's body. The so-called performance of the ape is purely determined by animation stripped to its most basic elements, similar to the so-called performance of a character in any cartoon. This purely simulated creation can be seen as what gives the original film its distinctly modernist feel (something created solely out of the frame-by-frame machinery of cinema), despite its narrative roots in nineteenth century adventurism and exploration. As Mark McGurl writes, 'Unlike the *techne* of the ape costume, the Kong model never hides a human actor. The Kong actor is pure artifice suggesting … an absolute merger of that artifice with the power of nature' (1996: 441). Thus, the original Kong, as an onscreen character, seems to pride itself within its unreality and non-humanity by forgoing the actor completely. It is a cinematic presence, but one distinctly based in the illusion of movement onscreen and not the aura of a body.

Let us consider a scene from both the original and remake that highlights the special effects performance of Kong. In the famous T-Rex battle of the 1933 version, Ann Darrow (Fay Wray), placed upon a tree by the ape, screams upon seeing the T-Rex approaching. Kong rushes to her rescue and proceeds to fight the giant beast. In an astonishing piece of stop motion animation that reportedly took seven weeks to complete, the battle exists as a fascinating hybrid of ape and human-like behaviour and movements. In some moments, Kong punches the giant reptile like a boxer or body-slams it like a wrestler, slinging the T-Rex over his hairy shoulders. At other times, Kong's behaviour is very animalistic, wrapping his body around the beast. Upon cracking the reptile's mouth open, the giant gorilla proceeds to pick up the head and playfully flick his broken jaw. He ends the fight by pounding his chest and letting out a triumphant roar. On the documentary *RKO Production 601*, various filmmakers and special effects wizards marvel over the original Kong's battle with the T-Rex, while also explaining how the process of stop motion actually works. In an interview, special effects make-up artist Rick Baker discusses how an animator has to 'act', stating that it requires 'performing in front of a mirror' to time the small model's movements and even consider its motivations. For example, O'Brien used his own movements to calculate the time frame of each of the ape's gestures. Randy Cook, a director and visual effects supervisor, goes further to suggest how the model reflects the animator's personality and creates intricate details within the special effects performance. Cook explains, 'Studying gorilla movement. Fine, that's great … but what makes him an über-gorilla, you know? The fact that it punches out the T-Rex. The fact that it grabs T-Rex and throws it over his shoulder.'

Cook's point is a valid one, since the ape during the sequence truly proves most fascinating through the movements that reflect O'Brien's personality – his interest in wrestling and background in boxing.[8] The artistic individuality of O'Brien helped to create the animated illusion of a special effect's performance, even though the actual process was far from a traditional form of performance. Despite the weeks of painstaking animation, the onscreen effect of the sequence is still highly cinematic in its fluidity of movement, depth and the illusion of individuality in the ape's behaviour. In this manner, the ape has a distinctive presence onscreen, something certainly illustrated by the cinephilic gushing over the original by various filmmakers and critics, as seen in the documentary. Given the animated illusion of presence created by stop motion, this cinematic engagement is far from surprising. As Sobchack writes, 'Cinema's animated presentation of representation constitutes its "presence" as always presently engaged in the experimental process of signifying and coming-into-being' (2005: 135). As cinematic subjects (and, equally, in defining us as viewing subjects), the figure onscreen finds its presence within a specific form of temporality based in 'the significant value of the "streaming forward" that informs the cinematic' (ibid.). The 1933 Kong, through an animated movement creating the illusion of performance, exists as a cinematic subject and can create empathy within the viewer. The effect is not accomplished with a preserved image of the actor's body, since the jerky model Kong feels removed from the reality of the 'flesh and blood' actors. The stop-motion gorilla is pure special effects artifice as cinematic subject – a bodiless ape. It is accomplished not from the aura of a real person but through an individualistic fluidity of movement, a constant 'coming into being'.

The remake's Kong also has a distinctly cinematic presence, but one based in something more considerable than just an individualistic fluidity of movement. The digital Kong as a cinematic subject can base its potency not only within motion itself, but within the kinetic aura of a real body. In the remake's version of the T-Rex battle, Jackson initially ups the ante by having three T-Rexes attack Kong as he attempts to protect Ann. The scene takes a variety of high octane diversions as Ann, the giant ape and the dinosaurs fall down a canon and become entangled in vines. But Jackson wisely ends this spectacular action sequence in a direct homage to the original as, now on solid ground, Kong finally battles one final T-Rex face-to-face. Ann cautiously backs away from the one last remaining dinosaur as a loud thud accompanies Kong as he jumps behind her. Jackson cuts to a close-up of Ann turning to look at her rescuer; her eyes are wide and express fear, though, also a definite relief at Kong's presence. Jackson then cuts to a close-up of Kong, furrowing his brow and flaring his nostrils. The comparison of these two expressive faces illustrates the seamless effect of the mo-cap performance beside a traditional one. As discussed in the examination of the capture process, the ape's facial expressions are a combination of key-frame animation and Serkis's recorded movements. Unlike in the original, Jackson, here and at other times, uses multiple cuts from Naomi Watts' face to Kong's face. Since the director shows a clear confidence in the realism of Serkis and the animator's collaboration, the film embraces a direct contrast of the human and artificial body image as both performances and onscreen presences. The fight itself takes on a more animalistic temper than the original as Kong roars at the T-Rex and pounds his chest as he lunges toward it. This time, he forgoes the wrestling and boxing moves and goes straight to prying the beast's mouth wide open. Then, he bends down and takes a savage bite at his tongue, ripping it out of its mouth. He wraps his body around the T-Rex's neck and proceeds to attempt to break its jaw, finally forcing it to the ground. When Kong finally succeeds in splitting it, the ape, in an ode to the original, playfully flicks the now dead beast's jaw. He then gives another chest-pounding roar. Throughout this fight, Jackson cuts to Ann watching her protector in amazement, shots that repeatedly suggest Watts' proximity to her digital co-star.

The T-Rex fight sequence was achieved more by animators than motion capture technicians, since the aggressive movements would be difficult for Serkis to actually perform. In these moments, Kong as cinematic subject feels based in movement more than anything material. As Serkis relates in an interview, 'The T-Rex fight sequence is predominantly, I would say, the animator's domain ... But the more emotional stuff was more heavily physically motion captured stuff' (in Fischer 2005). After the fight, the ape huffs heavily, as if tired from the battle. His rhythmic breathing is considerably more real than anything previously seen in animation – created, or at least heavily inspired, by Serkis's own rhythmic breathing on the mo-cap stage. Instead of just picking up the screaming Ann, as in the original, Jackson now goes further to contrast the performances of Watts and Kong. The ape, hurt by her previous attempt at escape, coyly walks up to Ann and turns his back on her. There is a precision of movement in Kong, less broadly conceived than Willis O'Brien's influences on the original model's gestures and fighting techniques. After turning his back, Serkis's ape gives just a slight peek over his shoulder to her. Ann responds by walking toward him, since her character is now aware that Kong truly is her protector on the savage Skull Island. It is within the smallness of these moments, purely physical in terms of Serkis's contribution, that a more bodily dimension feels added to the giant ape. Unlike the 1933 version, the mo-cap Kong has more of a corporeality onscreen. Both are certainly charismatic cinematic subjects, but motion capture allows the presence to feel more complete. The special effects performance comes closer to having an illusion of autonomy, since Kong adopts the intricate movements and even the heavy breathing of a real performing body. Therefore, in *King Kong*, Serkis becomes a major paradox as a performer. The process of motion capture exemplifies the rejection of physicality found in becoming the electronic subject. But the effect onscreen helps to humanise the special effects performance by 'ghosting' the actor as a tangible presence. Mo-cap provides a major step in supplying corporeality to the artificially animated by affixing the aura of a body to Kong.

As a result of this complicated position, Serkis's role in creating the ape forces us to reposition what the actor can mean as a cinematic subject. As a performer forced to emote in fragments, the film actor has always had less power in determining onscreen performance than what is promoted in the popular Stanislavski-influenced discourse on acting. With mo-cap, we see this discrepancy widen as the actor is literally stripped of his physical body to exist as pure kinesis – a marker cloud to be employed as a tool by the filmmaker. In this sense, we see that Serkis is only half-correct when he contends that there is no difference between 'flesh and blood' and motion capture acting. On one level, the technological process only continues to perpetuate the illusion of performance in film. But, more provocatively, mo-cap also illustrates how far this illusion can progress while still allowing the actor to have a presence onscreen, even if it is only spectral and kinetic in nature. The technology shows that now the performing body can be divorced from its physical presence, yet leave behind its aura – all in the pursuit of not just creating the illusion of onscreen performance, but doing so within cinema's most popular special effects gorilla.

AUTHOR'S NOTE

This article was originally given as a presentation at the 2007 meeting of the Society for Cinema and Media Studies on the panel 'Blockbuster Revisionist: New Frontiers in the Films of Peter Jackson'. I wish to thank my fellow panellists Barry Keith Grant, Cynthia Erb and Jenna Ng (along with those in attendance) for their interest and support of this chapter.

NOTES

1   Andy Serkis in Fischer (2005).

2   Peter Jackson's employment of motion capture was ground-breaking not necessarily in technological innovation as much as perfection of the technique. Part of the reason why Gollum and Kong's movements seem so realistic has much to do with the staggering number of cameras employed in the process (often upwards of fifty) and in the painstaking hours spent tweaking the digital images. See Stout (2003) and Wake (2005).

3   To Stanislavski, control of emotions was basically what constituted 'the main difference between the art of the actor and all other arts' (1974: 571) – since most other artists can wait for inspiration. Actors have to create as soon as they appear on the stage. Thus, his System was not a set of hard rules, but more so a number of experimental steps that can lead to a creative state of performance.

4   Serkis's comfort with the mo-cap technology might also have something to do with his education at Lancaster University – which was an Independent Studies degree covering theatre along with stage design, a skill that the actor suggests helped him with 'spacial awareness'. For more on his approach to other roles, see Ken P. (n. d.).

5   This appropriation of the cinematic cyborg as showing 'new subject-positions' was an outgrowth of Donna Haraway's famous feminist 'Manifesto of Cyborgs'. Among other qualities, Haraway saw late twentieth-century machines as making 'thoroughly ambiguous the difference between natural and artificial, mind and body, self-developing and externally designed, and many other distinctions that used to apply to organisms and machines' (1985: 69). In this sense, Stacey Abbott's association with Peter Jackson's use of mo-cap and the cyborg is understandable, since the process consists of using both the human body and the digital to create its effect. But this association becomes compromised when considering it beyond the process and as image itself.

6   Later, Naremore also suggested a similar importance upon 'making faces' and gestures as central to an actor's expressive technique in the montage-dictated process of filmmaking. See Naremore (1988: 34–67).

7   From research presented at a shared SCMS panel, Ng also has argued for the appearance of spectral elements in images derived from, among other techniques, motion capture. Though, unlike Ng, I am using the term 'ghosting' in direct reference to the actor behind the character (as derived from Willemen's point on Brando), I wish to credit her as originally developing the *ontological* possibilities of 'ghosting' in such scenes.

8   For more on O'Brien see Archer (1998).

REFERENCES

Abbott, Stacey (2006) 'Final Frontiers: Computer-Generated Imagery and the Science Fiction Film', *Science Fiction Studies*, 33, 10, 89–108.

Ammes, Ethan (2005) '1-On-1 Interview: Andy Serkis on *King Kong*', *Cinema Confidential*, 12 December. Online. Available at: http://www.cinecon.com/news.php?id=0512121. Accessed 20 December 2006.

Archer, Steve (1998) *Willis O'Brien: Special Effects Genius*. New York: McFarland.

Bazin, André (1967 [1945]) 'The Ontology of the Photographic Image', in *What is Cinema?* Volume 1, trans. Hugh Gray. Berkeley: University of California Press, 9–16.

Benedetti, Jean (2000) *Stanislavski: An Introduction*. Revised edition. New York: Theatre Art Books.

Blum, Richard A. (1984) *American Film Acting: The Stanislavski Heritage*. Ann Arbor: UMI Research Press.

Bukatman, Scott (1993) *Terminal Identity: The Virtual Subject in Postmodern Science Fiction*. Durham, NC: Duke University Press.

Carnicke, Sharon Marie (1999) 'Lee Strasberg's Paradox of the Actor', in Alan Lovell and Peter Krämer (eds) *Screen Acting*. London: Routledge, 75–87.

Dyer, Richard (1998) *Stars*. London: British Film Institute.

Fischer, Paul (2005) 'Interview: Andy Serkis', *Dark Horizons*, 5 December. Online. Available at: http://www.darkhorizons.com/interviews/624/andy-serkis-for-king-kong. Accessed 14 December 2006.

Grosz, Elizabeth (2001) 'From "The Body of Signification"', in Colin Counsell and Laurie Wolf (eds) *Performance Analysis: An Introductory Coursebook*. London: British Film Institute, 140–5.

Haraway, Donna (1985) 'A Manifesto of Cyborgs: Science, Technology, and Socialist Feminism in the 1980s', *Socialist Review*, 80, 65–108.

Johnson, Gary (2005) 'Movie Review: *King Kong*', *Images* December. Online. Available at: http://www.imagesjournal.com/2005/reviews/kingkong/text.htm. Accessed 20 December 2006.

McGurl, Mark (1996) 'Making It Gig: Picturing the Radio Age in *King Kong*', *Critical Inquiry*, 22, 415–46.

Morton, Ray (2005) *King Kong: History of a Movie Icon from Fay Wray to Peter Jackson*. New York: Applause Books.

Naremore, James (1988) *Acting in the Cinema*. Berkeley: University of California Press.

P., Ken (n. d.) 'Andy Serkis: Interview', *ING: Filmforce*, 27 January. Online. Available at: http://movies.ign.articles/383/38388.htm. Accessed 3 January 2007.

Sobchack, Vivian (2005 [1994]) 'The Scene of the Screen', in Andrew Utterson (ed.) *Technology and Culture: The Film Reader*. London: Routledge, 127–42.

Stanislavski, Constantin (1958 [c. late 1920s]) 'The Art of the Actor and the Art of the Director', in *Stanislavski's Legacy*, ed. and trans. Elizabeth Reynolds Hapgood. New York: Theatre Art Books, 170–82.

____ (1961) *Creating a Role*, trans. Elizabeth Reynolds Hapgood. New York: Theatre Art Books.

____ (1974) *My Life in Art*, trans. J. J. Robbins. New York: Theatre Art Books.

Stout, Andy (2003) 'Motion Capture Comes of Age', *IBE Magazine*, March, 12.

Thompson, John O. (1991 [1978]) 'Screen Acting and the Communication Test', in Christine Gledhill (ed.) *Stardom: Industry of Desire*. London: Routledge, 186–200.

Wake, Jenny (2005) *The Making of King Kong: The Official Guide to the Motion Picture*. New York: Pocket Books.

Willemen, Paul (1994) 'Through the Glass Darkly: Cinephilia Reconsidered', in *Looks and Frictions: Essays in Cultural Studies and Film Theory*. London: British Film Institute, 223–57.

Wuntch, Philip (2005) 'Movie Review: *King Kong*', *Dallas Morning Star*, 13 December. Online. Available at: *Guidelive.com*. http://www.guidelive.com/portal/page. Accessed 20 December 2006.

CHAPTER THIRTEEN

GESTURES AND POSTURES OF MASTERY: CGI AND CONTEMPORARY ACTION CINEMA'S EXPRESSIVE TENDENCIES
Lisa Purse

Action cinema is the site where two types of cinematic pleasure converge for the spectator. The pleasure of witnessing the perfect fantasy of empowerment, as the action hero or heroine shows off their physical and mental prowess to succeed against all odds, combines with the pleasure of experiencing the latest state-of-the-art special effects. Computer-Generated Imagery (CGI) is central to *both* pleasures in contemporary action cinema. But does the way in which the action film shows us the action body and its trials and successes change when that body is fully digitised, digitally enhanced or digitally composited with other image elements? How is the cinematic style of the action sequence changing, and how does this modified style of presentation communicate to the spectator – and perhaps communicate differently – the action body's progress, and other meanings that circulate around the body of the hero – such as power, strength and physical integrity? And where might our pleasure reside in this shifting cinematic territory?

This essay is part of an ongoing investigation into modulations in contemporary action cinema's presentational tendencies that seem to proceed from developments in digital imaging technologies. Indeed, these are modulations that are deeply linked to attempts to engage a more digitally-literate spectator of the action genre. The body in exhilaratingly purposeful physical action has long been central to action cinema's narrative operations, visual pleasures and affective dynamic. Action sequences provide an aspirational, empowering vision of the human body functioning at the extremes of what is physically possible. In the constant rush to produce the most breathtaking spectacles, action blockbusters now draw extensively on CGI to create perceptually realistic but clearly impossible bodies, physical feats and impact-filled interactions. At the same time, we should note that such movies are being watched by a digitally-literate generation of spectators highly aware of the computer-generated nature of key elements of action sequences. In my article 'Digital Heroes in Contemporary Hollywood: Exertion, Identification and the Virtual Action Body' published in *Film Criticism* (2007), I suggested that in recent years, Hollywood has been undergoing a period of negotiation over what kinds of cinematic bodies we can and want to identify with – pro-filmic, digitally 'enhanced', or fully computer-generated. Specifically, I explored the problem that fully computer-generated bodies and their lack of real-world materiality pose for the spectator's identification with the action body's visualised 'narrative of becoming'. I proposed that the spectator's extra-textual knowledge that the action bodies on show are inherently *virtual* threatens to result in an affective flatness to match the accusations of perceptual 'flatness' that still haunt discussions of digital images and digitally-enhanced film worlds.

In this essay, I want to consider some other significant presentational tendencies in contemporary action cinema that seem to similarly emerge from current CGI technologies' specific capacities and capabilities, and the ways in which these tendencies are linked to action cinema's particularly 'embodied' spectator. Using sequences from films such as the *Matrix* trilogy (1999, 2003, 2003) and *X-Men: The Last Stand* (2006) as illustrations, I will suggest that what we are seeing is a more expressive impulse emerging, which tries to find new ways to 'body forth' fantasies of physical achievement and mastery and the 'narrative of becoming' that is traditionally written across the body of the hero. How is the spectator being asked to engage with this 'expressive turn', and how might we critically evaluate it?

From cinema's earliest moments, physicality and bodily motion was framed for the camera's admiring or investigative gaze. The fascination with physiological motion that spurred on Eadweard Muybridge's famous multi-camera experiments is also evident elsewhere in the first decades of film production. The sensational melodramas made between 1900 and 1920 are the most obvious forerunners of the action film. From early one- or two-reelers to the serial films of the late 1910s, sensational melodramas were popular and often controversial for delivering 'abundant rapid action, stimulating violence, spectacular sights, thrills of physical peril, abductions and suspenseful rescues', as Ben Singer describes (2004: 52).[1] Nevertheless, even earlier, the frequency of sports (weightlifting, acrobatics, boxing, juggling) and dance spectacles in film output was already notable, with the Edison Manufacturing Company and others presenting vaudeville-style set pieces in single-reelers such as *Annabelle Serpentine Dance, Athlete with Wand, Unsuccessful Somersault* (a.k.a. *Amateur Gymnast, No. 1*), *Amateur Gymnast, No. 2* and *Souvenir Strip of the Edison Kinetoscope* which featured strong-man Eugen Sandow's feats of might (all released in 1894).

In his seminal essay on the temporality of the pre-1908 'cinema of attractions', Tom Gunning points out that the 'foregrounding of the act of display' was central: 'even the seemingly stylistically neutral film consisting of a single shot without camera tricks involved a cinematic gesture of presenting for view, of displaying' (1999: 73). There is a correlation here between a preoccupation with the moment of display (always inherently also a display of the cinematic technology itself) and a concomitant preoccupation with displaying the 'technology' (physiology, weight, momentum) of the body in motion. The 'pre-eminence of physical performances already organised into *acts*' that Laurent Guido (2006: 142; emphasis added) has observed in these early films points to the performativity of physicality within the frame, and the way in which a moment – a feat of physical strength or skill, an act – functioned as a revelation of the performer's mastery of his or her body. Supplying the opportunity to witness a body functioning at the peak of its powers, such spectacles seemed to speak to a fundamental human desire to exceed the bounds of everyday corporeality. The impulse to master our bodies and (through our bodies) master space, time and the bodies of others was projected onto the powerful pro-filmic body. By summarising, distilling, concentrating the revelation and sum of the performer's skill into a single moment or act that could stand in for the totality of that talented body's capacities, such spectacles constructed a visual shorthand for mastery as a condensed 'becoming-powerful'. I would like to term this a 'gesture of mastery' that was routinely gendered, racialised and class-inflected.

Thus what Gunning calls early cinema's 'cinematic gesture of presentation' (1999: 73), itself a technological 'becoming', becomes the presentation of a *gesture* of physical mastery, a body framed in the moment of 'becoming'. In subsequent decades, as Steve Neale has noted, the action genre has continued to be defined by its 'propensity for spectacular physical action ... [and] emphasis in performance on athletic feats and stunts' (2000: 52), providing a fitting outlet for our desire to witness and celebrate these physical gestures of mastery. Indeed, the process of 'becoming' encapsulated by such gestures of mastery has structured both the narrative and the visual presentation of the hero. That is, the action film constructs a visual 'narrative of becoming', of mastery as *process*. The action hero is transformed into a heroic body through events within the film's duration, where 'becoming' is the process of proving your heroic capacities through action the spectator witnesses. Periods of training and honing of physical and technical skills, strategic thinking and developing resolve are elliptically condensed into a series of moments – both the action sequences and the physical 'acts' within them – in which the body enacts its process of becoming, proving its heroism through the assertion of gestures of mastery. This series of acts, of bodily gestures, is also emphatically a *flow* of action. The action hero's agency and its becoming manifest themselves in the directional force of the body in motion. The speed of the narrative's forward momentum (punctuated at regular intervals by the action sequences) works with the fast rhythms of the action sequences themselves to communicate (visually and metaphorically) the flow of the body towards its inevitable and reassuring achievement of resolution-enabling mastery and control.

There is a tension in action cinema between this flow, this process(ion) of gestures and the static *postures* of mastery that function as attempts to consolidate our awareness of the heroic body's control. From the sword-pointing stance of the swashbuckling hero in films like *The Mark of Zorro* (1920), *The Adventures of Robin Hood* (1938) and *The Flame and the Arrow* (1950), to the cowboy's gun-toting posture in countless westerns, to the battle-ready poses of the muscle-bound 1980s action heroes in the *Rambo* films (1982, 1985, 1988), *Commando* (1985) and *Predator* (1987), these expansive, declarative poses attempt to assert the hero's mastery over his or her body, the space and, by extension, the situation. In their 'anticipatory stillness' or 'stilled-ness', to borrow Vivian Sobchack's terms (2006: 342), these postures signal the limitless potential of the body ready for action, a symbol of about-to-be-demonstrated potency. But in their very stilled-ness, they also point unwittingly to the other kinds of stasis the action body risks, which continually haunt the hero's narrative of becoming – a loss of momentum or control, injury or even death. Peter Lehman (1993) observes that this anxiety is present in all visual representations of active masculinity, which are polarised between the spectacular assertion of phallic power and the corresponding collapse of that power. But, in fact, within the representational framework of the action movie 'mastery and power' are always 'directly contrasted with the loss of control' whether the action hero is male *or* female, as Jason Jacobs has pointed out (2000: 12). Thus, the action body must anxiously enact a dramatic oscillation between power and weakness, intactness and the loss of physical integrity. Within this process, the progression towards or possession of power and control are asserted through a series of gestures and postures of mastery that attempt to point away from the possibilities of the body's failure.

As I have suggested, action cinema is traditionally visually and narratively invested in the physical 'work' of the action body and the explicitly-figured exertion, endurance and pain involved in its 'becoming-powerful'. The action film's embodied spectator is also invested in that work, and his or her identification with the physical processes and exertions on display is a central exhilarating pleasure of the genre. Especially relevant here is Vivian Sobchack's formulation of the spectator as a sense-making body 'that, *in experience*, lives vision always in co-operation and significant exchange with other sensorial means of access to the world' (2004: 59; emphasis in original). Writing within a phenomenological framework that characterises perception as inherently embodied, Sobchack describes the spectator's experience of watching a film:

> Reciprocating the figurally literal representations of bodies and worldly things in the cinema, the spectator's lived body in the film experience ... fills in the gap in its sensual grasp of the figural world onscreen by turning back on itself to reciprocally ·(albeit not sufficiently) 'flesh it out' into literal physicalised sense. (2004: 82)[2]

Sobchack's description is supported by other writers, including Laura U. Marks, who characterises spectatorship as always 'embodied and multisensory' (2000: 172; see also 222). Sarah Rubidge anchors a similar assertion in the evidence of, among others, a group of Italian neuroscientists who 'discovered a group of neurons in the frontal cortex called "mirror neurons" [within which] the same patterning of neuronal activity is activated … whether the action is being viewed or enacted by the subject' (2006: 114).[3] This responsive (if always incomplete) 'fleshing out', in Sobchack's terms, of the experiences depicted on the screen is precisely what makes action cinema's explicit displays of physical action and exertion so compelling. The spectator identifies sensorially with each success-ful move, leap and impact, and with the hero's physical and emotional trajectory towards achieving full occupation of the action body. And to make this possible, the depiction of action bears a relationship to realistic notions of the impacts and bodily consequences of exertion, collision and violence, in order to authenticate the active body in biologically credible terms. It is not a direct correlation, but a referencing towards real-world physical correspondences of weight, momentum, force and the materiality of bodies and objects[4] within a representational frame-work that allows those correspondences to be slightly exceeded in the interests of the fantasies of empowerment the genre is intended to supply.

In the Chesapeake Bay Bridge sequence in *Mission: Impossible III* (2006), for example, digital effects are used to convey the physical forces at work on the action body and that body's resilience in broadly 'realistic' terms. Ethan (Tom Cruise) sprints towards the camera away from a vehicle that is about to be hit by a rocket. The camera simultaneously dollies back, bringing a parked car into view frame right. As the rocket hits, a huge fireball rips the vehicle behind Ethan apart, and the force of the explosion slams him into the side of the parked car. Ethan falls to the ground, but amazingly springs straight back up as a helicopter crosses overhead, circling for the next round of rocket attacks. The bridge, explo-sion and Cruise's stunt-work were shot separately – with the actor's body, the car and the ground all padded for safe impact. Digital compositing brought these elements together in a single image. The padding was digitally painted out, and additional dust and shock wave effects were added (see Alducin 2006). Both the physiological resilience displayed by Ethan's body and the forces that work on him maintain a relationship to real-world correspondences that anchors the spec-tator's identification with the hero's physical exertions, a relationship forcefully asserted by the digital compositing work as much as by other filmic elements. Such sequences represent the impulse towards photorealistic verisimilitude that characterises some contemporary movies' articulation of action, in which digital imaging technologies become simply a further tool at the filmmakers' disposal for this purpose.

However, enabled by these same digital imaging technologies, an increasing number of movies have started to display an opposing impulse to articulate action in more expressive ways. This more expressive mode significantly pulls apart the relationship to real-world correspondences. Kristen Whissel has explored contemporary mainstream cinema's expanded use of the vertical axis to dramatise relations of power, a 'new verticality' as she calls it, which is made possible by digital effects and is much less concerned with sustaining 'realistic' real-world correspondences. Interestingly, Whissel also indicates the possibilities for meaning that are created by such filmic decisions, proposing that 'precisely by defying verisimilitude, the new verticality lends these films a *different sort of truth* – a symbolic or emotional one that mediates present geopolitical reality' (2006: 25; emphasis added). What are the implications of this kind of stylistic shift for the body-centred universe of the action film and the meanings that circulate within it? In foregoing verisimilitude, can action movies still provide us with a narrative of becoming that is rooted in the physicality of the body and still convey, sensorially, the work of the action body?

To answer this, I want to take a detour into a consideration of dance and the dance spectator. Action cinema has a relationship to certain dance-related forms in a number of ways. Its presentation of physicality as spectacle, and its structure, which José Arroyo pertinently notes is 'built around set pieces' (2000: 23–4), have invited comparisons with the musical. We might also note that it borrows the term (and arguably the principles of) *choreography* in its design of combat scenes and orchestration of different elements in action sequences. But dance itself might offer insights into the tendency towards the expressive use of movement, gestures and postures in contemporary action films. Mary Douglas has signalled the extensiveness of the body's symbolic potential, observing that the body is 'a complex structure' – the 'functioning of the different parts [of which] afford it a rich source of symbols for other complex structures' (1970: 138). Dance, as a body-centred art form, necessarily exploits this symbolic potential to the full. In her influential book *The Phenomenology of Dance* (1966) Maxine Sheets-Johnstone explains how this is achieved through a process of abstracting 'the forms of actual human feelings which are abstracted from their everyday context in order to be created and presented symbolically, and ... the movement which is abstracted from its everyday expressive context to become an expressive medium of dance' (1979: 58). More recently, Ted Polhemus roots dance's principle of abstraction in a more explicit socio-cultural context, stating that while 'physical culture' is 'the embodiment of society', dance functions as a kind of second stage, 'a scheme, an abstraction or stylising of physical culture' (1993: 7).

Both writers indicate how dance's abstract form is drawn from the ways in which bodies move and are moved, literally and metaphorically, within the spatial, social and ideological structures of culture. As a result, through the dancer's body arranged in space and time, in rhythm, motion and stillness, dance is able to achieve complexity of meaning despite the abstract nature of the form. Is this strategy – of deploying expressive movement in an abstract mode to convey cultural ideas about physicality and the body – transferable to other cultural forms, such as the action film? I think it is, and mapping out some of the correlations between action cinema and dance will help us to see this possibility more clearly.

For dancer and theorist Erin Manning 'our bodies are vectors of emergence that generate virtual embodiments in a future anterior we can only reach towards' (2007: 120), full of radical potential to exceed the bounds of fixed cultural definitions and categories. In the often rather politically conservative context of the action genre, the body is still celebrated for its potentialities, its 'virtual embodiments'. The action body vibrates with the future possibilities of its own becoming, the pleasures of anticipation rewarded as the action body subsequently fulfils or exceeds some of its imagined potentialities. If dance is, then, inherently a physicalised process of becoming, Sheets-Johnstone suggests that, for the dancer, 'consciousness exists its body in movement as a form continuously projecting itself toward a spatial-temporal future; hence, as a *form-in-the-making*' (1979: 36; emphasis added). This has its correlation in the action hero's corporeal process of becoming towards full occupancy of the action body across the narrative – what we might call a *body-in-the-making*. Sheets-Johnstone also resonantly describes dance as fundamentally a 'perpetual revelation of force' (1978: 88). In its presentation of the dancer as inherently agile, skilled and controlled, dance constructs images of force and fantasies of empowerment[5] that are rooted in the physical – conveying notions of strength, agency and control that are equally crucial to the construction of the action body. Moreover, this revelation of force creates 'a dynamic line … not an actual line, but "line" in the sense of an ongoing projection of forces from a beginning point' (Sheets-Johnstone 1979: 88). This approximates both to the visual line traced by the action body as it moves through space and time in each action sequence, and to what I earlier called the action body's 'flow' towards full mastery and control that structures the narrative.

Equally, from Sheets-Johnstone on, several writers have argued for an embodied 'spectator' for dance, close to the theories Sobchack and Marks have advanced for cinema. The dance spectator identifies with the corporeal experiences and movements of the dancer, her projection of force and her control in motion, through a mode of kinaesthetic identification – kinaesthesia being the sensation by which bodily position, momentum and movement are perceived. Cynthia Novack, for example, remarks, 'anyone who watches dance may feel kinaesthetic identification, simply because all people move with their bodies' (1993: 37). What is implicit in Novack's comment is that this kinaesthetic identification also depends on synaesthesia. That is, the dance spectator imaginatively responds to the images of the dance obtained through the sense of sight with his or her other senses (primarily the kinaesthetic, haptic and proprioceptive senses). Similarly, cinema, in Laura U. Marks' words, 'appeals to the integration and commutation of sensory experience within the body' through its basic, ever-repeating act of 'appealing to one sense in order to represent the experience of another' (2000: 222). Marks has pointed out that this sensual and sensory engagement is rooted in the ways we make sense of the world (figuratively and literally), and, significantly, that abstraction in itself does not prevent this embodied sense-making process from taking place:

> As [Walter] Benjamin and [Maurice] Merleau-Ponty argued in different contexts, a mimetic and synesthetic [sic] relationship to the world underlies language and other sign systems. Once that relationship is mediated through an image, multisensory experience is condensed into visual form ... We are constantly recreating the world in our bodies, even as our representational systems become more abstract ... cinema is a mimetic medium, capable of drawing us into sensory participation with its world even more than is written language. Images are fetishes, which the reader can translate – more or less, depending on how her own experience is embodied – into sensuous experience. (2000: 214–15)

Dance shows us how the body in motion might be deployed expressively or in an abstract mode to convey meaning without losing an embodied engagement with the body, since kinaesthetic identification can still take place. In action cinema, the literal work of the action body and its gestures and postures of mastery already stand in for more abstract notions of empowerment, assertiveness and agency that are also tied into issues of race, gender, sexuality and nationhood. Thus, a more expressive use of the body could be seen to build on certain existing strategies of meaning production. In the light of the preceding discussion of dance, we can say that the shift towards a more expressive style in a popular strand of contemporary action cinema consists of two interrelated presentational tendencies. Firstly, the use of digital imaging technologies to render action sequences which have a much more tenuous link with real-world correspondences, particularly in relation to the articulation of the action body. Secondly, a concurrent taking-on of the strategies for expressive use of the body that are present in dance – movement, rhythm, spatial arrangements, tableaux of momentarily stilled bodies, and so on.

But is there a particular reason why we see this development now? Certainly the martial arts film's significant influence on the articulation of the action sequences in films such as *The Matrix* (1999) and *Kill Bill, Vol. 1 & 2* (2003, 2004) has prepared the spectator for physical movements which sometimes have less direct reference to real-world correspondences. However, the main factors at work in the move towards an expressive mode are much more closely related to digital special effects' capabilities, and action cinema's desire to maintain the spectator's embodied identification with the work of the action body. If the fully computer-generated body incurs the digitally-literate spectator's incredulity, then it follows that digital effects' enhancements of the body's capabilities incur equal scepticism. While the spectator may well still enjoy the pleasures of the display of digital cinematic technologies that these digitally-enhanced action sequences provide, the verisimilitude of photorealist sequences does not have the same affective impact on the spectator as a pro-filmic event. The sensorial connection with the striving body of the action hero is in danger of dissipating, with a concomitant negative impact on the spectator's engagement with the hero's narrative of becoming. So in response, some films are no longer even attempting verisimilitude, instead adopting an expressive style that can still speak forcefully and dynamically of the action body's narrative of becoming – but in a much more abstract, more stylised form.

Earlier in this essay, I described how flow and stasis characterise the construction of the action body, implicit in his or her *moving* gestures and *static* postures of mastery. These notions structure his or her becoming across the film as a whole, in terms of the flow towards complete mastery and control punctuated at various moments by the stasis caused by obstacles that prevent progress. As I have already indicated, this flow and stasis also characterises the rhythm of the action sequences themselves: flow in the action body's projection of force and stasis in the hero's postures of mastery. So in the patterning of action into rhythms – that is, rhythmic oscillations between flow and stasis – the action sequence is already open to more expressive modulations of its basic shape. Is this the case with other aspects of film style conventionally associated with the action sequence? Traditionally, special effects have made possible the depiction of physical feats just beyond normal corporeal capacities. In the kind of contemporary action sequence that persists in trying to achieve verisimilitude, digital imaging technologies simply continue the work of traditional special effects. However, digital special effects have the capacity to provide a quite different kind of spectacle, indeed to jettison verisimilitude completely, thus opening up the possibility of a more expressive style.

Slow motion is another key aspect of film style with a long history in action cinema, slowing down time to emphasise a particular feat of speed or strength. It draws our attention to the striking athleticism inherent in physical motion, fetishising the workings of muscle groups, physiological extension, and the empowered exuberance of the powerful, agile body. While showing the body accelerating or moving at speed gives a sense of the body's momentum and *force*, slowing doesn't 'decelerate' those connotations but instead draws them into a more focused view. In other words, slowing simply fetishises the moment of force, the moment of becoming. Digital imaging technologies have modulated the deployment of slow motion in the action sequence. Digitally assisted slow motion takes traditional slow motion one step further, in that it allows a slowing of movement to the point of stillness without compromising the photorealism (or verisimilitude) of the film image. Contemporary action movies frequently deploy digital slow motion in this way and often modulate between different slow motion speeds within the same shot.

What are the consequences of this more expressive, more hyperbolic mode of slow motion deployment? Laura Mulvey observes that 'new moving image technologies, the electronic and the digital, paradoxically allow an easy return to the hidden stillness of the film frame' (2006: 66). She suggests that this has some implications for the spectator on a metaphysical level, a suggestion that requires unpicking in relation to action cinema's expressive use of digital slow motion. Mulvey points out that cinema's contradictory nature – consisting of a series of still frames but creating the illusion of movement, using filmed past events to create the illusion of events unfolding in the present – has always troublingly pointed to the final stillness of death, even as it insistently communicated present-ness of movement. 'As stillness intrudes into movement, the image freezes into the "stop of death" ... The blurred boundaries between the living and the not-living touch on unconscious anxieties that then circulate as fascination as well as fear in the cultures of the uncanny' (2006: 32).[6] For Mulvey, digital technologies return us to this metaphysical finality that the stilled film image can call up. And yet the stillness offered at the epicentre of a digitally assisted slow-motion shot or sequence is the 'before' of motion's 'after' – in that what will follow is the continuation of the flow of the action body's gesture of mastery. Digital slow motion may look as if it is bringing motion almost to a halt, but it is, as Sobchack suggests, 'hyperbolis[ing] movement by "forestalling" and "distilling" it to what seems its essence' (2004: 337). While the earliest body-focused one-reelers distilled physical mastery into a single 'gesture', digitally-assisted slow motion is doing the same with movement, distilling it to its essence. Since this is simply a 'forestallment', this essence resonates with its own potential – the potency of movement-about-to-happen.

We might recall Muybridge's multi-camera experiments here. In his analysis of physiological motion, Muybridge 'froze' the different phases of motion in a series of still photographs. And yet, what is most potent about Muybridge's chronophotography is that the subject registers not as a stilled entity (no longer moving) but as an entity whose movement is forestalled, the still image conveying the potency of movement-about-to-happen. For example, in *Human and Animal Locomotion* plate 626, 'thoroughbred bay mare Annie G. galloping' (1887), the horse's physical power and potential for graceful, vigorous motion was distilled into its essence in the still image series.[7] The stilled-ness of these images revealed the natural wonder of movement itself – perhaps this is one of the reasons why there has been such fascination with *re-animating* these series of photographs in recent years.[8]

More than a century later, digital slow motion invites us to take time out of the high speeds of contemporary life, to wonder anew at the corporeal technology of movement fetishised to the extreme. As Sobchack asserts, 'against the increasing accelerations of cinematic and social life, the operations and effects of [digitally-enhanced] slow motion visibly and sensually interrogate those accelerations in what seems a "revelation" – not of immobility or stillness, but of the "essential" *movement of movement* itself' (2006: 342; emphasis in original). Of course, this intense fetishisation of movement that digital slow motion gives rise to is by its very nature a disavowal of the 'stop of death' haunting the film screen, thus proving Mulvey's thesis in its underlying impulse. But it also fetishises movement rather than stillness, thus operating differently from more avant-garde responses to and explorations of digital technology's capacities to still and to freeze.[9] I want now to explore the consequences of digital slow motion's expressive fetishisation of movement (through the temporary stilling of the body) more closely, since it produces a kind of paradox in relation to the gestures and postures of mastery the body has traditionally adopted in action cinema. To illustrate this, I want to consider some key sequences from *The Matrix*, a film that is an originating moment in the history of this recent 'expressive turn' in contemporary action cinema. Through this film, we can identify some of the resulting stylistic tendencies.

Near the beginning of *The Matrix*, the resistance fighter Trinity (Carrie-Anne Moss) is cornered in a room by a squad of police officers. Despite being seated, her striking costume (of black, figure-hugging PVC), her straight-backed, confident posture and her composed, determined expression already hint at her physical potency. Minutes after the police lieutenant – waiting outside the building – confidently remarks, 'I think we can handle one little girl' (rebutted by an agent's assurance that 'your men are already dead'), Trinity proves her deadly power by bursting suddenly into action and dispatching each officer in the room with speedy efficiency. While the sequence as a whole functions as a *gesture* of Trinity's mastery (the flow of her force towards successful debilitation of all the officers) it is punctuated by the *postures* of mastery Trinity adopts at key moments. Indeed, in the most significant attack against the first police officer, her actions are broken into three clear postures of mastery, and one of these serves as a 'signature' posture symbolising Trinity's empowered physicality. The first two postures occur in real time, as the abrupt but devastating movements that disarm and then disable the officer seem to be held briefly at the point of impact. First a *chop* to the police officer's gun arm, next a further forceful extension of Trinity's arm to *smash in* the officer's nose with the flat of her hand. Then, in the movie's first use of the bullet-time special effect (for which it subsequently became famous), the camera rotates around Trinity as she rises up into the air in slow motion, extending her arms out and pulling her knees up to assume the most emphatic posture of mastery – that is, of about-to-be-demonstrated potency – in the sequence. A savage kick follows that sends the officer flying across the room and into the opposite wall. Digital effects achieve this spectacle as bullet-time digitally combines images from a series of still cameras arranged around the body to create the illusion of motion, captured by a notional camera traversing a path mapped out by a computer.

In the context of what I have discussed so far, two things are significant in the resulting onscreen images. Firstly, as Trinity gathers herself physically to unleash her deadly kick, the deployment of digital slow motion to emphasise (fetishise) the empowered body-in-motion converges with the presentation of a static stance of about-to-be-demonstrated potency, in a single moment of display. Trinity's body is still in motion but is slowed to the point that her gesture of mastery (the action of kicking the police officer) starts to signify also as a posture of mastery. Thus, digital imaging technologies have created the conditions to allow for a *conflation* of the gesture of mastery (the body in action, in motion) and the posture of mastery (a body stance). Secondly, the arrangement of bodies in space clearly articulates the power relations at work at this crucial point. As Trinity rises *above* the stunned police officer, her spatial positioning in relation to his earthbound stasis emphatically illustrates that she has the upper hand. This seems in line with the 'spatialisation of power' that Kristen Whissel notes as characteristic of the 'new verticality' she has identified in contemporary movies featuring digital effects (2006: 26). Whissel points out that current digital effects technologies 'have helped liberate many aspects of production from the laws of physics, allowing for much more pronounced and sustained exploitation of the screen's vertical axis' so that opposing forces are mapped onto the co-ordinates of 'height and depth' (2006: 25). Of course, as the term spatialisation implies, it is not just the vertical axis that is being used in digitally-enhanced action sequences. Digital effects are thus helping to arrange bodies spatially across various axes, and are generating more fluid articulations and conflations of the action body's gestures and postures of mastery.

For example, Neo's transformation into a heroic body in *The Matrix* is mapped onto a vertical axis. But in order to fully account for the way Neo's narrative of becoming is represented to the spectator, we need to consider how that becoming is spatialised and also take account of the communicative potential of the body positions adopted. In the opening action sequence already mentioned, Trinity's posture of mastery involves a rising into the air and an opening out of the body into an attack formation – arms frame (and thus claim mastery over) the space while legs pull into the body, ready to deliver her forceful kick. She is presented to us as an already fully-fledged action body, already a master of the technique she has adopted, and already 'assigned' a posture of mastery that sig-nifies that technique. It is against Trinity's declarative mid-air posture and forceful gestures of mastery that Neo (Keanu Reeves) is compared and declared at the start of the film as emphatically *not* an action body. He knows nothing about the matrix program that is holding him and millions of other humans prisoner in their own minds, but also significantly knows nothing about how to 'be' a heroic body. Thus, once 'unplugged' from the matrix program, the focus is on getting Neo to rise, literally within the matrix (for example the training test to jump between two high-rise buildings), and metaphorically to the challenge of being the 'One'. His training regime involves being taught numerous combat techniques that are recognisable by the postures they adopt, such as kickboxing and various types of martial arts, and it is clear that from these Neo will choose a posture that will signify his growing mastery.

As we move through the film, Neo's growing control of his action body is signalled in terms of his ability to rise. While his bullet-dodging during the res-cue of Morpheus (Laurence Fishburne) sees his feet still firmly rooted to the ground, later in the subway tunnel confrontation with Agent Smith (Hugo Weav-ing) he rises to a mid-air grapple several feet off the subway station's floor, having declared his intent with a martial arts-style posture of battle-readiness. By the end of the movie, Neo is punching the air with his fist in a posture of mastery that is emphatically declarative of his new powers, before rocketing up into the sky (and out of frame). So the very mechanics of the action hero's depiction – the gestures and postures of mastery – are incorporated rather self-consciously into the narrative itself through Neo's training, while the form these gestures and postures take onscreen is also directly informative. Neo's movement into the sky functions as a fitting visual signal that he has surpassed the vertical range of both Trinity and Morpheus (and, it follows, their levels of skill within the matrix). But the space within which Neo's mastery is defined is larger than Trinity's too, giv-ing a further clue to their future trajectories as action bodies. In Trinity's opening scene, the camera rotates around her, marking out the space within which she claims her position of mastery as about four or five feet square. In comparison, in the subway confrontation, the camera arcs around Neo and Agent Smith much more expansively, marking out a space of mastery that is much larger, and this is also true of the camera rotation around Neo as he dodges bullets during the rooftop rescue of Morpheus. So this is a declaration of empowerment that does not simply depend on verticality, but is figured spatially in very specific and rela-tive ways that can communicate a great deal about characters' relative status and narrative trajectories.

In my discussion of Trinity's conflated gesture-posture of mastery, I noted how her power over the correspondingly weaker police officers is signalled by her ability to literally rise above them. As bullet-time slows down the action, the

presentation of Trinity's spatial position in relation to the cowering officer functions like a *tableau vivant* of stilled bodies, frozen in a declarative clarification
of the power relations between them at this moment. This is one effect of the
slowing-unto-stilled-ness characteristic of digitally assisted slow motion in this
more expressive action cinema: over time the visual field becomes punctuated
by moments of slow motion that produce tableaux (often three dimensional, if
combined with a spatialising camera movement) of bodies and other scenic elements. Such *tableaux vivants* speak of the shifts in power relations that are taking place in the narrative between characters in confrontation with each other
and also, equally importantly, communicate the power relations that each body is
trying to *assert* in a particular encounter. Narrative information is thus 'imported'
into the action sequence, shaping its mechanics in expressive ways in terms of
the spatial arrangements and physical attitudes of the bodies depicted.

In *X-Men: The Last Stand* telepath Charles Xavier (Patrick Stewart) undertakes a dangerous meeting with Jean Grey (Famke Janssen), a telepath with
telekinetic powers of unknown magnitude who has been possessed by her evil
dark side, Phoenix. Charles' attempt to control Phoenix fails – she lifts him into
the air using telekinesis and then slowly vaporises his body. Digital slow motion
is used to decelerate movement at the crucial second when Xavier's powers can
clearly no longer protect him. The camera is initially positioned between the two
characters, and first frames Phoenix as her face darkens and contorts with the
final annihilating effort. This empowered moment is conveyed visually through
her raising of her arms. Like Trinity, she effectively frames the space with her
arms, thus claiming mastery over it. In contrast, as the camera pans round to
bring Charles into view, we see he is suspended in midair (verticality here reversing its connotative co-ordinates), his helplessness signalled by arms that hover
limply at his sides while the force of Phoenix's powers distorts his facial muscles like G-force in a fighter plane. This is a three-dimensional tableau that is not
framed in its totality initially, but is established gradually over a few seconds as
the camera moves around the stilled bodies – stilled at the point that the power
mismatch between them is most starkly drawn, the moment's 'becoming' elaborated at dramatic length.

As the preceding discussion should demonstrate, these tableaux of momentarily stilled characters give the spectator the time to absorb the details of the
scene. That is, they allow increased contemplation of each body's corporeal attitude and orientation, its projection backwards or forwards, each character's facial
expression and their spatial relation to other elements and bodies. In our interpretive task, we must be alive to the ways in which these details that we are invited
to contemplate so intently work expressively to produce meaning. Moreover, the
co-ordinates of such tableaux and the gestures and postures of mastery they are
so often grounded in can be expressively modulated in the service of the narra-

tive and its tales of empowerment gained and lost. For example, we might look at the expressive modulations evident in the depiction of Neo and Trinity's action bodies in the transition from *The Matrix* to its sequel *The Matrix Reloaded* (2003). The sequel quickly confirms that Neo has surpassed Trinity in ability and status, as plot developments early in the film explicitly relocate her as one of Neo's support team rather than distinguishing her as an empowered action body in her own right. However, this shift in status is conveyed much more powerfully through the design and orchestration of the action sequences in *Reloaded*, especially in relation to the key action sequences of *The Matrix*. In comparison with her definitively ascendant attacking pose in the opening sequence of the first film, Trinity's gradually declining status (concordant with a movement towards being 'only' a sidekick and love interest for Neo) is given emphatic and repeated visual expression in her spatial downward trajectory across *Reloaded*'s action sequences.

Near the beginning of the second film, Trinity uses a motorcycle to catapult herself into the air, but only in order to reach the ground quicker, to surprise security guards in a resistance operation to shut down a power station. She stays earthbound thereafter, running down corridors, walking through nightclubs, biking along the freeway. At the same time, her signature posture of mastery is being commandeered by others – by villains fighting Neo in the baroque lobby of the Merovingian's palace, and most explicitly by Morpheus in the freeway chase sequence. Directly mimicking Trinity's signature move, Morpheus rises above an agent in slow motion, arms raised, preparing to deliver a decisive kick in the fight atop a moving truck. And in a reversal of the process of becoming, Trinity's posture of mastery is literally turned on its head in her death fall towards the end of the film. Encountering an agent in an office block, Trinity delivers her signature kick, but it is not enough to disable the agent who begins to overpower her. In a desperate attempt to flee, Trinity leaps backwards out of the high-rise building, her guns still blazing at the agent as she goes into freefall. Her positioning and orientation underline her change of fortune: her upturned pose is a striking inversion of her original posture of mastery. Her legs are no longer drawn into the body poised to strike, while her arms are outstretched in front of her as if still trying to master the space, signalling along with her facial expression the defiance she feels even at this moment of defeat. Meanwhile, the agent has leapt out of the window after her, his body (and gun sight) bearing down on her. Shot in slow motion, this tableau clarifies the power relationship between them, subsequently confirmed by one of the agent's bullets finding its target and piercing Trinity's heart. Such expressive modulations between action sequences are thus communicative in themselves, while also building on the complexity of meaning achieved through each action sequence's communicative range of digitally assisted elements – which convey not just power relations, but characters' attitudes as they struggle for supremacy or control.

Thus far in my exploration of contemporary action cinema's expressive turn, I have focused on the ways in which the deployment of digital technologies in the expressive design and orchestration of action sequences has brought us into meaningful engagement with the action body's narrative of becoming. This is a result of the expressive mode's increased capacity to work on both abstract and literal levels in the construction of meaning. But occasionally, this mode is deployed in a way that problematises the action genre's central investment in the body as a locus (eventual or immediate) of power and control. The action body is expected to progress towards mastery of itself, its adversaries and the spaces and elements of the landscape. However, some expressive articulations of this process – in the ever-present context of the commercial imperative to pro-vide progressively ever more 'spectacular' sequences – can unwittingly mobilise meanings that counteract the primacy of the body. Perhaps as a response to the fact that the impacts and bodily consequences of exertion, collision and violence can no longer be realistically conveyed in a way that will not be knowingly decon-structed by the digitally-literate spectator, some films instead present large-scale clashes of opposing forces designed to pull the spectator into embodied engage-ment by their very *scale*.

Let us consider an example of this type of large-scale expressive articulation, the climactic battle between Neo and Agent Smith in *The Matrix Revolutions* (2003), which will decide (as seems always to be the case in these things) the future of mankind. Neo is at the peak of his powers, but it is not clear whether he will be able to overcome the seemingly unstoppable Smith. Their equally matched status is conveyed by their spiralling mid-air wrestling, which confirms through visual metaphor that neither is able to sustain the upper hand for long. The uncertainty of the outcome is dramatically prolonged over the duration of the confrontation using rhythmic repetition and visual mirroring of postures and gestures of mastery between the two characters. A series of tableaux punctuate the flow of the battle, symbolising the pendulum of fortune as it swings between them: Agent Smith landing a blow on Neo, Neo making contact with a kick, both frozen as their fists hurtle towards each other, and so on. Interestingly, they also mimic each other, or perhaps more accurately, exchange postures and gestures of mastery. Both rise into the air in an assertion of attempted mastery. Both throw each other into buildings and into the ground. Both recover and fly back into the fray with renewed vigour. The sequence uses scale to convey in more abstract terms the physical stakes the heroes are labouring under. As the fight increases in intensity, their impacts create shockwaves through the city and its environs that manifest as giant expanding bubbles of rainwater and debris. But there are consequences of depicting this confrontation on such a grand scale. The power struggle is so representationally overdetermined that the *mise-en-scène* becomes strangely bare as they fight each other in the empty spaces

between monolithic buildings and in the sky above the city. What is lost immediately is a sense of the exertion and agility required to move at speed through
a textured landscape of obstacles and bodies. Moreover, as the film tries harder
and harder to show the magnitude of the forces involved and the impact the
battle is having on the diegetic environment, Neo and Smith's bodies are often
reduced to dots barely visible in the distance. Our literal distance from the characters creates a correlative imaginative distance from their exertions – that is,
the work of the body that underpins the narrative trajectory of the sequence.
These overdetermined, excessive, inflated, rather grandiose images become – in
a sense – *too* abstract, and actually work against an embodied engagement with
the action body.

The final section of *X-Men: The Last Stand* similarly uses large-scale imagery
to convey the enormity of the task the action bodies are undertaking. 'Good'
mutants and their armed human allies are pitted against an army of 'bad' mutants
fighting to get to a young boy who has the ability to 'cure' any mutant. With hundreds on each side the battle initially unfolds as a series of infantry manoeuvres.
Gestures and postures of mastery come thick and fast as scores of mutants
assume combat-ready poses and throw themselves into battle. Later, as some
are penetrated by mutant-cure bullets, their bodies rearrange themselves into
limp configurations to convey their loss of mutant power. In the course of events,
not just characters but the larger structures of the scenery – cars, debris and
chunks of buildings – become drawn into the vortex of the battle. Perhaps aware
of the risks inherent in such a large-scale spectacle, the filmmakers try to engineer a direct return to the action body in the battle sequence's final moments.
The bad mutants have been defeated, but the powerful Phoenix is still standing
and enraged by the human soldiers' attempts to shoot her with their mutant-cure
bullets. She begins to vaporise everything and everyone in the vicinity. The only
mutant who can stop her is Wolverine (Hugh Jackman), whose powers include
the ability to quickly self-heal. In the centre of the smoke and debris-strewn battlefield, Wolverine edges painfully up towards Phoenix as she tries to vaporise
him too. Bits of skin and muscle fragment away from his metal skeleton and then
reappear again as his body repeatedly attempts to heal itself. The undulating revelations of Wolverine's insides under his skin are clearly attempts to return us viscerally to notions of corporeality, physical vulnerability and mortality. But in a film
where the distance from real-world correspondences is so pronounced, seeing
Wolverine's skin stripped away does not resonate with the body horror it might
have in another context. For the digitally-literate spectator, this is more likely to
be enjoyed as a neat bit of special effects work, rather than being experienced as
an emphatic return to the body – particularly since the expressive mode adopted
in the film as a whole constantly points *away* from the body.

Throughout *X-Men: The Last Stand*, mutant power manifests in large-scale effects – the manipulation of large structures, giant weather phenomena, massive shockwaves – that dwarf the bodies of those supposedly controlling such elements. In the most memorable sequence of the movie, where Magneto (Ian McKellen) rips the Golden Gate Bridge entirely from its original moorings and moves it to gain access to an island medical facility, the bodies of the characters are hardly visible. The film is careful to try to anchor the sequence in bodily risk by bookending it with shots of an endangered family in a car on the bridge. But the central segment of the sequence focuses almost entirely on the bridge itself – towering, creaking and buckling as it is wrenched from its moorings and loses its structural integrity. Bodies, where they are visible, are small by comparison with this massive structure and the giant forces that are controlling it. If we consider this alongside the film's recurring visual preoccupation with bodies obliterated into tiny fragments (Phoenix's killings of Scott (James Marsden), Xavier and scores of others), then what the expressive design seems most to reveal in *The Last Stand* – if unwittingly – is the *insignificance* of the body of the action hero.

Hollywood is grappling with its new powers – the expressive potentialities of the digitally-assisted action spectacle. The visual terrain of action cinema has always incorporated a symbolic 'language' of sorts, with physical action expressed in gestures and postures of mastery that reach beyond the acts themselves to speak of the action hero's becoming. But in the magic box of digital imaging technologies, contemporary action cinema has found a newly expanded visual language with which to articulate the action body's physicality, and its oscillation between power and its loss, integrity and penetration. In an expressive mode, action sequences work increasingly on the level of the abstract and the metaphorical as well as the literal. Thus, collectively and individually, such sequences become richly communicative, mapping out shifting hierarchies of power as well as characters' attitudes to themselves, their bodies and to other characters – in each environment and confrontation.

The expressive mode offers exciting possibilities for new and potentially radical articulations of the action body. But there are risks, as we have seen, for those filmmakers who would put large-scale spectacle before the body in this mode. And in amongst the inevitable stylistic cross-pollination between different strands of output in contemporary action cinema, we see the expressive turn starting to subtly infiltrate elsewhere. The incorporation of 'le parkour' performers and sequences in films like *Casino Royale* (2006) and *The Bourne Ultimatum* (2007) is one example. *Le parkour*, also known as 'free running', is a sport that involves traversing the urban landscape by running, jumping and climbing across rooftops, walls and other city structures. It requires athleticism, gymnastic ability and considerable nerve, and provides striking spectacles of graceful, fluid and seemingly gravity-defying physical motion. *Le parkour*'s appearance in certain action sequences feels like an attempt to mobilise the connotative potential inherent in the expressive mode by replicating 'for real' some of the expressive (and impossible) movements that the action body enacts with the help of digital special effects in other films. We must wait to see how these stylistic exchanges between different strands of contemporary action cinema will play out across our screens, but in the meantime we can celebrate the ways in which the expressive turn orients us differently in relation to our bodies and environments. If our pleasure resides in witnessing both the hero's narrative of becoming and the concurrent display of state-of-the-art digital effects, our pleasure also flows from the expressive mode's surprising and uncanny rearrangements of space and time and its metaphorical complexity as it structures action bodies' gestures and postures, rhythms and flows, and our own fantasies of becoming and empowerment.

AUTHOR'S NOTES

I would like to thank E. J. Rodican-Jones for her comments on aspects of this chapter in its initial stages of development, and Scott Balcerzak and Jason Sperb for their insightful editorial input.

NOTES

1   See also Singer (2001); Abel (2004: 31–51).
2   This essay builds on the theory Sobchack elaborated in *The Address of the Eye: A Phenomenology of Film Experience*, in which she points out that 'the activity and objects of vision have meaning only in relation to the *whole* that is the perceptive body all the senses constitute and share ... seeing is informed by perception in all of its modalities. What is visible is shaped from within by the intentional projects of the lived-body that does not merely see the world but also wholly inhabits it' (1992: 94; emphasis in original).
3   Rubidge refers to Vittorio Gallese, Luciano Fadiga, Leonardo Fogassi and Giacomo Rizzolatti (1996: 593–609).
4   See Stephen Prince's theory of correspondences (2002).
5   See Cynthia Novack's account of her admiration for the prima ballerina's power and agency, clearly an engagement with the fantasy of empowerment the prima ballerina offered, in Novack (1993: 35–48).
6   The phrase 'stop of death' is Raymond Bellour's (see 2002: 13).
7   Slide EM1105 of *The Eadweard Muybridge Bequest*, Kingston Museum, Kingston Upon Thames, UK. See www.kingston.gov.uk.

8   For example, see Hester Higton, 'Muybridge's Chronophotographs' web page, *The Bill Douglas Centre for the History of Cinema and Popular Culture*, University of Exeter (posted 13 June 2002 at: http://www.ex.ac.uk/bdc/young_bdc/movingpics/moving-pics5.htm), or User Waugsman's animation on *Wikipedia Commons* (posted 24 September 2006 at: http://commons.wikimedia.org/wiki/Image:Muybridge_race_horse_animated.gif). Both were accessed on 19 August 2007.

9   See Mulvey (2006) for a discussion of some of this avant-garde digital film work.

REFERENCES

Abel, Richard (2004) 'The "Culture War" of Sensational Melodrama, 1910–14', in Yvonne Tasker (ed.) *Action and Adventure Cinema*. London and New York: Routledge, 31–51.

Alducin, Manuel (2006) 'Todd Vaziri and *Mission: Impossible III*', *ILM Fan: the Unofficial Industrial Light and Magic site*. Online. Available at: http://www.ilmfan.com/articles/2006/todd_vaziri_mission_impossible_3/. Accessed 17 June 2007.

Arroyo, José (2000 [1996]) 'Mission: Sublime', in José Arroyo (ed.) *Action/Spectacle Cinema: A Sight & Sound Reader*. London: British Film Institute, 21–6.

Bellour, Raymond (2002) *L'entr'images: photo, cinema, video*. Paris: La Différence.

Douglas, Mary (1970) *Purity and Danger*. Harmondsworth, Middlesex: Pelican Books.

Gallese, Vittorio, Luciano Fadiga, Leonardo Fogassi and Giacomo Rizzolatti (1996) 'Action Recognition in the Premotor Cortex', *Brain*, 119, 6, 593–609.

Guido, Laurent (2006) 'Rhythmic Bodies/Movies: Dance as Attraction in Early Film Culture', in Wanda Strauven (ed.) *The Cinema of Attractions Reloaded*. Amsterdam: Amsterdam University Press, 139–56.

Gunning, Tom (1999) '"Now You See It, Now You Don't": The Temporality of the Cinema of Attractions', in Richard Abel (ed.) *Silent Film*. London: Athlone Press, 71–84.

Jacobs, Jason (2000 [1995]) 'Gunfire', in José Arroyo (ed.) *Action/Spectacle Cinema: A Sight and Sound Reader*. London: British Film Institute, 9–16.

Lehman, Peter (1993) *Running Scared: Masculinity and the Representation of the Male Body*. Philadelphia: Temple University Press.

Manning, Erin (2007) *Politics of Touch: Sense, Movement, Sovereignty*. Minneapolis: University of Minnesota Press.

Marks, Laura U. (2000) *The Skin of the Film: Intercultural Cinema, Embodiment, and the Senses*. Durham, NC: Duke University Press.

Mulvey, Laura (2006) *Death 24x a Second: Stillness and the Moving Image*. London: Reaktion Books.

Neale, Steve (2000) *Genre and Hollywood*. London and New York: Routledge.

Novack, Cynthia J. (1993) 'Ballet, Gender and Cultural Power', in Helen Thomas (ed.) *Dance, Gender and Culture*. London: Macmillan, 35–48.

Polhemus, Ted (1993) 'Dance, Gender and Culture', in Helen Thomas (ed.) *Dance, Gender and Culture*. London: Macmillan, 3–15.

Prince, Stephen (2002) 'True Lies: Perceptual Realism, Digital Images and Film Theory', in Graeme Turner (ed.) *The Film Cultures Reader*. London and New York: Routledge, 115–28.

Purse, Lisa (2007) 'Digital Heroes in Contemporary Hollywood: Exertion, Identification and the Virtual Action Body', *Film Criticism*, 32, 1, 5–25.

Rubidge, Sarah (2006) '*Sensuous Geographies* and Other Installations: Interfacing the Body and Technology', in Susan Broadhurst and Josephine Machon (eds) *Performance and Technology: Practices of Virtual Embodiment and Interactivity*. Basingstoke: Palgrave Macmillan, 112–25.

Sheets-Johnstone, Maxine (1979) *The Phenomenology of Dance*. London: Dance Books.

Singer, Ben (2001) *Melodrama and Modernity: Early Sensational Cinema and Its Contexts*. New York: Columbia University Press.

____ (2004) '"Child of commerce! Bastard of Art!" Early Film Melodrama', in Yvonne Tasker (ed.) *Action and Adventure Cinema*. London and New York: Routledge, 52–70.

Sobchack, Vivian (1992) *The Address of the Eye: A Phenomenology of Film Experience*. Princeton: Princeton University Press.

____ (2004) 'What My Fingers Knew: The Cinesthetic Subject, or Vision in the Flesh', in *Carnal Thoughts: Embodiment and Moving Image Culture*. Berkeley: University of California Press, 53–84.

____ (2006) '"Cutting to the Quick": *Techne, Physis*, and *Poiesis* and the Attractions of Slow Motion', in Wanda Strauven (ed.) *The Cinema of Attractions Reloaded*. Amsterdam: Amsterdam University Press, 337–51.

Whissel, Kristen (2006) 'Tales of Upward Mobility: The New Verticality and Digital Special Effects', *Film Quarterly*, 59, 4, 23–33.

SELECTED BIBLIOGRAPHY

Andrew, Dudley (2000) 'The "Three Ages" of Cinema Studies and the Age to Come', *PMLA*, 115, 3, 341–51.

Arnheim, Rudolf (2004a) *Art and Visual Perception: A Psychology of the Creative Eye*. Berkeley: University of California Press.

____ (2004b) *Visual Thinking*. Berkeley: University of California Press.

Barthes, Roland (1972) *Mythologies*, trans. Annette Lewis. New York: Hill and Wang.

____ (1975) *The Pleasure of the Text*, trans. Richard Miller. New York: Hill and Wang.

____ (1978) *Image, Music, Text*, trans. Stephen Heath. New York: Hill and Wang.

____ (1979) *A Lover's Discourse: Fragments*, trans. Richard Howard. New York: Hill and Wang.

____ (1982) *Camera Lucida: Reflections of Photography*, trans. Richard Howard. New York: Hill and Wang.

____ (1989 [1975]) 'Leaving the Movie Theatre', in *The Rustle of Language*, trans. Russell Howard. Berkeley: University of California Press, 345–49.

Baudrillard, Jean (1983) *Simulations*. trans. Paul Foss, Paul Patton and Philip Beitchman. New York: Semiotext(e).

Bazin, André (1967) *What is Cinema?* Volume 1, trans. Hugh Gray. Berkeley: University of California Press.

Belton, John (2002) 'Digital Cinema: A False Revolution' *October*, 100, 98–114.

Benjamin, Walter (1969 [1936]) 'The Work of Art in the Age of Mechanical Reproduction', in Hannah Arendt (ed.) *Iluminations*, trans. Harry Zohn. New York: Shocken Books, 217–52.

Bolter, Jay David and Richard Grusin (2000) *Remediation: Understanding New Media*. Cambridge, MA: The MIT Press.

Buckland, Warren (1999) 'Between Science Fact and Science Fiction: Spielberg's Digital Dinosaurs, Possible Worlds, and the New Aesthetic Realism', *Screen,* 40, 2, 177–92.

Bukatman, Scott (1999) 'The Artificial Infinite: On Special Effects and the Sublime', in Annette Kuhn (ed.) *Alien Zone 2: The Spaces of Science Fiction Cinema*. New York: Verso, 249–75.

____ (2003) *Matters of Gravity: Special Effects and Supermen in the 20th Century*. Durham, NC: Duke University Press.

____ (1993) *Terminal Identity: The Virtual Subject in Postmodern Science Fiction*. Durham, NC: Duke University Press.

Cavell, Stanley (1979) *The World Viewed: Reflections on the Ontology of Film*. Cambridge, MA: Harvard University Press.

Charney, Leo (1988) *Empty Moments: Cinema, Modernity and Drift*. Durham, NC: Duke University Press.

Cubitt, Sean (1988) *Digital Aesthetics*. London: Sage.

____ (1999) 'Phalke, Méliès, and Special Effects Today' *Wide Angle,* 21, 1, 115–30.

____ (2005) *The Cinema Effect*. Cambridge: The MIT Press.

de Baecque, Antoine and Thierry Frémaux (1995) 'La Cinéphilie ou L'Invention d'Une Culture' *Vingtième Siècle,* 46.

Deleuze, Gilles (1986) *Cinema 1: The Movement-Image*. trans. Hugh Tomlinson and Barbara Hammerjam. Minneapolis: University of Minnesota Press.

____ (1989) *Cinema 2: The Time-Image*. trans. Hugh Tomlinson and Robert Galeta. Minneapolis: University of Minnesota Press.

____ (1994) *Difference and Repetition*. trans. Paul Patton. New York: Columbia University Press.

Deleuze, Gilles and Felix Guattari (1987) *A Thousand Plateaus: Capitalism and Schizophrenia* trans. Brian Massumi. Minneapolis: University of Minnesota Press.

____ (1994) 'Percept, Affect, Concept', in *What is Philosophy?*, eds and trans Hugh Tomlinson and Graham Burchell. New York: Columbia University Press. 163–99.

____ (2000) *Anti-Oedipus: Capitalism and Schizophrenia* trans. Robert Hurley, Mark Seem and Helen R. Lane. Minneapolis: University of Minnesota Press.

Dinsmore-Tuli, Uma (2000) 'The Pleasures of 'Home Cinema' or Watching Movies on Telly: An Audience Study of Cinephiliac VCR Use', *Screen,* 41, 3, 315–27.

Doane, Mary Ann (2002) *The Emergence of Cinematic Time: Modernity, Contingency, the Archive*. Cambridge, MA: Harvard University Press.

Durgnat, Raymond (1971) *Films and Feelings*. Cambridge, MA: The MIT Press.

Elsaesser, Thomas (2005) 'Cinephilia or the Uses of Disenchantment', in Marijke de Valck and Malte Hagener (eds) *Cinephilia: Movies, Love and Memory*. Amsterdam: Amsterdam University Press: 27–43.

Elsaesser, Thomas and Warren Buckland (2002) *Studying Contemporary American Cinema: A Guide to Movie Analysis*. New York: Oxford University Press.

Epstein, Jean (1978a [1923]) 'The Essence of Cinema', trans. Stuart Liebman, in P. Adams Sitney (ed.) *The Avant-Garde Film: A Reader of Theory and Criticism*. New York: New York University Press, 24–5.

____ (1978b [1924]) 'For A New Avant-Garde', trans. Stuart Liebman, in P. Adams Sitney (ed.) *The Avant-Garde Film: A Reader of Theory and Criticism*. New York: New York University Press, 26–30.

____ (1984) 'Cine-Mystique', trans. Stuart Liebman. *Millennium Film Journal* 10–11, 192–193.

Erickson, Steve (1999) 'Permanent Ghosts: Cinephilia in the Age of the Internet and Video, Essay 1' *Senses of Cinema*. Available at: http://www.sensesofcinema.com/contents/00/4/cine1.html. Accessed 1 November 2008.

Flavell, Bill (2000) 'Cinephilia and/or Cinematic Specificity' *Senses of Cinema* . Available at: http://www.sensesofcinema.com/contents/00/7/cinephilia.html. Accessed 1 November 2008.

Foster, Stephen C. (1998) *Hans Richter: Activism, Modernism and the Avant-Garde*. Cambridge, MA: The MIT Press.

Gunning, Tom (1990) 'The Cinema of Attractions: Early Film, Its Spectator and the Avant-Garde', in Thomas Elsaesser (ed.) *Early Cinema: Space, Frame, Narrative*. London: British Film Institute, 56–62.

Harvey, Sylvia (1978) *May '68 and Film Culture*. London: British Film Institute.

Hillier, Jim (ed.) (1985) *Cahiers du Cinéma: The 1950s. Neo-Realism, Hollywood, New Wave*. Cambridge, MA: Harvard University Press.

Hills, Matt (2002) *Fan Cultures*. New York: Routledge.

Jarvie, Ian (1960) 'Bazin's Ontology' *Film Quarterly*, 14.1, 60–1.

Jenkins, Henry (1992) *Textual Poachers: Television Fans and Participatory Culture*. New York: Routledge.

____ (2006a) *Convergence Culture: Where Old and New Media Collide*. New York: New York University Press.

____ (2006b) *Fans, Bloggers, and Gamers: Exploring Participatory Culture*. New York: New York University Press.

____ (2006c) *The Wow Climax: Tracing the Emotional Impact of Popular Culture*. New York: New York University Press.

Keathley, Christian (2000) 'The Cinephiliac Moment', *Framework* 42. Available at: http://www.frameworkonline.com/42index.htm. Accessed 1 November 2008.

____ (2006) *Cinephilia and History, or The Winds in the Trees*. Bloomington: Indiana University Press.

Kehr, Dave (2006) 'The Real Web Critics' Available at: http://davekehr.com/?p=84. Accessed 21 May 2006.

Klinger, Barbara (2006) *Beyond the Multiplex: Cinema, New Technologies, and the Home*. Berkeley: University of California Press.

Kuhn, Annette (1999) 'Introduction', in Annette Kuhn (ed.) *Alien Zone 2: The Spaces of Science Fiction Cinema*. New York: Verso, 1–8.

Lambert, Jeff (1999) 'Permanent Ghosts: Cinephilia in the Age of the Internet and Video, Essay 4' *Senses of Cinema*. Available at: http://www.sensesofcinema.com/contents/00/4/cine4.html. Accessed 1 November 2008.

Lesage, Julia (2007) 'The Internet Today, or I got involved in Social Bookmarking' *Jump Cut* 49. Available at: http://www.ejumpcut.org/currentissue/links.html. Accessed 1 November 2008.

MacCabe, Colin (1976) 'Theory and Film: Principles of Realism and Pleasure', *Screen*, 17, 3, 17–27.

Mamet, David (1996) 'The Screenplay', *Make-Believe Town: Essays and Remembrances*. New York: Little, Brown, 117–25.

Manning, Erin (2006) *Politics of Touch: Sense, Movement, Sovereignty*. Minneapolis: University of Minnesota Press.

Manovich, Lev (2001) *The Language of New Media*. Cambridge, MA: The MIT Press.

Marks, Laura (2000) *The Skin of the Film: Intercultural Cinema, Embodiment, and the Senses*. Durham, NC: Duke University Press.

____ (2002) *Touch: Sensuous Theory and Multisensory Media*. Minneapolis: University of Minnesota Press.

Martin, Adrian (2007) 'Responsibility and Criticism' *Cinemascope* 7. Available at: http://www.cinemascope.it/Issue%207/Articoli_n7/Articoli_n7_05/Adrian_Martin.pdf. Accessed 1 November 2008.

Metz, Christian (1977) *The Imaginary Signifier*. trans. Celia Britton, Annwyl Williams, Ben Brewster and Alfred Guzzetti. Bloomington: Indiana University Press.

Michelson, Annette (1998) 'Gnosis and Iconoclasm: A Case Study of Cinephilia', *October*, 83, 3–18.

Mitchell, William J. (1992) *The Reconfigured Eye: Visual Truth in the Post-Photographic Era*. Cambridge, MA: The MIT Press.

Mittell, Jason (2004) *Genre and Television: From Cop Shows to Cartoons in American Culture*. New York: Routledge.

Modleski, Tania (1986) 'The Terror of Pleasure: The Contemporary Horror Film and Postmodern Theory', in Tania Modleski (ed.) *Studies In Entertainment: Critical Approaches to Mass Culture*. Bloomington: Indiana University Press, 155–66.

Moore, Rachel O. (2000) *Savage Theory: Cinema as Modern Magic*. Durham, NC: Duke University Press.

Morrison, James (2005) 'After the Revolution: On the Fate of Cinephilia', *Michigan Quarterly Review*, 44, 3, 393–413.

Mulvey, Laura (1975) 'Visual Pleasure and Narrative Cinema' *Screen*, 16, 3, 6–18.

____ (2006) *Death 24x a Second: Stillness and the Moving Image*. London: Reaktion.

____ Ng, Jenna (2005) 'Love in the Time of Transcultural Fusion: Cinephilia, Homage and Kill Bill', in Marijke de Valck and Malte Hagener (eds) *Cinephilia: Movies, Love and Memory*. Amsterdam: Amsterdam University Press, 65–79.

____ (2007) 'Virtual Cinematography and the Digital Real: (dis)placing the Moving Image Between Reality and Simulacra', in Damian Sutton, Susan Brind, Ray McKenzie (eds) *The State of the Real: Aesthetics in the Digital Age*. London: I. B. Tauris, 172–80.

Nichols, Ashton (1987) *The Poetics of Epiphany: Nineteenth-Century Origins of the Modern Literary Movement*. Tuscaloosa: University of Alabama Press.

Nin, Anais (1963–4) 'Poetics of the Film', *Film Culture*, 31, 12–13.

Norton, Bill (2003) 'Through a Glass Darkly', *Cinefex* 93, 88–111.

Panayides, Theo (1999) 'Permanent Ghosts: Cinephilia in the Age of the Internet and

Video, Essay 2' *Senses of Cinema*. Available at: http://www.sensesofcinema.com/contents/00/4/cine2.html. Accessed 1 November 2008.

Perkins, Claire (2000) 'Cinephilia and Monstrosity: The Problem of Cinema in Deleuze's Cinema Books' *Senses of Cinema*. Available at: www.sensesofcinema.com/contents/books/00/8/deleuze.html. Accessed 1 November 2008.

Pierson, Michele (2002) *Special Effects: Still in Search of Wonder*. New York: Columbia University Press.

Porton, Richard (2002) 'The Politics of American Cinephilia: From the Popular Front to the Age of Video', *Cineaste*, 4–10.

Prince, Stephen (1996) 'True Lies: Perceptual Realism, Digital Images, and Film Theory', *Film Quarterly* 49, 3, 27–37.

____ (2004) 'The Emergence of Filmic Artifacts', *Film Quarterly,* 57, 3, 24–33.

Purse, Lisa (2007) 'Digital Heroes in Contemporary Hollywood: Exertion, Identification and the Virtual Action Body', *Film Criticism,* 32, 1.

Rassos, Effie (2006) 'Everyday Narratives: Reconsidering Filmic Temporality and Spectatorial Affect though the Quotidian', Unpublished PhD Thesis, University of New South Wales.

Ray, Robert (1985) *A Certain Tendency of the Hollywood Cinema, 1930–1980*. Princeton: Princeton University Press.

____ (2001) *How a Film Theory Got Lost and Other Mysteries in Cultural Studies*. Bloomington: Indiana University Press.

Rehak, Bob (2007) 'The Migration of Forms: Bullet Time in Circulation', *Film Criticism,* 32, 1, 26–48.

Robnik, Drehli (2005) 'Mass Memories of Movies: Cinephilia as Norm and Narrative in Blockbuster Culture', in Marijke de Valck and Malte Hagener (eds) *Cinephilia: Movies, Love and Memory*. Amsterdam: Amsterdam University Press, 55–64.

Rosen, Philip (2001) *Change Mummified: Cinema, Historicity, Theory*. Minneapolis: University of Minnesota Press.

Rosenbaum, Jonathan and Adrian Martin (eds) (2003) *Movie Mutations: The Changing Face of World Cinephilia*. London: British Film Institute.

Sarris, Andrew (ed.) (1963) Special Issue: 'American Directors', *Film Culture* 28.

Shaviro, Steven (1993) *The Cinematic Body*. Minneapolis: University of Minnesota Press.

____ (1997) *Doom Patrols: A Theoretical Fiction about Postmodernism*. New York: Serpent's Tail.

____ (2004) 'The Life, After Death, of Postmodern Emotions', *Criticism,* 46, 1, 121–41.

Sobchack, Vivian (1998) *Screening Space: The American Science Fiction Film*. New Brunswick: Rutgers University Press.

____ (2000) *Meta-Morphing: Visual Transformation and the Culture of Quick-Change*. Minneapolis: University of Minnesota Press.

____ (2001) *The Address of the Eye: A Phenomenology of Film Experience*. Princeton: Princeton University Press.

____ (2004) *Carnal Thoughts: Embodiment and Moving Image Culture.* Berkeley: University of California Press.

Sontag, Susan (2001) 'A Century of Cinema', in *Where the Stress Falls.* New York: Farrar, Straus and Giroux, 117–22.

Sperb, Jason (2007) 'Sensing an Intellectual Nemesis', *Film Criticism,* 32,1, 49–71.

Stern, Leslie (2001) 'Paths That Wind Through the Thicket of Things', *Critical Inquiry,* 28,1 , 317–54.

Strauven, Wanda (ed.) (2007) *The Cinema of Attractions Reloaded.* Amsterdam: Amsterdam University Press.

Sterritt, David (1999) 'Permanent Ghosts: Cinephilia in the Age of the Internet and Video, Essay 3' *Senses of Cinema.* Available at: http://www.sensesofcinema.com/contents/00/4/cine3.html. Accessed 1 November 2008.

Tashiro, Charles Shiro (1991) 'Videophilia: What Happens When You Wait for It On Video', *Film Quarterly,* 45, 1, 7–17.

Taylor, Richard (ed.) (1999) *The Eisenstein Reader.* London: British Film Institute.

Trbic, Boris (2004) 'Contextualizing the Narrative: A Step Towards Classroom Cinephilia' *Australian Screen Education,* 34, 86–91.

Vogel, Amos (1974) *Film as a Subversive Art.* New York: Random House.

Willemen, Paul (1994) *Looks and Frictions: Essays in Cultural Studies and Film Theory.* Bloomington: Indiana University Press.

Wollen, Peter (1976) 'Ontology and Materialism in Film', *Screen* 17, 1, 7–23.

____ (2001) 'An Alphabet of Cinema', *New Left Review,* 12, 115–34.

INDEX